HORATIO ALGER, FAREWELL

The End of the American Dream

HORATIO ALGER, FAREWELL

The End of the American Dream

Celeste MacLeod

Seaview Books

NEW YORK

The author and publisher gratefully acknowledge permission to reprint:

Global Reach by Richard L. Barnet and Ronald E. Müller, copyright © 1974 by Richard L. Barnet and Ronald E. Müller. Reprinted by permission of Simon & Schuster, a Division of Gulf & Western Corporation.

The Self-Made Man in America: The Myth of Rags to Riches by Irvin G. Wyllie. Copyright 1954 by THE TRUSTEES OF RUTGERS COLLEGE IN NEW JERSEY. Reprinted by permission of Rutgers University Press.

"White Workers/Blue Mood" by Gus Tyler in *The World of the Blue Collar Worker,* edited by Irving Howe. Copyright © 1972 by Dissent Publishing. Reprinted by permission of TIMES BOOKS, a Division of Quadrangle/The New York Times Co., Inc.

Library of Congress Cataloging in Publication Data

MacLeod, Celeste.
  Horatio Alger, farewell.

  Bibliography: p.
  Includes index.
  1. Social mobility—United States. 2. Job vacancies.
—United States. 3. Migration, Internal—United States.
4. Success. I. Title.
HN90.S65M32   305.5'0973   80-5201
ISBN 0-87223-611-0

For David and Peter

Contents

PART THREE MAKING A LIVING: THE CURRENT IMPERATIVE

PART FOUR CHANGES

Acknowledgments

Every writer owes a debt to the works of others; this book has been enriched by materials from many authors, and I thank them all. Some works of in-depth research or original thought merit special mention because they added an important dimension to some part of the book: Irvin G. Wyllie, *The Self-Made Man in America;* Samuel Yellen, *American Labor Struggles;* Nels Anderson, *The Hobo,* and Kenneth Allsop, *Hard Travellin',* on American hobos; John Steinbeck, *The Grapes of Wrath,* and Thomas Minehan, *Boy and Girl Tramps of America,* on the Great Depression; David E. Smith and John Luce, *Love Needs Care,* on the hippie migration; Patricia and Brendan Sexton, *Blue Collars and Hard Hats,* and B. J. Widick, ed., *Auto Work and Its Discontents,* on alienation in the nonaffluent society; Walter Z. Laqueur, *Young Germany,* and John de Graaf, "Perils of Counterculture," on the German youth movement and its resemblance to the counterculture; and Richard J. Barnet and Ronald Müller, *Global Reach,* on the operations of multinational corporations. Thanks also to three authors whose beliefs differ somewhat from mine; their carefully articulated arguments were helpful, both to explain views that many Americans hold and as a springboard for my analysis of these views in the context of my thesis: Charles A. Reich, *The Greening of America,* which captured the mood of disillusionment with government and business that caused many Americans to turn inward in the 1970s, and Michael Korda's *Success!* which, along with Robert J. Ringer's *Looking Out for Number One* and *The Restoration of the American Dream,* presented the case for a revival of rugged individualism.

The many people I interviewed also provided essential material for this book, especially about the new migrants and the street people, because here little printed material exists. My thanks to: David Abel, Barry Balch, Dick Baltz, Jim Baumohl, Bob Blyth, Carol Bohnsack, David Brandon, Mark Brazas, Prof. Harry Brill, David Carrington, Boona Cheema, Ron Cole, Cathy Coyne, Peter Field, Rev. Bill Fitzpatrick, Peter Foldes, Nick Freeman, Teresa Ghilarducci, Cathie Greene, Rev. Bill Greer, Dr. Hyla Holden, Jude Horsefeld, Phyllis Hunt, Elsie Johnson, Irene Kudarauskas, Wayne Kwitny, Howard Levy, Roger Lewis, June Lightfoot, Jack McCloskey, Louise McCoy, Robert Martin, Prof. Henry Miller, Marjorie Montelius, Steve Mooser, Jean May, Brendan Nesbitt, Dr. John Newmayer, David Novogrodsky, Dr. Stephen Pittel, Barbara Poister, Connie Potts, Prof. Steven Segal, Ursula Sherman, Isabel Weissman, Jack Wieder, Ove Wittstock, Rev. Richard York, Sheri Glucoft Wong, and Elaine Zimmerman.

I would also like to thank the many others who told me about their own lives and situations—the people I call the new migrants, borderliners, and street people. In the book I have changed their names (and sometimes their geographical origins and occupations) to protect their privacy, so my thanks to them must be a collective anonymous one, but my debt is great.

A number of friends and fellow writers helped by reading and commenting on earlier drafts or by clipping relevant articles. My thanks to: Hilde Burton, Dorothy Bryant, Gae Canfield, Richard Katz, Arthur Lipow, Anita Lundquist, Carolyn Mohr, Elinor Richey, Hank Sanchez-Resnik, Lynn Snyder, and Dorothy Witt. Thanks also to Margaret A. Dorsey, economist of the Bureau of Labor Statistics in San Francisco, and to librarians at the University of California at Berkeley: Gwendolyn Lloyd and Clara Stern of the Institute of Industrial Relations, and the librarians of the General Reference Service and the Documents Department.

Finally, thanks to people who gave other help that facilitated the book's completion and publication: Carey McWilliams, who encouraged me to write it; Max Knight, for editorial help in Berkeley; Gail Kuhry, who typed the final draft; my agent, Elizabeth Trupin; my publisher, Charles Sopkin; and my editor in New York, Susan Friedland.

Celeste MacLeod, Berkeley
March, 1980

Part One

THE NEW MIGRANTS

CHAPTER ONE

The Dream and the Reality

Upward mobility was the essence of the American dream. In the new land of democracy and freedom, everyone who tried hard enough could rise and become rich—according to the dream. Individual initiative and persistence were automatic stairsteps to financial success. Horatio Alger, a nineteenth-century American minister, wrote more than 100 novels for boys that illustrated the dream in action; Alger's heroes invariably went from rags to riches through hard work and virtue.

Two interlocking premises supported the American dream—unlimited opportunity and an endless frontier to provide that opportunity. Without the frontier, the dream could not have survived.

The dream of riches for everybody originated in the United States, but it has become one of our most popular exports. The idea that everyone who works hard enough can become wealthy, regardless of social class or advantages (and irrespective of the economic and political situation in one's country), has universal appeal. It is a modern-day fairy tale wherein effort is the magic wand and every person turns into his or her own fairy godmother. The inherent justice of such a tale, its suitability as an inspirational piece for children, makes the story an unbeatable favorite. The American dream has helped raise expectations across the globe.

Belief in the dream has a special advantage for those who embrace its tenets: It serves as a screen that shuts out the real world, at least temporarily. The reality is that opportunity is shrinking, in the United States and elsewhere. When the frontiers ended, so did the basis of the dream.

Although a highly visible minority of individuals in the United States and other Western countries are better off financially than ever before, the common experience is that jobs are increasingly difficult to find. How to earn a living is becoming a dilemma instead of a choice for more and more people entering adulthood. Vast numbers of young people—ranging from unskilled laborers who quit school at sixteen through holders of doctoral degrees from prestigious universities—cannot find jobs. Their problem is not a lack of effort or individual initiative; it is a lack of jobs. More people are looking for work than there are jobs available for them to fill. Automation has been a primary factor in eroding the dream's promise of jobs for everybody; technological innovations have caused great numbers of unskilled and semiskilled workers to be replaced by machines.

In the past, migration was the trump card of the poor. If all else failed, you could leave home and seek opportunity in some other place. You could emigrate (leave your native land and enter another nation as an immigrant), or you could migrate (move within your own country, often from farm to city after the coming of the Industrial Revolution).

Today emigration is closing as an option for the poor. The countries that used to absorb large numbers of immigrants regularly (i.e., United States, Canada, Australia) are experiencing high rates of unemployment themselves, so they no longer want or need the poor and unskilled as immigrants. To the contrary, it is the rich and the highly skilled technicians who are welcome as immigrants these days.

Migration within one's own country is still open, and it remains a popular option. Whenever unemployment increases, so does migration, even though the areas people move to in search of work often have higher rates of unemployment than the communities they left behind. But the dream says that opportunity awaits them someplace, and so people keep moving, hoping to find it in the next town.

This book is about the end of the American dream. The focus is on young people and migration, because the young are hit the hardest by job scarcity, and they are also the most likely to leave home in search of the dream.

Part One introduces "the new migrants"—young adults eighteen to thirty years old, who have left their communities in hopes of finding a better life in a different part of the country. The new migrants come predominantly from poor or working-class homes and, like the majority of the American population, most of them are white. They are not new in the sense of being the first of their kind, because migration—especially westward migration toward the frontier—has long been a traditional way for young Americans to seek the dream; today's young migrants are new in that they reflect a resurgence: A combination of historical and economic events during the 1960s and 1970s caused the new migrants to leave home in renewed numbers.

The new migrants have been confused with "hippies," the middle-class youths (also predominantly white) whose rebellion against the dream in the mid-1960s brought them worldwide notoriety. A few critics of the American scene applauded the revolt, but the general public developed a deep revulsion toward the rebels, who were also closely associated with psychedelic drugs. These young people were too lazy to work, the popular argument went; they had been ruined by permissiveness and their immoral way of life.

When the new migrants went on the road in search of opportunity, they were thought to be running from affluence instead of looking for it, thought to be avoiding work instead of trying to find it.

Dr. Henry Miller, professor of social welfare at the University of California, takes a different view of the new migrants. Miller, whose specialty is "youth on the move," has studied youth migration patterns of the past as well as those in recent times, and he finds the new migrants closer in kind to the hobos at the turn of the century, or the migrants of the Great Depression, than to the beats or hippies. As Miller explained when interviewed at Berkeley:

> There's a popular myth floating around that the poverty of youth is self-imposed, but the fact is, we've produced a generation of young people for whom there are no jobs. The labor market cannot absorb them, so they seek other routes. Periodically in history there have been cataclysmic events

that coughed up great numbers of people and made them wander about looking for ways to survive. The Plague of 1386 is a classic example, but our own Depression is closer. In 1933 alone, the Southern Pacific Railroad apprehended six hundred thousand people riding the rails illegally. A quarter of them were under twenty-five. We're in the midst of another upheaval now, although we haven't acknowledged it.

Acknowledging this upheaval and its effects on young people from the bottom layers of American society would shake the dream at its foundations. The belief that a job exists *a priori* for anyone who really wants to work is a central tenet of the American dream.

Even the revelation in the 1960s that black Americans and other nonwhite citizens were being excluded from the dream was resolved in a manner that left the core of the dream's mythology untouched. Racial prejudice was isolated as the demon that was blocking their chances to climb the ladder of success. The remedy was simple: Remove the demon from the foot of the ladder, add some programs to compensate for past blockage, and then every American would enjoy unlimited opportunity for upward mobility.

The antipoverty programs of the Great Society did help some black people, but failed to eliminate poverty (and, in fact, made scant inroads on improving the lives of the poorest people). The programs, or the people they served, were blamed: The wrong incantation had been used to drive out the demon; the government bureaucracy was at fault; or the poor were not trying hard enough. To suggest that some people remained poor and jobless despite earnest efforts to succeed would have been blasphemous, for unlimited opportunity to get rich was considered a sacred natural resource that we could never run out of in the United States.

It is still so regarded by many an affluent American. Not only does the American dream include a job for everybody who wants to work, it also promises big money to those who try hard enough. A million dollars is just around the corner if you go after it. Horatio Alger will turn over in his grave if you say otherwise. Books and television specials about the few who do make millions reinforce this belief, but little is heard about those who tried and failed.

The grandiose expectations that the American dream instills in its young people make the reality all the more painful when the new migrants arrive in yet another city and cannot make it. They are not only poor and unemployed, they are also failures—in their own eyes and in the eyes of society.

Americans still have the highest expectations in the world, but other nations are catching up. In western Europe, young people from the working class are also leaving their hometowns in increasing numbers in search of brighter futures. In England they flock into London by the hundreds each month, coming mainly from areas of high unemployment such as the Midlands, Glasgow, or Ireland. In France they go to Paris, in Belgium to Brussels; or, because of the Common Market, Belgians may move to London, while British youths settle in Brussels. They expect good jobs to await them in their new locations, but, like their American counterparts, they are usually disappointed.

In every country the poor and the unskilled are the most adversely affected by the dwindling of economic opportunity. Well-educated people from middle-class homes are also experiencing serious job problems, because far more people aspire to professional or executive positions than any country can use in those capacities; but the highly trained can go down the job ladder, if necessary, while those who start out at the bottom can go no lower. They may find themselves pushed out of the job market altogether—and then castigated by society for not working.

The situation is bleak, but not hopeless. The final chapters of this book will discuss some possible directions for change and make a few suggestions, but no four-point plan for reshaping the world economy will be presented. The emphasis will be on readjusting our thinking to fit reality—changing the nature of the dream, as individuals and as nations. We cannot work out viable solutions to the world's growing unemployment problems as long as we cling to obsolete beliefs; it is like trying to win a sports-car race with a horse and buggy.

To start, we need to look at the tenets of the outmoded dream. This takes us back to the early days on the new continent, for that is where the dream began.

CHAPTER TWO

The Land of Opportunity

Money is the key word to the history of the United States. Long before the colonies became an independent nation, the desire for wealth was already a national obsession. "The only principle of life propagated among the young people is to get money, and men are only esteemed according to what they are worth—that is, the money they are possessed of," an observer in New York City reported in 1784.[1] A century later the French traveler Alexis de Tocqueville noted this same quality: "In America then everyone finds facilities, unknown elsewhere, for making or increasing his fortune. The spirit of gain is always on the stretch, and the human mind, constantly diverted from pleasures of imagination and the labours of the intellect, is there swayed by no impulse but the pursuit of wealth."[2]

Tocqueville viewed this scramble for wealth as a natural consequence of freedom under democracy coupled with the fortuitous discovery of a rich continent. Newspaper editor Horace Greeley echoed these same sentiments when he told a group of young people in 1867: "There is in this land of ours larger opportunities, more just and well-grounded hopes, than any other land whereon the sun ever shone."[3]

Everyone could succeed in the United States, because there was plenty of space on the undeveloped frontier. (The fact that numerous tribes of Indians were already living on that frontier was conveniently overlooked. The Indians were pushed out of the way of progress or killed.) Success or failure depended on the individual; if you were rugged enough, hardworking, and persistent, you were bound to get rich. Or so went the legend of the self-made man.

Success!

Rags to riches became the national success story. In the years that followed the Civil War, the lives of kings or dukes or even presidents could not excite the American imagination as much as stories of impoverished lads who pushed their way up to the top. Those who made it into the big money were revered as national heroes, living examples of the American dream brought to fruition. Authors found quick sales in adulatory biographies of any man whose worth ran into seven figures.

Manuals that told how to get rich were also brisk sellers. No knowledge of business or finance was required to write such books, because achieving wealth was considered a matter of moral character: Any young man who was honest, industrious, frugal, and sober could become a millionaire, the success manuals preached. (This advice was always addressed to men; aspiring young women of the nineteenth century were expected to marry big money instead of making it.)

Some manuals had the word "success" in their titles; others used "rich" or "money." Thus there were *The Foundations of Success* (1843), *Elements of Success* (1848), *Success in Business* (1867), *The Secret of Success in Life* (1873), *The Elements of Success* (1873), another *Success in Business* (1875), *Successful Folk* (1878), *How to Succeed* (1882), *Successful Men of Today and What They Say of Success* (1883), *The Law of Success* (1885), *Success in Life* (1885), *Keys to Success* (1898), *Successward* (1899), *The Attainment of Success* (1907), *How to Get Rich* (1866), *Money and How to Make It* (1872), *The Art of Making Money* (1872), *Money for the Million* (1872), *On the Road to Riches* (1876), *How to Become Rich* (1878), and *The Art of Money Getting* (1882).[4]

"Only a people mad with success could have endured the length and repetitiousness of these manuals," Professor Irvin G. Wyllie comments in his definitive study *The Self-Made Man in America*.[5] In his book Wyllie traces the close ties that business and religion enjoyed in the nineteenth century:

One of the impressive facts about the American cult of self-help is that many of its leading proponents were clergymen. The names of Henry Ward Beecher, Lyman Abbott, William Lawrence, Russell Conwell, and Horatio Alger were as familiar to readers of success tracts as to those who worshipped in the leading Protestant churches on the Sabbath. By teaching that godliness was in league with riches, such spokesmen put the sanction of the church on the get-ahead values of the business community. And by so teaching they encouraged each rising generation to believe that it was possible to serve both God and Mammon.[6]

Business was heralded as the moral avenue to wealth. The successful businessman was seen as a repository of exemplary values, so aspiring young men should worship their employers. "Let your eye light up at his request and your feet be nimble; be the arch upon which your employer may rest with safety," one manual said,[7] while an article advised, "Endeavor to become to your employer a thoughtful machine, and the meed of respect and confidence that will be yours will amply compensate."[8]

Not only was it possible to be devout and wealthy simultaneously, it was mandatory that the good Christian try for both, said *The Book of Wealth: In Which It Is Proved from the Bible That It Is the Duty of Every Man to Become Rich,* published by the Reverend Thomas P. Hunt in 1836.[9] Later that century, Russell Conwell, a leading Baptist minister, asserted that ninety-eight out of every hundred rich Americans were more honest than their less wealthy fellow men. "That is why they are rich," said Reverend Conwell in his famous sermon "Acres of Diamonds." Conwell preached this sermon at least 6000 times and made "a tidy fortune" from it, said Wyllie. With such praise from the churches, the super-rich could sleep easily. "John D. Rockefeller brushed off his critics with the simple assertion that it was God who had given him his money."

The Alger Myth

The profusion of success manuals in the Gilded Age suggests that every boy kept a copy by his bedside to dip into for inspiration, but the tedious preaching of these tomes suggests otherwise. The message that permeated American thinking—strive and succeed—came not from dull success manuals but from fast-moving adventure stories that were fun to read. Horatio Alger, Jr., became the popularizer of the myth of the self-made man. Alger was a minister who resigned from the pulpit to write full time, but his religious training stayed with him—his novels for boys were action-packed sermons on virtue rewarded with riches.

The Alger hero is remembered as the poor but honest lad who made it without help from anyone, the epitome of the self-made man; however, a look at some of Alger's novels shows that, although his heroes were indeed honest and hardworking, they never succeeded on their own. True, they had no wealthy fathers or uncles to fall back on, but a rich stranger always made a timely appearance to reward them for some heroic deed—such as stopping a train just before it plunged over a precipice, foiling kidnappers, rescuing a drowning child, or catching a pickpocket in the act. The reward was either cash or a job in the rich man's countinghouse—often both.

The benevolent rich man in Alger novels was as generous with advice as with money. In *Ragged Dick,* the story that made Alger famous, the opulent Mr. Whitney told the young bootblack Dick: "I hope, my lad, you will prosper and rise in the world. You know in this free country poverty in early life is no bar to a man's advancement. . . . Remember that your future position depends mainly on yourself and that it will be high or low as you choose to make it."[10]

Occasionally the widow of a benevolent rich man befriended the hero. In *The Store Boy: The Fortunes of Ben Barclay,* Ben stopped a pickpocket who was about to rob a woman. She gave Ben a $20 reward and told him, " 'In this country, the fact that you are a poor boy will not stand in your way of success. The most eminent men of the day, in all branches of business and in all professions, were once poor boys. I dare say, looking at me, you don't suppose I ever knew anything of poverty.'

" 'No,' said Ben.

" 'I was the daughter of a bankrupt farmer and my husband was a clerk in a country store. I am not going to tell you how he came to the city and prospered, leaving me, at his death, rich beyond my needs. Yet that is his history and mine. Does it encourage you?'

" 'Yes, it does,' said Ben earnestly.' "[11]

The possession of money alone could turn even a rude tramp

into a gentleman. A rogue who tried to extort money from Ben in the book's opening pages appeared later as a changed man, now immaculately dressed and well mannered. The transformation was caused by a $10,000 legacy left to the tramp by an old uncle. "It has led me to turn over a new leaf, and henceforth I am respectable, as befits a man of property," he told Ben. "I even keep a card case."[12]

Alger's theme of the benevolent rich man was contradicted, however, by his villains, especially country squires who held mortgages on the meager property of the heroes' families.

" 'But how could Squire Davenport so wickedly try to cheat us of our little property?' " Ben asked the tramp-turned-gentleman, who had revealed the existence of a promissory note from Davenport to Ben's dead father, worth more than the mortgage.

" 'My dear boy,' said the tramp, shrugging his shoulders, 'your question savors of verdancy. Learn that there is no meanness too great to be inspired by the love of money.'

" 'But Squire Davenport was already rich.'

" 'And for that reason he desired to become richer.' "[13]

Heroes of the Gilded Age

Squire Davenport had much in common with the heroes of the Gilded Age. In that period after the Civil War, great fortunes were made by numerous men, including John D. Rockefeller, Andrew Carnegie, J. P. Morgan, Phillip Armour, Jay Cooke, Thomas Mellon, Jay Gould, Jim Fisk, George Pullman, Leland Stanford, and Collis P. Huntington. Cornelius Vanderbilt and Daniel Drew, who started earlier, increased their holdings during this period. Conditions were highly favorable for amassing wealth: The transcontinental railroad had opened in 1869, the Industrial Revolution was in full swing, land and labor were abundant and cheap, and there was no income tax. The hallowed canon of business was laissez-faire. Rich men could do as they pleased to get richer, so they did.

Along with kudos from the clergy, the new millionaires were further vindicated by the works of British philosopher Herbert Spencer, who enjoyed a great vogue in the United States from 1870 to 1890. Spencer, expanding upon Charles Darwin's theory of natural selection, assured his gratified readers that the men who rose to the top in any age were inherently superior beings who would ultimately help to perfect the human race.[14]

During the years when rich men were deified as God's favorite sons and the fittest of the age, those most revered—because they accumulated the most wealth—often made their money by unscrupulous methods that ruined thousands of others. A favorite method was to gain control of a vital industry by forcing one's competitors out of business. You undersold your competitors, even if it meant a temporary loss, until they either sold out to you "voluntarily" or were driven into bankruptcy. Once you had a monopoly, you immediately raised prices, not only to cover your losses but to insure a handsome profit as well.

Using such methods, Cornelius Vanderbilt gained control of much of the nation's railroads.[15] John D. Rockefeller built the Standard Oil Company by working in collusion with railroad magnates who gave him secret rebates and preferential treatment; other refiners often could not get any railroad to take their oil to market, because the oil tanks were all leased to Rockefeller.[16] In ten years Rockefeller forced seventy-six competitors out of business in Ohio, Pennsylvania, and New York; by 1880 he controlled 95 percent of the nation's oil.[17]

Farmers and small businessmen had to pay the prices, however exorbitant and unreasonable, or do without essential services (railroads) and products (oil and steel) on which their livelihoods depended.

In classic American tradition, the new moguls were frugal on their upward climb, but in later years they often lived on palatial estates that made the castles of the European aristocracy look tawdry. Indeed, some moguls even bought European castles and had them shipped to America. The peasants who had flocked to America because it had no barons, kings, or czars to lord over the land with ancestral privilege found that men who made fortunes became the new land's aristocracy. Some even married their daughters to Europe's dukes and counts. These uncrowned monarchs bought up more than land, for agriculture was no longer paramount in an industrial age. The titans soon controlled the country's basic industries and natural resources and, in effect, the country. Today their grandchildren and great-grandchildren are multimillionaires by birth.

But the super-rich were not the only people who prospered,

one can argue; the average immigrant fared better in America than he or she would have back home. There is no doubt that immigration to the United States brought opportunity and money to millions at all points along the economic spectrum. But there is also no doubt that the wealth of the super-rich depended in large part on cheap labor. Millions of workers remained in poverty in order that a few people might prosper. The men and women who worked in the factories, mines, and railroads of the titans had scant opportunity to exchange rags for riches; they were lucky if they could feed and clothe their children on what they earned for ten to fourteen hours of labor each day. Frugality was a necessity, not a virtue, for these workers who were exempt from the American dream.

A look back at the first national railroad strike, for example, provides a startling contrast to the success literature that smothered the Gilded Age, by illustrating the plight of workers that Horatio Alger never mentioned.

The Railroad Strikes of 1877

The railroad strikes of 1877 erupted in Baltimore and spread spontaneously through several states, leaving more than a hundred workers dead before the strikes were quelled by state and federal militias. The immediate cause was a cut in workers' wages. In July the Baltimore and Ohio Railroad, following the lead of its competitors, cut wages of more than a dollar a day by 10 percent. This meant that first-class firemen would receive $1.58 per day, second-class $1.35, and brakemen even less. The men, who generally had only four days' work each week, would have to support their families on $5 or $6 a week, as well as paying their own living expenses on the job. They went on strike.[18]

To the surprise of railroad owners, crowds of sympathizers cheered the striking workers. Not only workmen in other trades supported them, but small farmers and businessmen as well. The small-time businessmen, and especially the midwestern farmers, viewed the railroads as the archenemy. In some cases farmers actually lost money if they paid the exorbitant freight rates they were charged to have their crops carried to market. Some farmers burned their crops instead. (It was a group of embittered Kansas farmers who coined the term "robber barons" to describe the railroad moguls, in an antimonopoly pamphlet of 1880.[19] That movement eventually led to the formation of the Populist party in 1891. Part of its platform was the nationalization of railroads.)

The farmers, like the railroad workers, were caught in an economic bind caused by years of shady dealing by entrepreneurs whose desire for wealth and power was limitless. In *American Labor Struggles,* Samuel Yellen describes the situation that led to the railroad strikes of 1877:

"By means of fake companies, improper consolidations, premium bonds and certificates, stock dividends and other maneuvers, the railroads had succeeded in erecting tremendous capitalization, as much as seven-eighths water, upon which they demanded their 'just and reasonable dividends.' " Similar maneuvering had taken place in other industries, "based too often on the wildest gambling and most corrupt scheming," said Yellen, with the result that the country's economic structure teetered with the Panic of 1873. "When the inevitable crash came, hundreds of thousands were thrown out of employment and many thousands lacked food, clothing, shelter, and medical attention. Even those still at work suffered, inasmuch as wages were cut nearly in half during the next six years."[20]

But even in the worst years the railroads never cut back on their dividends to stockholders. Instead they kept lowering wages.

Soon after the strike started, the *Baltimore Sun* said: "There is no disguising the fact that the strikers in all their lawful acts have the fullest sympathy of the community. The ten percent reduction after two previous reductions was ill-advised. The company for years has boasted of its great earnings and paid enormous dividends."[21]

But as the strike spread, the facts *were* disguised by newspapers and magazines throughout the country. Many citizens lost sympathy when the strikers were described as hoodlums who were disrupting the nation's business on orders from European Communists. Yellen found that in a single issue, July 26, 1877, *The New York Times* used the following words to describe the strikers: disaffected elements, roughs, hoodlums, rioters, mob, suspicious-looking individuals, bad characters, thieves, blacklegs, looters, Communists, rabble, labor-reform agitators, dangerous class of people, gangs, tramps, drunken section men, lawbreakers, threatening crowds, bummers, ruffians, loafers, bullies, vagabonds, cowardly mob, band of worthless fellows, incendiaries, enemies of society, reckless crowd, malcontents, wretched people, loud-mouthed orators, rapscallions, brigands, robber mob, riffraff, terrible fellows, felons, and idiots.[22]

When workers on the New York Central line threatened to strike, its president, William H. Vanderbilt (son of Cornelius), refused to believe that his employees were dissatisfied. The best mechanics were making $1.20 a day, while less-skilled workers got 80 cents to a dollar. Vanderbilt told reporters, "There is a perfect understanding between the heads of departments and the employees, and they appreciate, I think, so thoroughly the identity of interest between themselves and us that I cannot for a moment believe that they will have any part in this business."[23] A few days later he said, "Our men feel that, although I may own the majority of the stock in the Central, my interests are as much affected in degree as theirs, and although I may have my millions and they the reward of their daily toil, still we are about equal in the end."[24]

Vanderbilt, if not his employees, appears to have read the success manuals of the day and believed every word of them. Even when the workers on the New York Central did go on strike, Vanderbilt kept insisting publicly that his men were not on strike, that they were prevented from working by outside agitators. "Notwithstanding his assumption that there was no strike," says Yellen, "Vanderbilt asked for troops and Governor Robinson sent a militia force of 1200 to West Albany."[25]

Within two weeks, every strike in the nation had been crushed. The workers were forced back to their jobs at reduced pay. Little was written anymore about wage cuts, but much was heard in the years to come about the American laborer's right to work without organized interference, presumably to work even for nothing if his devotion to his employer extended that far.

Panics and Recessions

While railroad workers had their wages cut during the recession years that followed the Panic of 1873, other workers (estimates run as high as three million) lost their jobs altogether. With no unemployment compensation and only the most rudimentary relief system, the jobless often had no way to eat. Following the American tradition of migration, great numbers of unemployed people left home in search of opportunity. The transcontinental railroad made it possible for the unemployed to travel further than in earlier recessions, and to penetrate regions of the country that were not used to receiving masses of displaced urbanites. Their arrival caused a different kind of panic.

Wherever the unemployed went, they were regarded as bums. In a land whose credo has ever been "Anyone can find a job if he really wants to work," not working was equated with not wanting to work. And idleness was considered a sin.

In 1875, Ohio held a statewide "anti-tramp convention" in Columbus, at which delegates resolved "not to be gentle or generous to tramps" and called for the speedy construction of workhouses. A farmer wrote to the Cincinnati *Commercial* suggesting that tramps be rounded up and sent as forced labor to pick cotton in the South. "Some helpful hint, no doubt, could be taken from Russia's Siberia business," said the farmer. The *Cleveland Leader* advised its readers to "stop feeding the army of loafers who have taken advantage of hard times to inflict themselves upon people not too lazy to work."[26]

That same year the New Hampshire legislature passed an antitramp law; "for merely begging, any Justice of the Peace is authorized to put them to hard labor for six months at the county or town farm. If they cannot be profitably employed in these institutions, they are to be hired out to work for any citizen who may choose to bid for their services."[27]

Only a few people protested the ill treatment of unemployed migrants. Among them was Lorenzo D. Lewelling, the governor of Kansas. Lewelling, a Populist crusader, understood that lack of jobs, as well as wanderlust, was causing hordes of men to roam the country. In December 1893, the year of another major depression, Lewelling published an executive proclamation that became known as "The Tramps' Circular." In it he criticized the antitramp laws of Kansas:

"Thousands of men, guilty of no crime but poverty, intent upon no crime but that of seeking employment, have languished in the city prisons of Kansas or performed unrequited toil on 'rock piles' as municipal slaves, because ignorance of economic conditions had made us cruel. . . . The right to go freely from place to place in search of employment, or even in obedience of a mere whim, is part of the personal liberty guaranteed by the

Constitution of the United States to every human being on American soil. . . . Let simple poverty cease to be a crime."[28]

The Hobos

Poverty remained a crime, or at least a cause for ostracizing people from the community. The Protestant work ethic, growing from Puritan and Calvinist roots, thrived in America, spreading its message that everyone must work and prosper. Wealth was a sign that God was satisfied with one's performance.

The hobo worked, but he did not prosper in the sense of accumulating money and property. The reward for his labor was to be classified as a pariah. The hobo was America's migrant worker.[29] He went wherever he was needed, and left as soon as his services were no longer required, a pattern that ideally suited his employer's requirements. He was a prime worker in building the cities of the western frontier. He dug the country's great mines and dams and canals. Along with Chinese immigrants, he built the western sections of the first transcontinental railroad. He also worked seasonal trades, cutting ice and timber in the North, harvesting wheat in California and the Midwest, shearing sheep in the Southwest, and picking cotton, hops, fruits, and vegetables in many frontier states.

His transportation was the railroad—not a seat on the day coach but a free ride in the boxcars of freight trains. Riding the rails gratis became a hobo tradition; men in that occupation would no more have purchased a train ticket than they would have reserved a suite in a first-class hotel. Along the route their hotel was the "jungle," an informal camp set up near the railroad tracks in most cases, where traveling hobos and tramps cooked their meals, washed their clothes, and slept.

Although the hobo generally received good wages on the job, so much of his time was spent traveling from one job to another, or sitting around in big cities during the winter months when his work was out of season, that often his yearly income was barely enough to live on. His life-style also excluded a family or permanent relationships with women. He lived apart from the main currents of American existence, with his own hangouts, newspapers, cultural life, and organizations.

In America the terms "hobo," "tramp," and "bum" have been

used interchangeably to describe the man who regularly goes on the road. But Nels Anderson, who gave us the first accurate picture of hobo life in his 1923 study *The Hobo,* made distinctions. He divided the men living in Chicago's "Hobohemia" section as follows:

Hobos: casual migratory workers who came to live in Hobohemia between jobs and to seek new jobs there through the employment agencies that lined the streets.

Tramps: men who traveled regularly but did not work. A smaller group than the hobos.

The Home Guard: men who stayed in Hobohemia permanently instead of going on the road periodically. They made their living from unskilled day labor and odd jobs.

Bums: men who stayed in Hobohemia but did not work. This category included alcoholics, drug addicts, beggars, and petty thieves, as well as men who were too old or sick to work anymore but had no means of support.

Some men might fit all these categories at different times in their lives, Anderson said, whereas others were clearly bums or hobos. He also pointed out that many people labeled bums or tramps were unemployable because of physical or mental handicaps.

Chicago had the nation's largest Hobohemia section, but several other cities, including St. Louis, Kansas City, Minneapolis, Seattle, and Spokane, had similar districts. In each city the men congregated in their special section of town around the "main drag" or "the stem," as its central area was called. Along with cheap hotels, flophouses, restaurants, bookstores, saloons, brothels, religious missions, burlesque houses, and secondhand-clothing stores, there were numerous employment agencies. They were clustered together in an area hobos called "the Slave Market." Here dozens of agencies put placards in their windows or solicited on the streets to attract the hobo to temporary jobs in the West or the Midwest. There were few calls for workers to go south, because that part of the country had a seemingly inexhaustible supply of cheap black labor. Many black men, however, came north in search of jobs during depression years.

The majority of hobos were white, and usually American-born. The newly arrived immigrant was likely to stay close to

family and ethnic ties, working in sweatshops or on farms for
whatever wages his employer would pay. The second generation,
nurtured on Yankee soil and Yankee ideas of freedom, was often
more independent. If working conditions were miserable, he
might walk off the job.

Anderson, who studied 400 homeless men in Chicago, found
that their reasons for ending up in Hobohemia were as varied as
the men themselves, but that their arrival was usually preceded
by a series of defeating and disappointing events in their lives.
Some were victims of industrial hazards, forced to quit work
when they developed lung disease in the coal mines or were
adversely affected by dust and dyes in the New England textile
factories. Others were physically crippled, or had psychological
handicaps that made it impossible for them to be employed at
full-time jobs.

There were some, however—especially many of the younger
men—who had no special problems. "The American tradition of
pioneering, wanderlust, seasonal employment, attract [sic] into
the group of wanderers and migratory workers a great many ener-
getic and venturesome normal boys and young men," said Anderson.[30] He disputed contemporary studies in France, Italy, and
Germany which concluded that the vagabond was a psychopathic
type, and cited studies done on unemployed hobos and on the
general population in army camps which showed that "the intelligence of the unemployed is not lower, but, if anything, higher
than that of the adult males tested in army camps."[31]

The question of how many men adopted the hobo life as a
conscious choice and how many drifted into it inadvertently after
prolonged unemployment cannot be answered with certainty, but
the size of Chicago's Hobohemia in boom and bust times gives
us a clue. Anderson reported that in good times the population
of Chicago's Hobohemia averaged 30,000 men, but during recession years, when great numbers of people were thrown out of
work, its numbers swelled to 75,000. Clearly, becoming a hobo
was frequently not a matter of choice.

Whatever the reasons that led men to become hobos in the
nineteenth and early twentieth centuries, those who adopted that
life could survive economically, on a modest scale, because there
was a steady need for migrant labor. The man in good health who
was willing to accept the rigors of riding the rails and eating
bunkhouse food could find seasonal employment on the Ameri-

can frontier. Maybe the jobs turned out to have more drudgery than glamour, but they paid and ended, leaving the hobo free to take a breather in the stem and then sign up for another job.

A few generations later, in our own time, the country no longer needs the hobo's seasonal labor. But so great is the legend of the endless frontier that young men—and women as well, today —still head west expecting to find the kinds of outdoor jobs that sustained the hobos.

Even more people go west with the traditional aim of finding riches there. Belief in the West as the quintessence of opportunity has persisted to the present day, although a long line of migrants have stumbled over more rocks than gold nuggets on arriving in the promised land.

CHAPTER THREE

Westward Ho!

Migration, as we have seen, increases during hard times. The hardest time in the United States to date was the decade of the 1930s. The stock-market crash of 1929 and its aftermath, coupled with severe dust storms and droughts that plagued large segments of American farmlands during the early Thirties, put one-third of the country's labor force out of work at one time or another during that decade. From twelve to fifteen million people were unemployed.

In retrospect we call that period the Great Depression. But at the time, the millions who lost their job or their land because of the crash or the dust storms were blamed for their sudden poverty. The tenets of the American dream had no exception clause for depression years—it was your own fault if you couldn't make it. And for the most part the unemployed accepted that blame, because the poor as well as the rich clung to the myth of the American dream.

The dream had one saving grace—one escape clause that compensated the poor for their misery. No matter how great their current failure, the dream said they could still make it big. All was not lost. If they migrated westward where opportunity lay, and worked hard enough, they could get rich.

The Golden State

Of all the land that stretched to the west, California was the favorite. Its lure began in 1849 when gold was discovered there and people rushed in from America, Europe, and Asia, expecting to get rich overnight. Only a few succeeded, but the legend of the land of gold refused to die. California became the apotheosis of the American dream.

From the beginning, migrants without capital had difficulty making it in California. While many other states had plenty of land available for homesteaders, opportunities were scant in California. There was plenty of land there, too, but it was already taken. The vast land grants of the Spanish period were transferred (through bogus documents and back-room deals) into the hands of a few Americans. Later, huge land grants to the new railroads intensified the land monopoly in California, leaving little space for the small farmer. By 1860 agribusiness was flourishing in California.[1]

At first, growers used the labor of the hobos, who would come in when they were needed and leave as soon as the picking season ended. But when the American-born hobos began to organize and demand better wages and working conditions, they were replaced by newly arrived immigrants from poverty-stricken backgrounds. In turn growers played Chinese, Japanese, Filipino, and Mexican immigrants off against each other to insure a plentiful supply of cheap labor for the harvest.[2]

Little word of this situation wafted eastward, however. When migrants headed west during the Great Depression, the Golden State was their number-one choice. Soon the migrants of the 1930s outnumbered the old gold seekers in California.

In his novel *The Grapes of Wrath* (1939), John Steinbeck took the wealth of information he had collected about the experiences of the "dust bowl" migrants and fashioned it into a composite portrait of a family—the Joads—that has come to symbolize these migrants.

When bank officials rode out to Tom Joad's Oklahoma farm to foreclose the property and order the family off the land, Joad asked: " 'But if we go, where'll we go? How'll we go? We got no money.'

" 'We're sorry,' said the owner men. 'The bank, the fifty-thousand-acre owner, can't be responsible. You're on land that isn't yours. Once over the line, maybe you can pick cotton in the fall. Maybe you can go on relief. Why don't you go on west to California? There's work out there and it never gets cold. Why, you can reach out anywhere and pick an orange. Why, there's always some kind of crop to work in. Why don't you go there?' And the owner and men started their cars and rolled away."[3]

The Joads piled their family and their belongings into a jalopy and headed west. They arrived in California to find that the supply of migrants seeking agricultural work greatly exceeded the demand. Wages were rock-bottom. When the Joads were lucky enough to find work in the fields for a short time, the labor of the whole family, including the children, did not bring in enough money to fill their empty stomachs. In addition, wherever they went, the Joads were scorned and hated as "Okies," as the dust-bowl migrants were called. They were treated with a contempt similar to that doled out to migrants who ventured into Ohio or Kansas after the Panic of 1873. Yet there were differences between the two periods.

Federal Help: Now You See It, Now You Don't

The Great Depression of the 1930s made the panics and recessions that came earlier look like warm-up exercises. This time, rich and middle-class Americans suffered along with the poor. At first the nation tried to persevere cheerfully in Alger tradition, singing "Happy Days Are Here Again" during some of the worst years and rejoicing when President Hoover announced that prosperity was just around the corner. But as the incidence of misery increased, there were widespread cries that the government should help the unemployed.

In time the government did help, under the New Deal of the Roosevelt administration. But programs appeared and disappeared or changed content in midstream with a schizophrenic unpredictability.[4] The concept of government help was anathema to the American traditions of rugged individualism and the self-made man. And if a third of the nation was unemployed and most of the population was adversely affected in other ways by the depression, there were millions of people who did not suffer; some, in fact, increased their wealth and holdings during those years. In the 1930s prices fell as unemployment rose (unlike the 1970s, when steady inflation persisted, regardless of the employment rate), so people with money to spare during the Great Depression experienced good times indeed.

Some Americans who were not hurt by the depression protested against every government program to help the poor and accused

President Roosevelt of treason. They saw infamy in the act of a government helping its people; people worth their salt would help themselves as they had always done in America, the affluent pointed out.

In 1933 the government set up the Federal Transient Service under the Federal Emergency Relief Act (FERA). Administered by the states but wholly supported by federal funds, it provided housing, food, medical services, education, recreation, and public-service jobs for migrants of all ages. By the end of 1933 there were 261 transient-relief centers and 63 transient camps in 40 states; a few months later, every state except Vermont had a transient program.[5]

At the end of 1935 the Federal Transient Service was discontinued, thrown out with the entire Federal Emergency Relief Act. All along there had been intense opposition from citizens who viewed the FERA as a giant giveaway to lazy people. They thought direct relief—that is, giving money to destitute people to buy food and other essentials—weakened the moral fiber of the poor.

Los Angeles had one of the largest federally funded centers for transients because California was receiving so many migrants. When the news arrived that the government was closing the Federal Transient Service in September 1935, citizens of Los Angeles panicked. How would they cope with the hordes of penniless people who kept arriving, when there were no jobs or housing facilities for them? A group of citizens formed the Los Angeles Committee for Indigent Aliens, with the local chief of police as their leader, and tried to solve the problem by devising a way to prevent indigents from entering Los Angeles.

The committee set up patrols at border stations in counties hundreds of miles from Los Angeles. From November 1935 to April 1936 these patrols, with 125 employees, stopped all cars whose occupants looked like "unemployables" and sent them back. This illegal action, known as the "Bum Blockade," was eventually halted through litigation initiated by the American Civil Liberties Union. The irate Californians did not give up so easily, however. As Carey McWilliams recounts in *Factories in the Field:*[6]

Recourse was had to other time-honored stratagems to stem the tide of migrants. A bill was introduced into the

Legislature to bar all transients from the State; stiff vagrancy
sentences were given "alien transients"; transients failing to
meet the three-years' residency requirement for relief were
left to starve; many were rounded up by the relief officials
and shipped out of the State; and, in the rural counties,
transients were shifted back and forth from one county to
the other, in the vain and foolish hope that, somehow, in
this elaborate reshuffling process, they would suddenly disappear.[7]

After the Federal Transient Service closed, the direct relief of
the FERA was replaced by work relief through a new program,
the Federal Works Progress Administration (WPA), which ran
from 1935 to 1939. Millions got jobs through the WPA, but millions of others were excluded. Transients were among those who
had difficulty getting into WPA projects. Josephine Brown, a
social worker on the staff of Harry Hopkins (who directed both
the FERA and the WPA), said of the period after the FERA was
terminated, "Plans were made to transfer the employable transients to the Federal Works Program (WPA), but local prejudice
against outsiders made this process slow and unsatisfactory."[8]
And, of course, throughout its existence the WPA was harshly
criticized by Americans who thought work relief interfered with
the free-enterprise system.

Young Migrants of the Depression

Young people are among the first to leave home during hard
times. They have stamina, idealism, and a thirst for adventure,
and they lack the commitments (small children and elderly parents) that may keep older people at home until circumstances
force them to leave. In the next two sections we will look back
at the young migrants of the 1930s and 1940s. Information about
these migrants is scant, since, as with their counterparts today,
little notice was taken of them. But two men—George Outland
and Thomas Minehan—did study these migrants; their writings,
covering different segments of the young migrant population,
provide a picture that resembles the young migrants of the 1960s
and 1970s who will be discussed in the chapters ahead.

George Outland, a California educator, studied 5000 boys, aged

15 to 20, who registered with the Federal Transient Service in Los Angeles between December 1933 and July 1934.[9] He published several articles based on his studies, trying to fight the "wild boys of the road" stereotype by describing the situation as he found it. In 1934 he wrote:

> The statement has frequently been made that all transients, boys included, are "bums" and "hoboes," and the Federal Government has often been condemned for attempting to care for them. Those closest to the field of transient work realize that such a statement is grossly exaggerated; whereas there are a few transients who might properly fall into one of the above listed undesirable categories, a great majority of them are individuals who have lost their jobs on account of economic difficulties over which they have no control, and who are extremely anxious to rehabilitate themselves. Especially this is true of the army of minor transients, boys under 21 years of age, who had left an undesirable situation at home in order to set out for themselves and make a new start in life.[10]

Outland's statistics showed that the boys who migrated to California came from every state plus a few foreign countries; their background was urban more often than rural; their average education level was ninth grade; and their main concern was to find a job and get ahead. "It has been interesting . . . to observe these boys and to note how eager they are to find work and help the folks back home," said Outland.[11]

Minehan's Migrants

Some of the young migrants that Thomas Minehan studied had no folks at home. They shared economic and family problems with Outland's migrants, but they were a different breed—or they became one. During 1933 Minehan lived and traveled with these youngsters who rode the rails, while he collected material for his doctoral dissertation. By day he was one of them, participating in their lives; at night, or whenever he was alone, he wrote up his notes in secret. He reported on 468 transients, 95 percent male, aged 12 to 21. Minehan was so amazed by what he saw that after completing his thesis he wrote a book for the general public, *Boy and Girl Tramps of America* (1934). As he explained in the introduction:

> I had seen pictures of the Wild Children of revolution-racked Russia. I had read of the free youth of Germany after the World War. I knew that in every nation, following a plague, an invasion, or a revolution, children left without parents and homes became vagrants. . . . Before my own experiences, I had always believed that in America we managed things better. And yet in the face of economic disorganization and social change our own youth took to the highroad.[12]

The young transients Minehan described traveled mainly in railroad boxcars, living in makeshift jungle camps along the way and staying in urban jungles or religious missions in the cities. Often ten or twelve young people traveled together, a solid enough group to protect themselves from attacks by the railroad police, yet not so large that a town would panic when they arrived and send a sheriff's posse to raid their camp.

Jumping on and off freight trains and tramping for miles in the dust wore out clothing and shoes quickly, hence finding clothes was a constant problem. Some were able to beg clothes from housewives or steal some off clotheslines; others bought secondhand clothes in the stem when they could scrape together a little money. In the jungle camps, washing and repairing one's clothes was as important an activity as cooking. But most of the young transients were ill-clothed for the cold weather. Bronchial troubles and pneumonia were common.

The youngsters did not starve, but they rarely got enough to eat; most showed signs of malnutrition, Minehan said. On the road they ate what they could scrounge or beg, while in cities they could usually get one meal at a religious mission or a relief station. Typical fare was "a bowl of beans, two-thirds water, two slices of bread, two donuts, very stale, and a cup of dunking coffee —coffee used only for dunking because it has such a vile taste."[13] Transients had to work two to four hours in the relief kitchens for such a meal, but they preferred this to the forced religious services of the missions. The proselytizing on skid row was wasted on the young migrant of the depression.

"He has no background of sinful experience and dissipation to which the preacher may appeal as justification for his present need," Minehan explained. "None of his money was squandered upon harlots and riotous living. Unlike the older man, he knows little of gambling joints and houses of booze and sin. Nor of bonanza wages and foolish sprees."[14] The young transients did not regard begging or stealing food as a sin; these activities were seen as a necessity in a society that offered them no opportunity to earn a living.

Minehan's migrants gravitated toward the cities, because they felt at home there—most came from large industrial cities. Their six most common home states were Pennsylvania, Michigan, Ohio, New York, Illinois, and Texas. "Few farmer boys and girls are on the bum. It is the city youths who have been forced into vagrancy, and they wait around cities for a job."[15]

If they waited longer than a day, the migrants stayed in the jungle camps near the railroad tracks, because relief groups would not keep them. In religious missions and community relief stations alike in cities and also in small towns, young transients received the same treatment in this regard: They were given a meal or two and a place to sleep overnight in return for agreeing to leave the next day.

This system of forcing transients to remain on the road was not limited to young people, nor was it confined to America. George Orwell described a similar system in England in *Down and Out in Paris and London,* published in 1933. In England the "spikes" (relief shelters) also offered overnight food and lodging to the homeless and then forced them to move on. In both countries the relief systems operated on the assumption that transients were worthless people who refused to work; they must be kept moving or they would become a burden on the communities they settled into.

At the time Minehan and Orwell wrote their books, there were virtually no jobs for these chronic wanderers in either country. If there had been, the constant travel forced on these people by the system would have prevented them from finding such jobs.

Minehan's migrants became alienated from the mainstream of American life and turned into bitter cynics. "They do not have any more feelings of loyalty to America than they have to the South Pole," he reported.[16] Yet when they first left home, some were not much different from the hopeful boys whom Outland interviewed at the Federal Transient Service in Los Angeles.

There was "Texas," nicknamed for his home state. "It wasn't so bad at home before the big trouble came," Texas told Minehan. In the service during World War I, Texas's father had developed an illness that later continued to flare up sporadically, keeping him out of work for a month or so. But he always found another job after he got well, and the family managed although there were seven children. Texas shined shoes after high school, his brother delivered newspapers, his sister was a baby-sitter, and his mother sewed for the neighbors.

Suddenly his father could not find another job, no neighbors wanted his mother to sew for them, his sister lost her baby-sitting job, and his brother stopped his paper route because customers were not paying their bills. "I cut the price of shines to a nickel, but it didn't help much," Texas said.

The big trouble—the Depression—engulfed the family. They began living on mush, staying in bed all day when it was cold. Texas left home to get a job with a man in Forth Worth whom his mother thought would help. "But he was as hard up as anybody else. I didn't want to return home and pick bread off the kids' plate, so I tried to get work from a farmer for my board. Instead I got a ride to California. Near Salinas I worked in the lettuce fields, cutting and washing lettuce. I made $32 and I sent $10 home. But that was my first and last paycheck. I got chased out of California in June. . . . Since then I just been traveling."[17]

Jenny's father, a Hungarian immigrant in Pennsylvania, was promised a lifetime job by his company after he was crippled in an industrial accident; but when the big trouble came, they laid him off. Then her mother, who cleaned office buildings at night, collapsed and died. "Dad tried to keep a home for the four of us kids. . . . But what could he do? I was willing to work but nobody hired me and the rest of the kids were too young. So a home took the three kids, my married sister in Allentown took my father, and I just sort of scrammed. . . . I never had much chance to go to school or anything, and I wish I could learn a trade, but hell, I'll get by."[18]

Often troubles at home had included worries other than

money. Al was raised by grandparents. He didn't know much about his father and barely remembered his mother. "My mother never came to visit us after she left for Pittsburgh when I was a little baby during the war." After his grandparents died, he stayed at different places near home, and than "I scrammed for California. On the way I had some hard luck in Texas." Al lost a leg between two boxcars in Texas; he had made himself an efficient peg leg and said that being crippled was an asset when panhandling.[19]

Hank went to live with his aunt when his new stepfather didn't want him. His aunt tried to be nice, but not his uncle. "You know he was always throwing hints—saying how it was hard enough for a man to support his own kids, and asking me every day how old I was and then acting surprised when I'd say "Sixteen" and shaking his head and saying 'Sixteen! God, I was earning my own living when I was twelve!' " So Hank went on the road.[20]

California: War and a Population Explosion

World War II ended the peripatetic existence of Minehan's migrants and of families like the Joads. Able-bodied men went off to fight, war industries boomed, and the unemployment problem disappeared for the duration.

In California there were more jobs than there were people to fill them. The state became a center of the wartime aircraft and shipbuilding industries, and numerous military bases were situated there as well. In the early 1940s workers from all parts of the country—especially the South—poured into California, where women as well as men could enjoy the double satisfaction of performing their patriotic duty at a good rate of pay. Rosie the Riveter was celebrated in song.

Then the war ended, and with it the war jobs. Old-time residents assumed that those war workers would all go home and life would return to normal; but "normal" meant bigger now, for the workers stayed. On top of that, soldiers returned to their homes in California and went back to work, and other servicemen who had been stationed in California during the war returned after discharge, often bringing with them wives and children; if they found jobs, their brothers, sisters, and parents might join them in the years to come. Although women workers in

California left the job market in great numbers after the war to embark on the suddenly sacred occupation of raising three or four children, their departure alone could not balance the number of people seeking jobs with the number of jobs available. By 1949 the unemployment rate in California was 14 percent, double the national rate.[21]

The high unemployment was part of an accelerated western migration. In the first quarter of 1949, the three westernmost states—California, Oregon, and Washington—had one-fifth of the nation's unemployed. California had the greatest unemployment because of the continuing intensity of its migratory onslaught. In 1949 California had more than ten million people. By 1964 it had passed the eighteen-million mark, edging out New York (population leader since 1820) as the state with the most people. In 1974 California had nearly twenty-one million residents. The state had doubled its population in twenty-five years. Although new industries opened continuously during those years and services kept expanding, there were always more people than there were jobs for them.

But the myth of California's endless economic opportunities lived on. Apparently no one gave out the advice "Don't go west, young man or woman, unless you have highly marketable skills or plenty of money. The frontier days are over."

The 1947 California Study of Transient Youth

In the early 1940s California became concerned about the numbers of young transients who were entering the state. The governor appointed a youth committee to consider such questions as: "Is California being flooded by ne'er-do-wells and incorrigibles who in any event should be sent packing to their homes?"

World War II interrupted the inquiry, but in 1947 a special subcommittee made a study of transient youths.[22] For two days the personnel at eighteen border-patrol stations kept tabs on the numbers of people aged 18 to 22 who came into the state without parents (1335); while in fifteen cities, social agencies, including the police, asked the 1079 transients who came into their offices on those two days to fill out questionnaires.

The resulting data showed that these migrants were not "ne'er-do-wells and incorrigibles"; instead, they were typical American youths from the lower economic echelons. Three-fourths were white, and they came from every state but from predominantly urban backgrounds; only one in ten came from a rural area. Their average age was 19. Most of them were looking for work or fleeing from an unhappy home situation; often they were doing both. They chose California over other states because of its reputation for a mild climate and excellent job opportunities.

At that time unemployment was higher in California than in most of the states they had left, and these migrants had little going for them: Less than half had completed high school, and "little more than one in five was reported as having any training for a vocation, or having acquired any specific skill that might make a living for himself or herself, although three out of four had had some sort of job before leaving home."[23]

The results of the survey were printed in a report called *Transient Youth in California* (1948) with the telling subtitle "A National, State, and Local Problem." The report stressed that transient youths needed increased services rather than restraints.

Services, however, take money and effort, and neither social workers nor transient youths had much political clout. Assured by the report that transient youths were not a criminal threat to California, the state ignored them. The report was filed and forgotten.

The Hippies—A New Kind of Transient

California and other states continued to ignore migrant youths until the mid-Sixties, when a different kind of youth took to the road. They were called "hippies."* Their appearance created such an uproar in America that, at the height of their prominence, they received more publicity in a week than all the earlier young migrants had received collectively in a century.

The hippies startled the nation by rejecting the tenets of the American dream. Instead of searching for the dream, they were fleeing from it. They contradicted America's value system by saying that money was not important and material possessions would not bring happiness. The credo of the hippies was particularly upsetting to the nation because these young people came from families that had made it into the upper third of society in terms of income and had provided their children with the comforts,

---

* The word "hippie" was a variation of "hipster," the self-proclaimed outcast of the "beat generation," idealized by Norman Mailer in *The White Negro* (1957).

privileges, and opportunities that other Americans were striving to achieve. They came, in short, from the affluent society.

In a nation of 220 million people, a third of the population is a sizable chunk. It is roughly 70 million people, larger than the population of Britain, enough to form a society within a society. But this division, it should be noted in passing, leaves 140 million other Americans in the nonaffluent category.

Members of the affluent society in America come predominantly from what we call the "middle class"; but the upper third of the nation also includes people who are above the middle class economically—those smaller groups (decreasing in numbers as we approach the apex of wealth) that are variously called "upper-middle-class," "upper-class," or the "super-rich." In order to encompass all members of the affluent society and distinguish their children from the young migrants who form the main subject of Part One, we need a term other than "middle-class."

A new word, "optionaires," makes this distinction. Optionaires are defined as people who grew up in the affluent society—that is, the upper third of the nation—and have options in life and privileges in society as a result of their upbringing. (For more information about the optionaires, see Chapter 11.)

Only a small segment of the nation's young optionaires rebelled against the American dream in the 1960s; the segment that did rebel became the hippies. The hippies dropped out of the mainstream by choice, but they did not risk their futures when they deserted the Establishment, because they walked away already equipped with the skills and know-how that would allow them to reenter at a later date. Most of them had good verbal skills, some higher education, access to money, and contacts (through their families) in the Establishment.

If some hippies kept themselves spaced out on drugs for a while, it was because they chose to do so. Life-style was a matter of personal decision, selected from the panoply of options and opportunities that beckoned. They opted to become hippies; but if they changed their minds at any time, they could return to their parents' homes, accept a job, go back to college, travel around Europe for a while, or fly off to get high in Katmandu.

The times also played a role in their rebellion. The hippie movement flourished in the 1960s, a period when the national economy seemed destined to boom forever. Incessant prosperity was one of the Establishment fixtures that the hippies were rebelling against. In those days no one dreamed that in a few years industries would be laying off workers regularly, newly trained schoolteachers would find themselves a surplus commodity, cities like New York and Cleveland would be struggling to stave off bankruptcy, and prices would skyrocket in a seemingly endless spiral of inflation. But that is getting ahead of our story.

The Haight-Ashbury District—Hippie Capital of the World

Between 1965 and 1969 the hippie movement flourished in enclaves that sprang up across the country, in Europe, and beyond. In time, small groups of optionaires in virtually every industrialized nation identified with the hippies and formed a similar movement of their own.* But the epicenter of the hippie movement was San Francisco, where a once obscure neighborhood near Golden Gate Park—the Haight-Ashbury district—suddenly emerged as the hippie capital of the world. It became so famous that in the summer of 1967 an estimated 100,000 young people poured into the Haight-Ashbury district. Close behind them was an army of reporters, photographers, and television cameramen ready to record the hippies' every movement and opinion.

Although the hippies differed from previous migrant-youth groups in terms of family background and economic goals, those who came to California shared some geographic characteristics with their predecessors. They, too, came largely from urban centers in the eastern half of the United States; and they, too, viewed California as a magic territory where they could forge a new life, divorced from what they had known before.

The hippies arrived in the Haight-Ashbury district expecting to develop a society based on the humanitarian ethos of brotherhood and love, a utopia where money and social status would be irrelevant. In keeping with their goal of eradicating every trace of the hated Establishment from their midst, they set up their own social agencies—called "alternative agencies"—to help one another. The Haight-Ashbury Switchboard, founded in the summer of 1967, served as a prototype for hundreds of other alternative agencies that opened in America and abroad during the next few years.

* The word "optionaire" also refers to people in the middle classes and above in other countries, but there are likely to be fewer of them; less than a third of the citizens of most countries fall into the optionaire category.

The original aim of alternative agencies such as the Haight-Ashbury Switchboard was to provide social services for fellow hippies who'd opted for a new life-style. A few years later, however, a recession hit the United States and the hippie movement evaporated as former hippies quietly melted back into the Establishment. But the remaining alternative agencies found that they still had plenty of clients, although they were different from the hippies. Their clients were poor, but not by choice. They were the new migrants.

The new migrants had been around throughout the hippie period, but only a handful of people had noticed them.

CHAPTER FOUR

The New Migrants

The new migrants have remained so obscure that there is no adequate terminology to describe them; but without terms it is difficult to explain their situations clearly and differentiate the groups of young adults from the nonaffluent society who are now on the move. A few definitions and pigeonholes are necessary.

People, of course, do not fit into pigeonholes as neatly as pigeons, so there will be some overlap; to those few who work with the new migrants, the definitions that follow may seem oversimplified. But just as a painter may distinguish two dozen shades in the spectrum between red and purple, to the child first learning colors, "red" and "purple" are useful designations; and if the child does not pursue a career in art, he may never need to distinguish two dozen shades. To follow the analogy a step further, those who recognize red and purple are unlikely to mistake them for yellow and green; perhaps readers who learn about the new migrants will no longer categorize them as hippies, bums, or affluent dropouts.

Who Are the New Migrants?

At the end of Chapter 3 we divided the United States into two socioeconomic divisions—the affluent society (the upper third) and the nonaffluent society (the lower two-thirds). The new migrants are transient youths from the nonaffluent society.

They are young adults, 18 to 30, from working-class or poor homes, without marketable skills or college training, who leave their communities hoping and expecting to find jobs and a better life somewhere else. This definition fits at least 60 percent of the new migrants.*

The remaining 40 percent form two subgroups within the broad category of new migrants: street people and borderliners.

The street people, who comprise perhaps 15 percent of the new migrants, are deeply alienated individuals who harbor a strong hatred of the Establishment; some are loners who cannot fit into any group. Most street people are unemployable in the current labor market.

The borderliners, at the other end of the spectrum, grew up near the border that separates the affluent and nonaffluent societies; they expected to become affluent as adults. Borderliners, who make up about 25 percent of the new migrants, may have a year or more of college and some marketable skills. Their self-esteem and expectations are higher than those of other new migrants. When borderliners left their homes during the 1960s, they assumed that their options were as great as those of the affluent hippies. But they soon learned otherwise.

Age: Juveniles Not Included

The term "young migrants" refers to people who are legally old enough to be on their own and support themselves—who, in fact, are expected to do so by society. In most states the legal age of adulthood is 18. Younger people (juveniles) are also on the road, but they have a special legal problem, because juveniles are supposed to be under the care of parents or guardians who are required by law to support them. The juvenile on the road is considered a runaway and is breaking the law, regardless of the circumstances that caused him or her to leave home. Thus the situation of juvenile migrants is a separate subject, not within our purview here.

Many new migrants left home when they were still juveniles, but our interest in them here begins when they reach the age of 18 and are transformed overnight by law from teen-agers too

---

* The percentages given here are not statistical data—none exist—but impressionistic estimates to give a general picture of the people who make up the new migrants.

young to be self-supporting into adults who are expected to work. It should also be noted that the marked increase of runaways during the hippie period has long since subsided; there are still runaways, but the new migrants on the move greatly outnumber them.

Racial Makeup

Most new migrants come from urban areas, and most are white.* In small hotels in downtown slum areas, in dilapidated apartment houses scattered throughout our major cities, in vast housing projects, old duplexes, and tiny houses that somehow escaped the developer's bulldozer, poor white people live in our cities along with those who are black and brown. They are less noticeable, because discrimination does not force them to live crowded together in designated areas with other poor whites; but they exist.

On the periphery of cities, there are even more whites from the bottom of the working class who are barely making it. Our cities are ringed with small towns that were incorporated into growing metropolises, and with layer after layer of suburbs. Some suburbs have stately homes, but many more consist of drab, low-cost tract houses in endless subdivisions. Some children who grew up in crackerbox tract houses are not finding the jobs they need to purchase their own little boxes, so they are leaving home. They are not as poor as blacks living in the inner cities, but they are as far from the world of the affluent society as a peasant from a king. Yet the mythology of the American dream tantalizes them with promises of kingly riches if they seek opportunity and persevere in their quest.

The fact that young people from the "Third World" (as blacks and members of other nonwhite groups in America are referred to in the current vernacular) are in the minority among new migrants may seem surprising in view of the fact that black teenagers have the highest rate of unemployment in the nation. One reason for their smaller participation in the migration relates to the American dream—they are less likely to believe in it.

Inherent in the peripatetic existence of the new migrants is the

* The number of nonwhite new migrants increased throughout the 1970s. (See p. 250.)

belief that life *can* be better somewhere else. But urban blacks and other nonwhites who have grown up in poverty often lack that optimism. They cannot believe that other cities will offer them more than where they are now. Didn't their parents or grandparents once head north with that illusion? Whenever they leave the ghetto, they encounter prejudice. At home, however dismal their futures, they are likely to be part of a family and a familiar community where they feel accepted; they may also belong to a close-knit group of their peers.

Thus, if they tend toward activism, they are more likely to work on local projects or do politicking near home, as the Black Panthers did in Oakland. If they hang out on the street, the streets are usually near home—in Chicago, New York, Detroit, Philadelphia, Los Angeles. If they migrate, it may not be far: from Newark to Manhattan, from Oakland to San Francisco. They seek jobs in the nearby big cities—the cities where experienced older workers may already be facing layoffs and where new migrants with white faces are also arriving daily from both near and far.

Two Centers of the New Migrants

From the mid-1960s through the 1970s, the new migrants clustered in two centers: hippie enclaves and central-city slums. The hippie enclaves were the centers of the hippie movement and included special areas like the Haight-Ashbury district in San Francisco and the village of Woodstock, New York, which became a hippie center after a famous music festival of that name was held some fifty miles away. Most hippie enclaves, however, grew up around large universities, in places like Ann Arbor, Michigan; Austin, Texas; Berkeley, California; Boulder, Colorado; Cambridge, Massachusetts; and the area around New York University in Manhattan's East Village.

The central-city slums were the downtown slum areas in large metropolitan areas, which have the cheapest housing facilities in town, as well as a tradition of absorbing society's outsiders and the poor. New migrants of Third World origin generally came here rather than to the hippie enclaves.

By 1980 the migrant population of nonaffluent youths in search of work was so firmly anchored in the central-city slums that the memory of sizable groups of new migrants in the former hippie enclaves seemed like ancient history. But to understand the new migrants, we must look back at the days when they did frequent the hippie enclaves in large numbers. For that is where they were first recognized as being different from the affluent hippies around them. They were noticed in Berkeley, California, and at first they were called by a different name.

THE EVOLUTION OF THE NEW MIGRANTS

Berkeley, California, a quiet university town that had long enjoyed a reputation as a scholarly oasis, erupted into political action in the early 1960s, when hundreds of students joined the Free Speech Movement (FSM) to protest the impersonality of the multiversity system and press for reform. In December 1964, Berkeley made national and international headlines when police arrested 733 FSM demonstrators on the campus. The student activism kindled at Berkeley caught on and spread across the nation and beyond. But for a few years after the FSM, Berkeley remained the center.

In those years, although Berkeley attracted many students who were interested in political change, especially in ending the Vietnam War and extending civil rights to all Americans regardless of skin color, the city soon attracted even more young people who were not students at the university and who had little interest in politics. Instead, they sought personal fulfillment. They were the hippies, and, as noted earlier, their appearance attracted widespread attention from the media because they came largely from affluent homes and had rejected the American dream and vociferously disparaged its values of the Establishment. And they took drugs.

The four blocks of Telegraph Avenue that adjoined the Berkeley campus became a popular hippie enclave. Soon the area was so crowded, and the problem of feeding and housing the new transients so manifest, that various groups of Berkeley citizens began going down to the Avenue to help out. To their surprise, they discovered that large numbers of the nonstudent transients on Telegraph Avenue did not fit the media image of the hippie dropout at all. To the contrary, these young people were genuinely down-and-out, they had little education, and they apparently came from homes well below the middle class. They seemed more like pushed-outs than dropouts.

This newly identified group was dubbed "the street people," because they lived and often slept on the street. They were, in fact, the same people that this book calls the new migrants. When alternative agencies opened near Telegraph Avenue to feed the hungry, find crash housing for them, and provide medical care, this nonaffluent group of migrants, who had few resources, were among the heaviest users of these services.

Alternative Agencies

Although the Haight-Ashbury Switchboard in San Francisco was started by hippies, alternative agencies in Berkeley, as in most university communities and in some central-city slums, were started mainly by community residents to provide emergency facilities for the penniless young people who kept arriving in their cities. Strictly speaking, these services were not "alternative," because they did not exist before for this population. But the name "alternative agencies" caught on, and provides a useful label here.

In Berkeley, which again is typical in this regard, the alternative agencies near the campus were founded largely by ministers, university professors, businessmen who had stores along Telegraph Avenue, and a variety of other Berkeley citizens from the affluent society. Most agencies were located near the campus in the basements of churches whose liberal members were receptive to projects that helped the street people. One church, the University Lutheran Chapel, housed the Emergency Food Project, a supper program that served as the location for the one major study of the street population in the 1970s.

The Baumohl-Miller Study

Professor Henry Miller of Berkeley's School of Social Welfare and Jim Baumohl, then a graduate student with several years' experience working with the transient population on Telegraph Avenue, did the study together. During the week of March 26–30, 1973, they surveyed 295 people who ate supper at the Food Project at least one night and were willing to fill out a questionnaire about themselves in return for a special dessert of pie and ice cream supplied by the researchers. (The regular supper, which cost 25 cents or a work shift in the kitchen, always had fruit for dessert.) Using the questionnaires, whose answers were tabulated by computer, the researchers also selected a smaller group at random who were interviewed in depth, and paid $2 for their time. The results of the study revealed what many people in Berkeley had known for years: that the street people—that is, the new migrants—were different from the hippies.[1]

Nearly three-quarters of Baumohl and Miller's subjects came from the nonaffluent society. Asked to identify their fathers' occupations on the scale devised by the U.S. Census Bureau, 25.5 percent classified their fathers as unskilled or service workers, 49.2 percent checked one of the categories for blue-collar and other skilled workers, and the remaining quarter had fathers in one of the professional or business categories.[2]

Their average age was 22; 19 percent were female, 81 percent were male; 89 percent were white, 11 percent black, the remainder a sprinkling of Chicano-Latinos, North American Indians, and Asians.

They came from every state, but especially from the eastern half of the country; nearly 40 percent came from cities in New York, New Jersey, Pennsylvania, Ohio, Illinois, and Michigan. Comparing their home states with those of the migrants whom Thomas Minehan studied in 1933, we find a remarkable similarity: Five out of the six states listed as the most frequent states of origin were identical in both studies. (New Jersey had replaced Texas.) Forty years later, young migrants to California were still coming predominantly from the large industrial cities of the East and the Midwest.

Although 79.7 percent of the subjects had retained contact with their families—usually a tenuous contact, such as an occasional letter or phone call—returning home permanently was rarely a viable option. "Slightly less than half (48.5%) indicate that their parents would allow them to come home and live with them, and only 6.5% of the subjects express any intention or desire to do so. It seems that, for better or worse, street people are on their own."

In education, the people surveyed at the Food Project were below the national average. While 6 percent had completed two years of college and 9 percent were college graduates, 27.2 percent had ended their schooling with high-school graduation, and 32.5 percent had not finished high school. They generally had less education than their fathers.

Nearly two-thirds of the people in the survey lived on $100 a

month or less. Common sources of money were friends and panhandling. Welfare accounted for the income of 15.8 percent, and
2.5 percent were receiving unemployment compensation, while
13.3 percent had jobs, including part-time work. Of those with
jobs, "81.3 percent worked only at short-term or casual-labor
jobs, never being employed for longer than a few months at a
time." Among those without jobs, 77.3 percent said they had re-
peatedly tried to get work in the past year but without success.

In evaluating the results of their study, Baumohl and Miller
said:

> Today when even college graduates have difficulty finding
> employment, street people appear to have grim occupational
> futures. From our canvass of subjects' occupational endeav-
> ors, we glimpsed how ominous their futures might be. Street
> people are, with few exceptions, unemployed, and more sig-
> nificantly, unemployable in the context of today's labor
> market. Their employment has been part-time, unskilled,
> erratic or episodic in nature. Most are dependent on a fast
> disappearing casual labor market. The sad fact is that they
> have little in the way of marketable skills, and without ref-
> erences or "presentable attire," have few salable virtues.
>   . . . In short, our subjects are cut off from this country's
> primary source of personal income.[3]

THE STREET PEOPLE

In the years after the Baumohl-Miller study, the meaning of the
term "street people" gradually changed. Originally a general
term for new migrants, it became a specialized one that described
the 15 percent of "hard-core" street people—that is, the most
deeply alienated (and in some cases mentally disturbed) people on the street. Today this usage is prevalent in former hippie
enclaves throughout the United States.

Although street people come predominantly from the nonaffluent society, a handful of former hippies also remained on the
streets and became street people. These hippies, who came from
well-to-do homes in some cases, were too alienated or disturbed to
return to the mainstream. They were often well educated and
highly articulate and their presence has contributed to the mis-
conception that the street people are ex-hippies.

The current street people appear to be greater in number than they are, because they remain on the street day after day, year in and year out. They live there. If they find housing, it is usually temporary, like crashing in a new friend's hotel room until their welcome wears out, or staying in an emergency shelter or hostel for a few nights, in cities where such facilities exist, when the weather is bad and they can scrape together the small fee. But most often they sleep on the streets. They live by scrounging, panhandling, drug dealing, and occasional odd jobs. It is rare for them to receive General Assistance or food stamps—either they are too opposed to the Establishment to accept it, or they are ineligible because they have no address or rent receipt, and no cooking facilities. Their hostility to organized groups, including alternative agencies in many cases, cuts them off from any chance of aid.

Today's street people are predominantly male and they are largely unemployable. Even if they want to work full time and get off the streets, they cannot in most cases. Who would hire them? Perhaps a third of the street people are chronically disoriented and go in and out of mental hospitals and sometimes jails. Street people may eventually get on Supplemental Security Income (SSI), a federal/state program for the permanently disabled, and receive enough money to rent a small hotel room. Some street people are alcoholics or heavy drug users and resemble the "winos" of Skid Row; the difference is that the street people are generally in their twenties or early thirties.

The street people have no faith in anybody. If they ever dreamed of making it, such dreams faded long ago.

THE NEW MIGRANTS

The new migrants, to the contrary, are eager to make it; they left home with economic advancement squarely on their minds. They may also dream of a life-style different from that of their parents —as many young people their ages do; but what pushes the new migrants onto the road is the belief that they will find better opportunities to make a good living in another part of the country. This section will explore the main group of new migrants, who will now be called simply "the new migrants."

New migrants are generally high-school dropouts or high-school graduates; they rarely have even a year at a community college behind them. Their lack of language skills, both written and verbal, and their frequently low self-esteem mean that the dearth of options that stymied them at home follows them wherever they go. When the new migrants compete with borderliners for jobs, as they frequently do these days, the borderliners consistently win.

In good times, employers may hesitate to hire someone who is overeducated or overqualified for a job, afraid that their new employee will soon get bored and leave to seek more challenging and interesting work—and higher pay. But when challenging and interesting jobs are at such a premium that college graduates are fighting to get them, employers can hire a borderliner for a routine job with impunity, knowing that the overqualified employee is likely to stay, bored or not. The employers, in essence, get more for their money by hiring a borderliner.

For the new migrants, this means that the kinds of jobs that were once their province—waiters/waitresses, salespeople, bus drivers, file clerks, and the like—may no longer be available to them. In the former hippie enclaves they compete with borderliners (and today with recent college graduates as well), while in the cities they compete with the much larger numbers of people with a year or two of college who never left home. In both cases, the new migrants are being pushed out of unskilled jobs by those with more education and poise.

But unlike the street people, the new migrants are not ready to give up. Assured by the dream that if they persevere they will eventually succeed, they keep moving, always hoping that in the next city they will make it.

Stan and Margaret Watson

Stan and Margaret Watson (not their real names) are new migrants.* They have been trying to make it for years.

Those who saw the Watsons in Venice, California, in the late 1960s at the height of the hippie period probably assumed they were ideological dropouts who had fled from wealthy parents: Stan had long hair and a beard, while Margaret wore long skirts and kept her babies nearby when she took her turn at the switchboard of the communal house where they lived for a while.

---

* All information about the "Watsons" is drawn from author's interviews with "Margaret Watson."

Actually, both came from families firmly rooted in the non-affluent society. Margaret's mother quit high school to marry, but her husband deserted the family when Margaret was eight months old. She worked at whatever job she could find and married again—three times. Margaret found life with her last stepfather so difficult that she ran away when she was 14, obtained a false ID, and got a job. She met Stan and married him before she was 16.

Stan's parents came from the bottom ranges of the nonaffluent society. After his parents divorced, Stan's mother married a man who was an alcoholic and seldom worked. The family moved from city to city, settling into abandoned houses until they were discovered and thrown out. Stan began working at 12; at 14 he was a steeplejack in the Oklahoma oil fields. As soon as he was old enough, Stan joined the army to get away from his family. When he got out and married Margaret, he always found some kind of job because of his skills and experience. But after their two daughters were born, the pay was never enough. The family kept moving, hoping to find a better job elsewhere, perhaps on the West Coast.

In Oregon, Stan hurt his back on the job and could no longer do strenuous work. He got workmen's compensation until a new doctor, noting his long hair and beard, started screaming about longhairs cheating the government, and said there was nothing wrong with Stan's back. The workmen's compensation stopped.

The Watsons knew nothing about legal appeals; they didn't even know they could appeal. And they couldn't turn to their parents for help: Margaret's mother, who had left her husband, was a clerk at Sears and had a child at home. Stan rarely saw his parents—and besides, they had less money than he did. So the Watsons packed their children and their belongings into the car and headed for California.

They came to Berkeley, where an alternative agency helped them find temporary housing in a summer youth hostel. The Watsons and their daughters often ate supper at the Food Project, and Stan found some one-day odd jobs to tide them over while he looked for full-time work. When the summer hostel closed and Stan still had no job, the staff at the alternative agency suggested that the Watsons go on welfare so they would have a place to live while he job-hunted. They rented a tiny apartment, their daughters started school, and Stan continued applying for jobs. He hoped to start a new career in light assembly work, perhaps electronics. But his background in heavy labor and his frequent changes of address and job did not impress employers who already had plenty of job applications from longtime residents of Oakland, Richmond, and surrounding suburbs.

The Watsons liked Berkeley and wanted to settle there, but when spring came and Stan still had no job, they grew discouraged. Then some people they met told them that jobs were easy to find in Utah. They packed their children and their belongings into the car and headed north. No one in Berkeley has heard from them since.

THE BORDERLINERS

Borderliners have more education and skills than the average new migrant. Their parents, who worked in white-collar or unionized blue-collar occupations for the most part, expected their children to make it into affluence. Their children had the same expectations, although some of them did not realize it at first.

In the late 1960s and early 1970s, many borderliners left college after a year or two under the influence of the hippie movement or the counterculture movement that grew out of it. When borderliners went on the road, often they were not concerned about making a living, the way the new migrants were, because borderliners took it for granted that a good job would await them when they were ready to work.

Some borderliners were looking for fulfillment outside the Establishment; others were enjoying a space of freedom and travel between school and the job world. Their reasons for going on the road were as varied as the people themselves, but eventually they found themselves at the same terminus. The day came when they had traveled enough. They decided to take a job. To their amazement, they could not find a good full-time job.

Around 1973, alternative agencies began to notice an increase in the number of borderliners who were turning up at their offices for help. Some were almost in shock. These young people had been indoctrinated with the belief that, in the United States, anyone who really wanted to work could find a job. They had accepted it as gospel. The realization that unemployment could be more than a statistic in the newspaper overwhelmed some of them.

For their parents, the situation was even harder to accept. Mom and Dad had looked for jobs twenty-five years earlier, during the postwar boom. They made it, so why couldn't Betty and John? "It's because they smoke marijuana," said Mom. "They're bums," said Dad.

Borderliners are chameleons of circumstances. When times are good, as in the 1950s and early 1960s, with a little effort they manage to sprint over the border into optionaire affluence. They think they will stay there forever, and that their children and their children's children will continue the thrust of upward mobility. When times are bad, their children (or they themselves) may be tossed back to the other side.

Individual initiative will of course determine to some extent who gets tossed back, but the nation's economic situation—especially the availability of jobs—is an equally crucial factor. Yet, in the perspective of the American dream, borderliners are viewed as people whose fate will be wholly determined by their own efforts. Awareness of borderliners and their precarious position remains scant; the borderliners themselves had little understanding of their predicament when they first left home.

Henry

Henry is a borderliner who grew up in Chicago.* His father, an appliance salesman in a large department store, and his mother, who stayed home with the children, realized that Henry was the brightest of their three children and they made sacrifices to send Henry through college; he would become a professional and buy a large house in the Chicago suburbs with a spacious lawn for their future grandchildren to play on, they thought.

Henry, a shy, introverted person, had other ideas. As soon as he got his degree, he headed for Berkeley; he planned to teach English in a private school for a while and then get a Ph.D. at the university and become a college professor.

But Henry couldn't find a teaching job in Berkeley, or in any of the surrounding communities he tried—and when he got to know students on campus, he learned that people with doctorates in English were as much in demand as the mumps. For several years he did a variety of jobs—selling, general handyman, paint-

* Information in this section is drawn from author's interviews with "Henry."

ing houses. When he was nearly thirty he took up cabinetmaking, "by a process of elimination," as he puts it. He found that he had a special skill for the work and became an excellent cabinetmaker.

By now Henry was married and had a son. But although he worked full-time at cabinetmaking (when he could get enough jobs) and his wife worked part time, together they could not earn enough money to rent a small house with a lawn in back for their son to play on. Nor could they look forward to a day when they would have more. They were, and are, cemented to an income just above the poverty level.

Henry's parents are disappointed that he did not become a professional or an executive. They are appalled that, with a college degree, Henry earns less than his father. What went wrong with Henry? they ask one another over the dinner table.

One guesses, from Henry's quiet, gentle manner, that this is a man who has accepted his fate and his country as they are. But he is bitter. His visits to spacious houses in the Berkeley hills where he installs his custom-made cabinets reinforce the gulf between their owners' standard of living and his. Asked what he sees as the solution to the economic problems of people like himself, he replies calmly, "I think a revolution is the only answer." Henry has no confidence that the optionaires who run the government will yield to his needs of their own accord.

Henry does not belong to any revolutionary group. In his spare time he writes poetry. But he smiles with satisfaction when he reads in the newspapers that some terrorist group has blown up a bank or threatened the lives of industrialists.

The Borderliners Settle In

Borderliners no longer expect opportunity to await them; the rough times of the late 1970s have dissolved the rosy haze through which they once viewed the future. They know they are "caught in the job scrunch," as one person put it. Although they win out over new migrants for routine jobs, when they seek more interesting, well-paid work they find themselves in a losing competition with optionaires from the affluent society—graduates of prestigious universities whose parents can and do pull a few strings if necessary to secure desirable jobs for their children.

Many borderliners have settled in and around the former

hippie enclaves, where they rent apartments or have other stable living arrangements. Borderliners live as couples—married or not—with or without children, as heads of single-parent families or, less frequently, alone or communally.

Those who remain in the former hippie enclaves eventually do find jobs as postmen, waitresses, salesclerks, craftspeople, and the like. They manage to eke out a living in most cases, but their incomes remain well below the level of affluence. There is no way they will ever be able to save up enough money to buy their own homes, as—like most Americans—they dream of doing one day. Even opening a savings account is an accomplishment. They can scarcely cover the rent, food, shoes for the children, and other necessities on their monthly paychecks. They stay where they are because they don't know of other places in the country where they could find better-paying jobs.

They are disappointed—sometimes, like Henry, they deeply resent the economic straitjacket into which they are strapped—yet borderliners rarely become active radicals; at least they have not thus far. Most of them are too caught up in the daily routine of living and working to have energy left for political action. Besides, they have lost their earlier idealism.

Their lives are a far cry from what they originally envisioned, and eons away from their parents' expectations; yet the borderliners get by. They have jobs, apartments, and enough money for their basic needs—assets that the new migrants may not enjoy.

These days fewer borderliners go on the road in the first place. It is the new migrants who still leave home in sizable numbers, because the areas where they grew up have so little to offer them. They now head for the big cities.

CHAPTER FIVE

Job Hunting
in the City

When the new migrants arrive in an unfamiliar city, they cannot check into the Hyatt-Regency or even into middle-priced hotels geared to tourists and traveling salesmen. Having little or no money, they must go to the section of the city that has the lowest prices for food and lodgings. And, they soon learn, they must go where they will not stand out as anomalies—where hotel doormen will not turn up their noses as they pass and policemen will not eye them suspiciously for simply being on the streets. They must go to the area that is found in every city—the central-city slum.

In some cities, such districts were once the Hobohemias of yesterday's migrant workers; the districts may be called "Skid Row" because of the high incidence of alcoholism among its permanent residents. Metropolitan areas generally have more than one central-city slum area, each attracting a different segment of the nation's outsiders.

San Francisco's Tenderloin district is the central-city slum where the new migrants cluster. Along with cheap hotels and short-order eateries, the Tenderloin also offers some free facilities and services of use to new migrants, such as a free lunch served by members of a religious order (set up for elderly homeless men but open to all), a branch of the state employment office, a day center for transient young adults, and an office of the Travelers Aid Society. The Tenderloin can serve as the prototype of central-city slum areas where new migrants gather in cities across the nation.

Long before the new migrants arrived, the Tenderloin had a steady population of people outside the mainstream of society. It was home to alcoholics and drug addicts; to elderly men and women existing on welfare or Social Security checks in small hotel rooms; to homosexuals rejected by their families; to former mental-hospital patients and paroled prisoners; and to Third World people who could never find jobs. It was the workplace of people whose jobs—as pimps, prostitutes, and hustlers—were outside the legally acceptable framework of employment. The Tenderloin housed people whom no other area wanted as neighbors, as well as those who could never scrape together enough money to pay their first and last months' rent plus a security deposit in advance for an apartment. Room rates in Tenderloin hotels were the lowest in town, payable by the day or at the economical weekly rate.

The new element in the Tenderloin in the 1960s and 1970s, as in its counterparts throughout the country, was the increased numbers of people under thirty who were moving in, young people who had never experienced affluence. Their major stigma was being down-and-out.

What happened in the 1960s to cause this great increase of young migrants who were similar in kind to the migrants studied by Outland and Minehan in the Thirties? The answer is the hippie movement. The media told us only about middle-class youngsters fleeing from middle-class values, but in fact, large numbers of the young people who were influenced to leave home by publicity about the hippie movement came from the non-affluent society. Hippie philosophy said that money and social position were not important; that people should live together as brothers and sisters, helping one another instead of competing. Such ideas were music to the ears of young people cemented to low-paying jobs in communities where they and their families were considered nobodies. Likewise the philosophy of the hippies appealed to young people who had serious problems at home and were looking for a way to escape the family nest. As with young migrants of previous generations, it was usually a combination of economic factors and family problems that caused the new migrants to head for a hippie enclave.*

---

* The Pittel-Miller study of middle-class hippies in the Haight-Ashbury who were heavy drug users showed that family problems also played a major role in causing young people from the affluent society to become hippies.

Why were the new migrants ignored by the media? It was not a conspiracy against them or even a deliberate exclusion. When reporters rushed into the Haight-Ashbury district or New York City's East Village in 1967 in search of a story, they were looking for hot copy. Their best material came from upper-middle-class dropouts—well-educated, articulate, angry young men (those quoted at length were usually male) who were as eager to expound their views as reporters were to record them. The well-phrased statements of these young men, filled with pungent jabs at the Establishment as well as ecstatic descriptions of communal living in hippieland, provided reporters with lively copy that readers and viewers devoured with gusto. The new migrants either were overlooked, or information gathered from them was discarded in favor of more interesting material.

The Travelers Aid Project for Transient Young Adults, 1966–68

A project for young adults in the Tenderloin, which ran from 1966 to 1968, provides a look at the migrant youth whom the media never mentioned.

When Marjorie Montelius became director of San Francisco's Travelers Aid in the 1960s, her first action was to move their office from the YMCA building into a run-down building in the Tenderloin, just off Market Street, an easy walk from the Greyhound bus depot. She wanted the agency to be less formidable and more accessible to the people who needed its services most. Montelius and her staff soon noticed that increasing numbers of young people were coming in for help, so she obtained a grant from a local foundation to run a special program for transient young adults.[1]

Travelers Aid kept records on 800 young people, aged 18 to 21. Of them, 75 percent were white and 65 percent had not completed high school. No Princeton or Harvard dropouts came to their office during those years, but they saw plenty of young people who had left low-paying jobs to head west. "The work history of almost all those seen had been in unskilled occupations: busboys or stockboys; waiters-waitresses; cook's helpers, domestics, factory workers, dishwashers; a small number were from more skilled occupations such as machinists, welders, drill press operators, telephone operators, clerical workers."[2]

Many Travelers Aid clients, especially those who arrived during the summer of 1967, went to the Haight-Ashbury district first. They expected to be welcomed into a commune, where they could live without the burdensome necessity of finding a job.

Some people from working-class backgrounds did find a niche in the Haight—those who were "street wise" or had flamboyant personalities or good verbal skills and plenty of self-confidence; but for most young migrants from the nonaffluent society, sanctuary in the Haight turned out to be one more dream that failed them. They were the prey of local hustlers and con artists who had a field day ripping off the naïve "flower children." After a few days in the Haight, the new migrants often turned up penniless at Travelers Aid in the Tenderloin, having learned that the hippie credo of caring and sharing was not meant for the likes of them.

These new migrants found themselves in the same position as other new migrants who came straight to the Tenderloin—less sophisticated youths who would have been terrified or repelled by the thought of going near Haight-Ashbury and meeting the infamous hippies face to face. Both groups of new migrants came from similar backgrounds and had similar economic aspirations: They wanted more out of life than a dead-end job with pay that would never rise much above the minimum wage. They believed that the West would offer them opportunities that were unavailable back home.

When they didn't find jobs in San Francisco, many new migrants moved on. Of the 800 young people in the Travelers Aid study, 608 (76 percent) had already moved more than once before they came to San Francisco, and 91 of them had been in at least six places previously. Montelius characterized their flight as "the constant search of the undereducated and the unskilled for the job they know exists for them somewhere."[3]

New Migrants at Travelers Aid in the 1970s

By 1973, more than half the people who came to the Travelers Aid office in San Francisco for help were between 18 and 30 years old. That trend has continued.

Cathie Greene, casework supervisor at Travelers Aid, interviews many of the new migrants. She is amazed that people still regard San Francisco as a good place to look for jobs. "They simply don't realize that San Francisco is a very unionized city." Even those with past experience in a skilled trade, such as construction work, will have difficulty finding a job in San Francisco, she says, because local men in the unions are already competing for the available jobs. But the great majority of her clients have no skilled trade. Says Greene:

"The people we see are marginal in every sense of the word. We see more and more people who are truly desperate in many basic ways. They're not on the road for a lark; they want jobs. But often they lack the most elementary knowledge about what to say at a job interview to make a good impression, or how to dress. They have little education, perhaps eighth to tenth grade. Some will put down that they've finished high school, and maybe they have, but they can barely write well enough to fill out the forms."[4]

Greene mentioned a newspaper article with the headline "23 Million Incompetent Americans," which discussed results of research done by a team at the University of Texas. Their study showed that one in five American adults "lacks the basic know-how to function effectively in a complex society." The researchers found that 13 percent (15 million adults) could not address an envelope well enough to assure delivery by the postal service, and 14 percent (16.5 million adults) could not make out a personal check correctly enough for a bank to process it.[5]

"I can really get behind that article," she said, "because that's what we see every day. A large number of people who are invisible to most Americans are in deep trouble. Most of them would need a lot of help before they became employable in today's market."

In recent years, as the last vestige of hippie influence has disappeared, the percentage of young people of Third World origin who come to Travelers Aid has increased, especially the numbers of single, black males without training in any trade. The office has also seen more families traveling with small children, most often white families—married couples in their mid-twenties, or single parents, who thought they would find better economic opportunities out west.

Whatever the family constellation or the ethnic background of new migrants who come to the cities seeking work, they face special problems as migrants. In a nation that makes no provision to meet their special needs—that does not even acknowledge the existence of this population—the going can be rough.

PROBLEMS OF JOB HUNTING AS A NEW MIGRANT

The new migrant who looks for work in an unfamiliar city first of all has the same difficulties that unskilled and poorly educated residents face when they hunt for jobs on their home turf: Both generally lack "contacts" with the people in the Establishment who hand out jobs; they may not know how to fill out a job application, prepare a résumé, or present themselves in a favorable light during a job interview; and they may lack the skills and experience that available jobs require. Even if they have the required skills, the fact that they are unlikely to belong to a union (in many cases, they can't get into one) keeps many jobs out of their reach. But the new migrant additionally faces another set of problems.

At home even the poorest job hunter usually has a bed and a meal of some sort available. He has access to bathing and laundry facilities. He has an address, and often he has a telephone. If there is no telephone at home, some friend, relative, neighbor, or perhaps the man who runs the liquor store around the corner, may be willing to take messages from prospective employers who phone to say "You're hired."

The new migrant may have none of these. Call him Bill Jones. Bill, a single man in his early twenties, arrives in a new city hoping to find work quickly, because he is broke. But his lack of money may prevent his finding employment. It takes money to job-hunt.

In large cities the offices, factories, and institutions with job openings at any given time may be miles apart. If Bill has ten job interviews in one day, they may be in five or six different areas of the city. If he lacks the money for five sets of carfare and can't borrow it, he walks. (In some cases he may be able to hitchhike.)

If Bill is job-hunting in New York City, his first interview may be in the Wall Street area, the next in Queens or Brooklyn. In Chicago, one job opening may be in the Loop and another near the University of Chicago. In downtown Los Angeles, if Bill hears of an opening for a busboy at a restaurant in Woodland Hills out in the San Fernando Valley but he has no car, he might as well forget it. Even if he could borrow money for public transportation, by the time he arrived the job would be filled by someone who drove there or lived close by.

Within the central downtown sections of large cities, walking is feasible. But if it is windy, raining, or snowing, Bill may not look too good on arrival after a two-mile trek. He may not look presentable anyway if he hasn't changed clothes or taken a shower in more than a week because he has been sleeping in a doorway. And if he hasn't eaten anything but a loaf of bread and three apples in the past few days and feels like collapsing on his prospective employer's floor on arrival, the prospective employer is unlikely to be impressed with Bill's energy and verve. The employer may also be wary of that hacking cough that Bill has had for the past week.

But suppose an employer does decide to hire Bill for a casual-labor job that would give Bill enough money to rent a room and eat regularly? Where can the employer reach Bill if he lives on the streets? Alternative agencies provide some help here by serving as message centers, but their services are limited by their hours. Suppose the employer phones them and says, "Tell Bill Jones to be at my warehouse tomorrow morning at eight and I'll have a job for him." Bill has already stopped by the office that day to check for mail and messages. The office closes at 5:00 P.M. and won't reopen until 10:00 the next morning. No one knows where to find Bill, because he sleeps in the streets.

When Bill fails to show up for work the next morning by 8:30, the employer assumes that he has found another job or is unreliable, so he calls someone else—probably someone who lives at home. By the time Bill gets the message and arrives at the warehouse, the job is gone.

Basic requirements for the new migrant as job hunter are: a room with a bed; food; access to washing facilities for self and clothes; enough money for carfare and telephone calls, and for clothes that are presentable and protective; and access to a telephone, or at least a mailing address where the job hunter can be contacted.

How the new migrants can acquire these basics, and the consequences they may suffer without them, will be explored in chapters ahead. Now we turn to the question of where the new migrants can look for jobs in the city.

How and Where to Look for Jobs

The ways in which new migrants can find jobs are limited by their status as newcomers; many of the methods available to young people at home in their same age and education range will not be available to the new migrants.

If you queried a few hundred young adults in a metropolitan area who had grown up, finished high school, and found jobs in their home cities, their answers to the question "How did you get your job?" would evoke a wide variety of responses.

Typical replies of one type might be: "My aunt heard about an opening in her office and told my mother about it"; "My father worked in this factory for twenty years, so when I finished school I came here, too"; or "Our neighbor had a friend who was managing a hamburger place and needed a busboy."

In all the situations above, contacts played a significant role in helping the young person find work. The importance of contacts in job hunting cannot be overstressed. Whether the job is pumping gas or managing a hospital, knowing the right people—or having the right people know of you and your qualifications—is the easiest way to find a job; it is a method that is used regularly at all levels of the work pyramid. Indeed, sometimes people who are not qualified for a job, or who have fewer qualifications than other applicants, will be chosen because they know the right people. But the new migrant, who generally has no contacts whatsoever in an unfamiliar city, is cut off from this popular method of finding a job.

Contacts that come from courses taken in high school, or from part-time jobs that later expanded, account for a number of other full-time jobs that are filled by young people who live at home. Replies here might be: "I took the secretarial course in high school, and the teacher helped me find a job"; "This man visited our high school and said his company had openings for people with computer skills. I talked to him afterward; he said to take all the computer and math courses I could, and then come to see him when I graduated. So I did"; or "I used to work on Saturdays as a stockboy in a large grocery store; when I finished school they offered me a full-time job as checker."

A handful of people might have been successful using the direct approach: "I just walked into this large office and asked if they had a job for me. By luck, one of the file clerks had announced an hour earlier that her husband was being transferred and she was leaving. I got her job." The chances of new migrants using this method successfully are much smaller; they will not know of the existence or locations of large offices, factories, or institutions in the area that have frequent job openings. If new migrants make the rounds of restaurants and stores in the area where they are staying, they will be canvassing the same territory that other new migrants, as well as unemployed local residents, are trying.

Answering employment ads in the newspapers is yet another method of job hunting that may prove fruitful for many young people at home. Newspaper ads are also a possibility for the new migrant, except that the costs involved may be prohibitive for those with little or no money. Not only must they buy a newspaper every day, but they will also need a ready supply of change for telephone calls to answer the ads, and bus or subway fare to get to job interviews. Young people job-hunting from the family home can check the newspaper to which their parents subscribe and get right on the family phone to apply for the jobs they want before others get to them. If they can borrow Daddy's car for the job interview, they are almost certain to edge out any new migrant who applies for the same job.

Finally, employment agencies may be the vehicle through which many young adults at home find jobs. For the new migrant, an employment agency is a feasible method of job hunting in an unfamiliar city; but even here there are limitations. Commercial private agencies can be intimidating while alternative agencies and other small job programs run by nonprofit groups can generally offer only casual jobs—a day's work washing windows or weeding a garden, or, at best, a three- or four-day job painting a few rooms.

A government-run employment bureau, which charges no fee and offers full-time jobs, is the place where the new migrant is most likely to find a job in an unfamiliar city—if he finds one at all. In America, such offices are usually state-run, supported in part by federal money.

State Employment Offices

The advantage of a state employment office, aside from the obvious one—that it is free—lies in the great number of current job listings it provides daily. Employers regularly list their job needs here because the state's services are also free to them and the listings will reach the widest segment of job seekers. These days, job listings in state offices are processed and coordinated by machines, such as Teletypes or computers (microfiche cards), so they reach the job market quickly.

But the typical state employment office may also have its disadvantages and problems for the new migrant who goes there in search of work. There is the complicated application form to fill out, with its numerous blank spaces asking for detailed information about past employment—including specific dates, job titles, amount of pay, and the names and addresses of former employers or established community members who can serve as references. For the new migrant with a checkered job past, or one who has been on the road for months or years without more than casual, part-time work, the application form itself may appear to be an insurmountable obstacle, placed there to keep him from gaining access to the job openings. If the new migrant is semiliterate, he may feel like a pupil at school who has failed once again, and be ashamed to even turn in the application.

The office may be so crowded with job seekers that the new migrant (like other applicants) has to stand in line for several hours before he can get an interview—and a chance to hear about the job openings. Many a new migrant, feeling out of his element to begin with in an institution of the Establishment, may interpret standard delays and routine red tape in state offices as a personal rebuff. After a fruitless morning standing in line and a frustrating afternoon where a harried counselor bluntly points out the lack of basic information on his application blank—e.g., references and details of past employment—the new migrant may decide that the counselor is against him and it is useless to expect any help from a government source. He rushes out, feeling a profound sense of relief when he reaches the street, and never returns to the one place in the city that might have helped him find a job, had he persisted.

Some of the inadequacies of state employment offices may be inherent in the operation of large institutions, so new migrants who can't cope with them will simply have to remain unemployed. But a search for innovative ways to make state employment offices more helpful to new migrants could result in more job placements, as a special outreach program in San Francisco has shown.

JOB OUTREACH FOR THE NEW MIGRANTS

In the heart of the Tenderloin, a small job bureau has been helping the new migrants for several years. Its informal atmosphere suggests an alternative agency run on a shoestring by altruistic citizens; in fact, it is a branch of the California State Department of Employment, and it has an advantage that the most well-meaning private groups in the state could never match: Twice a day a large stack of slips describing current job openings are delivered to the office, hot off the Teletype machines. In addition, Dick Baltz, who runs the Tenderloin office, has tailored the operation to the needs of his clients.[6] Standard procedure in most employment offices, public or private, is to fill out an application blank and be interviewed by an employment specialist. Only then will you hear about job openings, and they will be limited to those the interviewer deems suitable to your qualifications. Baltz reverses this process. In the morning and again after lunch, when copies of current job listings are delivered to his office, he puts them out in a wire basket. People looking for jobs go through them and pass them around; if they find a job they feel qualified for and want to apply, then they fill out an application blank and Baltz phones to set up an interview for them.

"My way gives people a little dignity, and it saves time for all of us," he says. "Most people know what they can or can't do, so it makes sense to give access to the job openings. You have to trust people a little. Of course, I use my judgment, too. If a person obviously doesn't qualify for a certain job, I'm not going to send him out for an interview. But that's rarely a problem."

The result of Baltz's method is that he consistently places two or three times as many people in jobs each month as any worker in the main office. Another reason his method works, Baltz believes, is that it shows people the reality of the job situation. There are no secrets in the office, so people don't suspect that he has hidden plums reserved for special people. Twice a day they see all the full-time jobs that are available. In addition, Baltz has developed a liaison with a few local companies who phone in when they need temporary or short-term help.

Baltz began his outreach work for the state in 1969, working from an upstairs office in Hospitality House, a day center in the

Tenderloin for people 18 to 30 years old. In 1975 he moved across the street to the Northeast Community Care Center, where his office on the first floor is easily accessible from the street. During these years he has seen thousands of people from all over the country who were looking for work. Their education ranged from first grade on up through master's and doctor's degrees, he says, but the heaviest concentration of job seekers are those who have never been to college. He is angered by reports that young people don't want to work anymore.

"People want to work. They beg to work," Baltz says. "They'll say to me, 'All I want is an honest day's work; I'll do anything.' "

Many job seekers stop by his office daily to check the new listings. Some come by twice a day, waiting outside until the door opens so they can have first crack at the openings and get to potential employers before anyone else does.

On a spring day in the late 1970s, nearly a dozen people were clustered outside the office door, waiting for Baltz to return from lunch and distribute the afternoon listings. Once inside, several people left as soon as they had finished reading through the day's job openings. It was easy to see why: More than half of the listings called for skills, qualifications, and past experience that no one in the room was likely to have—qualifications such as "three years supervisory experience necessary," or "must type 70 words per minute."

More people kept coming in to read the job listings and talk with Baltz. They were of different skin colors and both sexes, but the majority were male and there were more whites than blacks. No one looked under 21, and only a few people appeared to be past 35.

Sam and Ellen had arrived recently from Nebraska and their money had run out. Sam was a Vietnam veteran who'd returned home after he got out of the army but had not been able to make it there. He was hoping for better luck in San Francisco. "Don't you have any custodial work?" he asked Baltz. "I've done custodial work."

There were no listings for custodial work that afternoon, but Baltz mentioned a survey job with the telephone company; it would only last for a few months. Yes, Sam was interested. Baltz phoned the company and learned that the openings had been filled. The only other job he could suggest to tide them over until they found full-time work was distributing handbills; but for this work, one had to be there at 4:45 in the morning.

A man sitting near the desk chimed in, "They only pay you two dollars an hour. They can get away with less than the minimum wage by saying it's seasonal work."

Sam was interested. "I'll work for almost anything right now." Ellen also wanted to distribute handbills. Baltz phoned the handbill office; they were filled up for the next few days, but he signed Sam and Ellen up to work the following Monday.

In another chair, Wayne, a man past 30 whose well-developed muscles gave him the look of a longshoreman or a lumberjack, was studying the job listings. He stopped at an opening for a chambermaid in a downtown hotel. It paid $2.90 an hour. "Do you think they'd hire a man?" he asked. Baltz said he'd try to find out. He explained that sex discrimination is illegal, so the manager probably wouldn't state his preference openly. Baltz phoned the manager and then told Wayne: "He says he'll talk to you, but he thinks the job is more suitable for a woman. It's a waste of your time to go down there." Wayne nodded in agreement. He went through the rest of the listings and left, saying he'd be back in the morning.

A few minutes later two young women walked into the office. "Hey, maybe one of these gals wants that maid's job," someone in the room said. One woman was interested; she had worked as a maid back home in Texas. Baltz phoned the manager again, someone else got out a map of San Francisco and showed the woman how to get there, and off she went.

To many new migrants, the office was more than a job bureau; it was a community, the only place in the new city where they could sit and talk with other people and be part of a group. A few people stayed there most of the afternoon. Job seekers offered each other help and advice. A man who was about to leave for an interview about a painting job said he had no money for bus fare; the person next to him quietly pressed some change into his hand.

One young man, John, did not take part in the discussions, nor did he read through the job listings. He was white, in his twenties, and wore glasses with thick lenses. Baltz told John he would go over the job listings with him in a few minutes. Then a businessman phoned in to say he needed someone to pack boxes for a few hours that afternoon. Baltz suggested that John take the job. Two other people gave detailed directions on how to get there, and he left.

"John can't read or write," Baltz explained later. "He's having a hard time. That job will at least give him a little money."

"Where is he living while he job-hunts?"

"On the streets, I guess."

A few of the job hunters that afternoon had college degrees. Alan was an elementary-school teacher from New Jersey. His credentials were not applicable here, he said, so he hoped to find tutoring jobs or work in a private school. Simon, who looked at least 40, was an ex-teacher who had also worked as a businessman. Most recently he had been a florist in Michigan. He hoped to find work in San Francisco as a florist. There were no listings for florists that afternoon, but Baltz explained that one might come in some other day. When Simon learned how the office operated, he said, "I'll be back first thing in the morning; I'll bring my sleeping bag."

All afternoon the office was filled; Baltz went from telephone to people to forms and back again.

In Haight-Ashbury, where Robert Martin runs another out-reach employment office, the pace is slower. Martin used to work out of the Haight-Ashbury Switchboard, but now his office is in the basement of Aquarius House, a small house for transients on a quiet residential street on the outskirts of the Haight. With fewer clients, he operates a bit differently, spending a lot of time with each applicant to get a good idea of his or her qualifications, so he can match the person with the right job. (He, too, places more people in jobs than those in the main office, though his tally is lower than Baltz's.)

Martin has also developed part-time work for his clients by circularizing the neighborhood in much the same way as alternative agencies do. "No job is too big or too small—from cleaning your garage to setting up a bookkeeping system," says a letter he mailed out to the neighbors. "We have a large pool of skilled and unskilled job applicants who can be referred to you promptly upon request." Almost all of his clients want full-time work, but one-day and short-term jobs help keep them going until they find permanent jobs.[7]

Job Questions

Are the job problems of the new migrants caused primarily by their lack of skills, combined with the added difficulties of transience? If so, would more job training programs, along with employment services and temporary housing facilities for transients in a city, mean that new migrants would be able to find work as easily as young people who grew up in that city? But with so many local young people already seeking jobs in their communities, should city governments make a special effort to help the new migrants? Or should they instead encourage the new migrants to go back where they came from? And is the real job problem of new migrants (and that of local jobless youth, too) perhaps that they don't try hard enough to find jobs in the first place—that their expectations are too high, and they give up too easily?

In the United States, the popularity of discouraging new migrants from settling in new cities is evident from the virtual lack of facilities for them, as compared with those provided for new migrants in other nations, such as Britain. And the pervasiveness of the belief that joblessness is primarily the fault of the unemployed is clear from the considerable criticism that public job-training and job-creation programs encounter, even in times of high unemployment.

Once again the Alger myth rises to the surface. Its belief in unlimited opportunities for rugged individuals smothers consideration of the possibility that some people may need a little help in order to help themselves. The dream of riches for all who try hard enough squelches the urge to provide services for those in need; in fact, the American dream has made "welfare" a dirty word.

CHAPTER SIX

Welfare
and Other
Social Services

"Welfare" is a loaded word in the United States. It evokes images of freeloaders sitting in the park all day eating candy bars while hardworking citizens are toiling to earn their bread and support these loafers as well.

Undoubtedly some freeloaders do get welfare, just as some swindlers exist in the business community along with honest people. But curiously, a newspaper story about a mother of six who has cheated the government out of $30,000 a year by applying for welfare in several states simultaneously will produce greater feelings of outrage in American bosoms than an article about a wealthy businessman who has swindled the government out of $500,000 a year by taking large tax deductions for the expenses of a nonexistent corporation. The man's success in business gives him status, while the act of applying for welfare—even in one state—brands the woman as an inferior type.

The belief that any American who is sufficiently motivated and persistent can triumph over adversity without government help is so deeply rooted in the American psyche that even the new migrants accept it. No matter how desperate their circumstances, many of them will fight the suggestion that they apply for welfare to obtain enough money to live on while they hunt for a job. To many new migrants steeped in traditional American values, accepting welfare payments would be tantamount to acknowledging themselves as personal failures. They would turn into one of "those people" whom their parents scorned. Ron felt that way.

Ron: Determined to Be a Self-made Man

Ron came out to Berkeley from New York City in 1973, planning to find work and settle in the area.* He was 20 years old, white, and had a year of college behind him. By a stroke of luck he walked into the local state employment office just after an employer had phoned in to request a night watchman for his factory in east Oakland. A jubilant Ron got the job. But a few days later, on his way home from work in the early morning, he was approached by drug pushers; when he refused to buy, they beat him up. By the time Ron got out of the hospital, his job was gone.

Again he looked for full-time work, but this time luck was not with him. Before long his money ran out, and since the youth hostel was closed in the winter, he began living on the streets. He went to the Berkeley Streetwork Project (an alternative agency) seeking suggestions about where he could look for work, but they had no special leads on full-time jobs; all they could offer Ron was an occasional odd job, information about survival services in the area, and moral support.

Ron got free dinners at the Emergency Food Project in exchange for helping out with food preparation, but there was no cheap housing available to him. Elsie Johnson, a social worker at the Streetwork Project, suggested that he apply for General Assistance (welfare) so he could rent a room in a cheap hotel while he continued his job hunt. But the idea was repugnant to Ron. He thought he was not the type to apply for welfare—he saw himself as being different from the other down-and-out people on the streets. Ron felt sure he could make it on his own if he just kept trying. Eventually someone would offer him a job when they realized how eager he was and how hard he would work.

After a few weeks Ron began to look scroungy, because he slept in his clothes every night in Tilden Park, at the Berkeley Marina, or on the streets. Then he began to smell. Finally he started sneaking into a small hotel off Telegraph Avenue to take a

---

* Information about "Ron" from author's interviews with Elsie Johnson, former staff worker at the Berkeley Streetwork Project.

shower when the manager wasn't looking. But still he found no job. He was job-hunting during the major recession of the decade, a time when the national rate of unemployment was to climb as high as 8.9 percent, but he did not know this.

Ron often dropped by the Streetwork Project, where the sympathetic response of Johnson and others on the staff provided his only personal support system in Berkeley. They noticed that Ron seemed more discouraged each time he came in, but he refused to give up.

One day a short article in the local newspaper reported that the body of a young man in his early twenties had been found at the Berkeley Marina. Police said he had been stabbed several times, apparently in the middle of the night. Elsie Johnson felt sick when she realized that the murdered man was Ron. Lacking a room to sleep in, he had been at the marina at a time of night when most Berkeley citizens would consider it unsafe to venture out alone.

William: Persistent but Ready to Accept Help

Social workers in agencies that serve the new migrants often view welfare as a stepping-stone to employment because it provides the job hunters with enough money for basics while they look for a job. William was a new migrant who agreed.*

William came west with a company that sold magazines and Bibles door-to-door. In his hometown of Baltimore, Maryland, the company promised travel, adventure, and big money. On the job he worked ten to twelve hours a day, six days a week, and was paid by commission after his employers deducted expenses for his room and board. He cleared $200 to $300 a month.

When he arrived in San Francisco, William decided he could do better on his own and left the company. He was 22 years old, a high-school graduate, well dressed, personable, and black. A woman he met on the bus told William about Travelers Aid; it housed him temporarily and sent him around to employment bureaus.

When William hadn't found a job after a couple of weeks, his social worker at Travelers Aid, Carol Bohnsack, suggested that he apply for welfare so he would have money to live on while he

---

* The story of "William" is drawn from author's interviews with him and with Carol Bohnsack, former staff member at Travelers Aid.

continued job-hunting. The year was 1975, a time when people like William could still get onto General Assistance in San Francisco.

To William, accepting welfare payments for a while did not seem a disgrace—it was what poor people did when they had no money and couldn't get a job. Perhaps because he was black and had grown up in poverty, he lacked the expectations of new migrants like Ron, who were sure they could make it on their own. William knew that people could want jobs and yet not find them, because of prejudice or lack of available openings. Back home his father had a steady job as a chef in a large restaurant, but William's brothers and sisters were having a hard time making it. One married sister and her husband had moved in with his parents to save money. Another brother had recently been laid off from his job and couldn't find another one. William was glad to accept any help he could get.

With the help of Travelers Aid, William was approved for GA —General Assistance, the term for temporary welfare payments to people who can't find jobs; he received $83 a month, plus food stamps. With the money, he rented a small room in a Tenderloin hotel for $15 a week, ate inexpensive meals, and continued job-hunting. Every few days he would drop by Travelers Aid to chat with Bohnsack and report his progress. When he had been job-hunting for three months, he talked about his experiences with the author.

"I get up at seventy-thirty and go out all day; then I get back at six-thirty or seven. It's like having a job, except that I'm looking for one," William said. "I keep putting in applications all over town, but no one will hire me." He shook his head. "I didn't realize it was so bad out here."

His parents still thought he was on the road selling magazines. He was ashamed to write and say that he was broke in San Francisco, or to return home with no money when his brothers and sisters were already in a bind. After he found a good job he would write to them.

Yes, he had worked at home after he finished high school. He had been a stock clerk in a department store. "But it got so boring counting scarves and pocketbooks all day, folding eight hundred scarves a day into little piles." After two years, he quit. His father was mad about that, although they usually got along.

Being young, William wanted to live a little, and the traveling job had sounded ideal when he heard about it in Baltimore. But he found he hated trying to pressure people into buying magazines he could see they couldn't afford. And he lost twenty-five pounds on the road. When a woman who answered his ring said to him, "Young man, why are you selling magazines? You can do better than that," he thought he could.

"But I can't even get a job as a dishwasher in San Francisco. Come to tell you, I'd much rather be working than getting GA, but what can you do when nobody will give you a job?"

William had no plans to move on. What good would it do to try other cities when he didn't know whether they'd have any jobs there either? It was better to stay where he was. At least here he had a room to live in. "I don't know what I would have done if I hadn't gotten on GA." But he also didn't know what he'd do if his shoes wore out, because he couldn't afford to resole them again. "All I need now is some work," said William.

Several months more went by, and still William could not find a full-time job, although every morning he went to the employment office run by Dick Baltz in the Tenderloin, read over the day's job openings, and applied for every job he seemed qualified for.

Then one month he attended a job-search program run by a local group with funds from the federal Department of Manpower. The course helped unemployed people aged 18 to 25 identify their skills and learn job-hunting techniques, such as how to answer questions during an interview and how to dress. Soon after he finished the course, William was hired as a runner for the Stock Exchange. He and a coworker rented an apartment together, and William left welfare and the Tenderloin behind him. Now he could write to his parents and tell them that he had made it in San Francisco.

APPLYING FOR WELFARE

Critics of the welfare system may believe that anybody can get money from the government by simply walking into a welfare office and demanding it. In fact, it is not that easy. The ease or difficulty of getting financial assistance from government sources may vary radically from state to state or even county to county;

but in general, those who are likely to encounter the most difficulty getting onto welfare are physically fit people under 30 who
have no children. This includes most new migrants.

Families with children are eligible for welfare if the parents
are unemployed and have little or no money. This form of welfare
is called AFDC, Aid to Families with Dependent Children. Should
you blame a hungry six-year-old because his parents are penniless? In nineteenth-century England, children of paupers were
sometimes forced to work full time in factories at the age of six
or seven. And in the United States during the 1930s, migrant
families like the Joads could not get financial relief even if the
parents couldn't find work and their children were starving, because they hadn't lived in the new area long enough to meet the
residency requirements. But today, in the United States and
England, as in most industrialized nations, legislative bodies and
courts have formulated or upheld policies supporting the belief
that children should not suffer hunger and deprivation when
their parents are unable to support them.

Thus in 1977 when a family of new migrants climbed off a
Greyhound bus in San Francisco one night, they were eligible for
relief because they were traveling with their four small children.[1]
The Millers (like the Joads) had come from Oklahoma in search
of agricultural work, but, to their surprise, Mr. Miller could not
find a job in California. They arrived in San Francisco on a bus
from Fresno (center of one of the state's richest agricultural
areas), broke, hungry, and "kinda desperate," as Mrs. Miller
put it.

Luckily for the Millers, Travelers Aid had a social worker on
duty that night at the bus depot. He took the Millers to a nearby
McDonald's for hamburgers, found them a hotel room for the
night in the Tenderloin, and set up some appointments for the
morning.

Although it is doubtful that Mr. Miller did find work in San
Francisco, the Millers at least were assured of a roof over their
heads and some food in their stomachs while the father hunted
for a job—because the family had children. If a 19-year-old
nephew of the Millers had left Oklahoma with his wife in 1977
in search of work, but they had no children, their chances of
qualifying for General Assistance in San Francisco would have
been slim.

Once again the familiar mythology rears its head: If you are young and persistent, you can find a job regardless of your qualifications or the local rate of unemployment. Earlier in this chapter we met Ron, the job seeker who refused to apply for General Assistance and was murdered in the night. Had Ron applied for such assistance, to get money for a hotel room, it is debatable whether he would have been approved.

At that time Alameda County, where Berkeley is situated, was paying $125 per month for General Assistance, compared with San Francisco's $83, but it was harder to qualify in Alameda. It was especially hard if you were a young, white, childless migrant living in Berkeley and thus fit the "hippie" stereotype. Even if you could qualify, the work requirements attached to the money were often untenable.

In those years male recipients judged physically fit were required to report to an office in downtown Oakland five mornings a week at 4:30 A.M., in case farmers or other employers could use them as casual laborers. The money they earned—$2 an hour—went to the county to help pay the cost of their welfare allotment. (Women were not required to come down then, because of the danger of rape if they were on the streets alone at that hour.) Welfare recipients were unlikely to own cars, and buses ran infrequently at that hour, if at all, so getting to downtown Oakland, several miles from the center of Berkeley, at 4:30 A.M., presented a major obstacle to would-be recipients.

One welfare specialist believes these regulations were set up as a form of punishment, to discourage people from applying for General Assistance. There is little organized effort to fight such regulations, he says, because the affected people have no political clout: They are not a part of any voting constituency and have little support in the larger society.

Residency requirements also keep new migrants from receiving General Assistance. Theoretically, residency requirements for welfare have been struck down by the courts in the United States, but there is a Catch 22 that helps keep the poorest people off the rolls: Transients are ineligible for General Assistance. In order to qualify, you must show that you actually reside in the city in which you are applying for assistance. A rent receipt from a landlord is a standard proof of residency, but if you're homeless, penniless, and jobless, obviously you can't pay a week's rent in advance to get a rent receipt. Even if you've been living on the streets of a city for months, eating out of garbage cans and hounding employment agencies in vain, until you come around with that rent receipt you are classified as a transient and are thus ineligible for General Assistance.

There are ways of getting around this requirement, as in everything else, but the person in such straits is likely to be the last one to know about them. This is one reason why welfare counseling has become a vital component of programs that serve the new migrants and other poor people. Staff members become familiar with the eligibility rules and the exceptions for various programs; they know whom to contact in which office for what, how to fill out the forms, what papers are required, how long it usually takes, and whether a person, given his or her situation, has a chance of qualifying. In short, they know how to work the system. Social workers in county welfare and federal Social Security offices also benefit from the work of welfare counselors and often welcome their help. It means they deal with clients who come to the right office with the necessary papers, know how to apply, and have realistic expectations about what the government can and cannot do for them.

But even with the help of specialists, there may be obstacles. One is the requirement that applicants have personal identification. Often the new migrants don't have any. If they've never driven a car, they have no driver's license. They are unlikely to have credit cards, and some do not even have a Social Security number. They may have had some identification once, but it was stolen along with their packs on the road.

The know-how of welfare specialists includes explaining how to write for a duplicate copy of your driver's license or birth certificate. But it takes money as well as time to get such documents; in California, for example, you need a copy of your birth certificate plus $3.25 to get a nondriver's identification card. "Many of our clients are too poor to get on welfare," a worker in one alternative agency explained.[2]

In 1976, San Francisco, which had a more flexible policy on General Assistance eligibility than nearby Alameda County, tightened up its requirements in an effort to save money and discourage new migrants from moving into the city. GA recipients, who formerly had to show that they had sought work from at least five employers each month, now had to prove that they had sought work from twenty to twenty-five employers per month, and that the business or agency they contacted was actually looking for employees. For new applicants, requirements for verifiable identification were increased.

In less than ten months the number of people on General Assistance in San Francisco dropped from 9047 to 4240—a savings of more than $3 million to the taxpayers, social-service workers pointed out.[3]

To the staff at Travelers Aid, the new regulations spelled disaster. Most of their clients would now be relegated to the streets if they stayed in San Francisco.

"I don't know what they expect us to do for people who have no money and can't find jobs," Marjorie Montelius said. "Just let them starve to death slowly, I suppose."

Carol Bohnsack was also discouraged. "It gets so depressing when you see people day after day who lead marginal lives. You know they'll probably spend the rest of their lives that way, because they have nothing going for them, and you can't offer them any real help."

SOCIAL WORK POLICIES—PAST AND PRESENT

Although the kinds of social services provided for the poor in the United States have been influenced by the myth of the American dream, the origins of the country's social-service system reach back to England. From the days of the thirteen colonies, the United States copied Britain's system. Workhouses for debtors and indigents, immortalized in the novels of Charles Dickens, were also abundant in the United States, some surviving until as late as the 1930s. And in the United States as in Britain, a controversy once raged over the merits of "outdoor" relief—that is, giving money or goods to the poor so they could remain in their own homes, as opposed to "indoor" relief, which meant committing indigents to workhouses or "poor farms."

In both countries, social work as a profession emerged in the latter half of the nineteenth century as an organized method of giving outdoor relief to the deserving poor—and of making sure that those considered "undeserving" did not get anything. The originators of social casework were members of the Charity

Organisation Society (COS) which started in 1869 in Britain and spread to America in 1877.[4] In both countries the COS was organized by altruistic members of the middle and upper-middle classes. They followed the prevailing philosophy of the day in believing that poverty was the result of a moral failure within the individual, and that help should be given only to people of good character who fell on hard times through no fault of their own—through illness or a serious accident—people who would appreciate the help and use it to pull themselves out of poverty.

Techniques of social casework were developed by the COS to determine who was worthy of aid. The COS preferred giving moral rather than financial support, and sent volunteers into the homes of the poor to instruct them in habits of cleanliness and thrift. Any money given had to be accounted for by the recipient, for it was thought to be a disservice to poor people's moral development to give them money which they might squander.

One American COS leader believed that outdoor relief did great "moral harm because human nature is so constituted that no man can receive as a gift what he should earn by his own labor without a moral deterioration."[5] This reasoning led the COS to lobby against outdoor relief; in some American cities the COS helped the poor by eliminating winter distributions of food and coal to them.

The COS believed that it was the duty of private charity to look after the poor. In Britain the COS vigorously opposed government help for poor people, including soup kitchens, free school lunches, and old-age pensions. Free school lunches "weakened the duty of the family and encouraged the mother in lazy habits, since, if the children got a good meal at school, she might give up cooking and feed them on scraps, using the money saved for bad purposes."[6] Pensions were dangerous, because the workingman should learn to save for his old age; dangling a pension in front of him invited idleness.

A clergyman, Canon A. S. Barnett, was initially an enthusiastic supporter of the COS. But after he got a parish in the East End of London and lived among poor people, he changed his mind. How could the workingman save for his old age if he didn't earn enough to feed and clothe his family? Barnett asked. He came to the conclusion that the government must step in and help with the problems of unemployment and old age among the poor.[7]

The Rise of Social-Work Advocacy

The civil-rights struggles and the black-power movements of the early 1960s played a role in discrediting traditional concepts of social work in the United States and in leading the profession toward changes. The belief that poverty was the result of moral failure in the individual was challenged by black leaders: A nation that discriminated against black people, keeping them from decent education, housing, and jobs, assured the perpetuation of poverty among them, they said. At the height of the black-power movement, leaders such as George Jackson and Eldridge Cleaver declared that all black people in prison were political prisoners who could not be held responsible for their actions because their shameful treatment by society was the cause of their troubles. That viewpoint did not remain popular for long, among blacks or whites (in the 1970s the Reverend Jesse Jackson of Chicago launched his "Push for Excellence," advocating more individual effort to achieve among blacks), but the impact of the accusation helped dislodge the moral dichotomy of the deserving and the undeserving poor from its unquestioned position.

In America that dichotomy was hard to dislodge, because it merged neatly with the cardinal belief in unlimited opportunity. If everyone had the chance to be president, or could at least become a millionaire, then people of sound body who could not make a living must be the scum of the nation. Even if laws pushed through by do-gooders made relief for the poor mandatory, the money could be doled out in a way that showed the agency's scorn for its clients.

This attitude was far from universal among social workers, of course. There were social workers who were constantly frustrated because their budgets and the regulations of the system prevented them from giving their clients enough help, but sometimes their compassion was hidden behind the endless forms asking personal questions and the home investigations they were required to make. There were also plenty of social workers pushing for changes long before the 1960s. But the inheritors of the COS tradition still dominated the system.

During the 1960s, a reverse reaction occurred: Increasing numbers of poor people refused to be served by any Establishment agency, public or private; some would literally die before they would go near one. People whose past lives had brought them into frequent contact with social agencies—the poor and the children of the poor—viewed the system with hostility and saw all social workers as enemies who pried into their lives and took away their dignity. Some could not understand the language of social workers, so different from the way people spoke at home; others resented the workers' efforts to mold clients into their own image, stressing the importance of filling out forms correctly and arriving on time for appointments. They hated the social worker's image, so where was the motivation to copy it? Instead they clung all the more to what they were—and kept out of sight.

As civil-rights demonstrations escalated, some social workers became aware of the contempt their clients had for them, especially Third World clients who lived in abject poverty in inner-city ghettos or barrios. In those years, reformers, including professional social workers and recent graduates of schools of social work, as well as grass-roots community workers without specialized training, began to practice a new type of social work. It was called "advocacy."

"Advocacy" means that the social worker speaks and acts for the client's interests in the same way that a lawyer does. Instead of passing moral judgment, the worker offers practical help geared to the person's needs. Advocacy may take the worker out of the office to help the client deal with the system. For example, if a client is seriously ill but is afraid of doctors and receptionists, instead of merely handing him the phone number of a clinic, which the client might be too intimidated to use, the worker may make the appointment for him and perhaps even accompany him on his first visit.

Social-work advocacy does not mean that the social worker relieves clients of all personal responsibility for their own lives, any more than a lawyer who helps a client fight a criminal charge takes on responsibility for every aspect of the client's life. The function of both lawyer and social worker as advocate is to provide the client with real help in a crisis. It is not to run the client's life. Nor is it to lecture the client on how to live.

Alternative Agencies and Advocacy

The people who formed the first alternative agencies during the hippie period were all for advocacy—or perhaps it is more accurate to say that they were against all traditional practices of social work. The Haight-Ashbury Switchboard's manual of office procedures stated its feelings about traditional social work on page 1:

> No matter why people may call or visit the Switchboard, the most important service an operator can render is to be *human*. Keep in mind that Switchboard defeats its own purpose if it cannot offer an alternative to service organizations which give automatic, impersonal responses to human problems. We don't deal with problems here; we deal with *people*. Never allow these procedures to govern your behavior to the extent that you become just like the robot clerks and agents who are unable and unwilling to deal with anyone who will not play *their* game on *their* terms.[8]

At the Haight-Ashbury Switchboard the motivation to give real help to clients was great, but the resources available were not. At first, staff members tried to use only alternative services, because they were as alienated from the Establishment as their clients were; they hated traditional social services, whether government-run or sponsored by private or religious charities. The problem was that few alternative services existed. Organizing hospital facilities and a welfare network was beyond the scope of alternative agencies, and survival services—such as temporary housing, free food, and job bureaus—were grossly inadequate if they existed at all.

Initially the Switchboard met the need for transient housing by organizing its own crash-housing program. People who volunteered to house transients overnight free in their own places were listed along with their telephone numbers; every evening a Switchboard volunteer got on the phone and matched the available beds for the night with those who needed one. It seemed like an ideal system. But unexpected problems occurred, even during the heyday of the hippie period when numerous people were still ready to open their homes to strangers.

The originators of the crash-housing plan assumed that people would invite travelers into their homes in a spirit of brotherhood, and most of those who volunteered *were* motivated by such ideals; but a few men, the Switchboard discovered to its consternation, were offering to house young women in order to seduce them. This made it necessary to check out people who offered free crashing space, which went against the grain of the Switchboard's philosophy of trust.

The Switchboard also knew that while one night's free housing was fine for young people who came to visit San Francisco, it was not enough for those who hoped to find work in the city and settle there permanently. Over the years, as the numbers of new migrants increased, and more of them were families traveling with young children, the Switchboard kept looking for additional places to house migrants without money. The question of whether a facility was run by a traditional or alternative group became irrelevant—the crucial questions were how many beds they had and how many nights they would let people stay.

In the early 1970s the Haight-Ashbury Switchboard began publishing an annual four-page newspaper of basic resources in San Francisco, called *Survival Manual*.[9] (Other organizations have sometimes collaborated with them.) The opening page gives lip service to the old philosophy—"Once you get your trip together, don't leave your brothers and sisters behind—get involved with alternatives to the system"—but the resources listed in the newspaper lean heavily on government-run operations, such as hospitals, the welfare network, and state employment offices. Most of the private agencies it lists (traditional or alternative), particularly in the areas of legal help, medical or psychiatric help, child-care facilities, and women's services, have been able to remain open only because they got a grant from a foundation, have tapped into the United Way (the cooperative fund-raising network for charities in the community), or, most often, have received some type of government funding. The hue and cry is for alternatives to the system, but the reality is that the government is the prime provider of funds to agencies that help the new migrants.

At the height of the hippie movement in the 1960s, the government was the last place where alternative agencies in the mold of the Haight-Ashbury Switchboard wanted to look for funds. To them, the government was the enemy. As a further ironic twist, a decade later the mass of the nation's population, the people who had hated the hippies, were loudly echoing the hippies' blanket condemnation of government and its services. And yet, as Canon Barnett of London realized in the nineteenth century, self-sufficiency is not possible for all people during every period of their lives. Who but a nation's government has the motivation and the resources to help its people avoid lives of deprivation?

CHAPTER SEVEN

A Place to Stay

Housing is the prime survival need of the new migrants. Young transients in America are unlikely to starve to death (there is good food in city garbage cans if all else fails), but, as we saw in the story of Ron, they have died from lack of a place to stay. Other results of homelessness are more common. Young women and men who come to the big cities may be led into prostitution because it offers them a way to get off the streets and earn some money—and they can find no alternative method of survival. More frequent, though less remarked on, are new migrants who are doomed to perpetual unemployment because they lack the basic housing facilities needed to job-hunt with success. No matter where they go, they have no place to stay.

In the United States there are virtually no government-sponsored temporary housing facilities and services for new migrants or older adults who move to new cities in search of work but have no money. In the private and nonprofit sectors, the numbers of low-cost or free facilities for transients are minuscule. As the director of one alternative agency remarked, "There's little available in this country between Holiday Inn and the flophouse."[1]

Americans are famous for their mobility, so it may surprise people in other countries that so few facilities exist for migrants in transition. Some cities do have emergency shelters geared to elderly alcoholics or the mentally ill who become public nuisances, but other people are expected to find their own emergency housing.

Once, during the Great Depression, the federal government did set up a network of temporary housing and other social services for migrants. As we saw in Chapter 3, between 1933 and 1935 the Federal Transient Services (part of the FERA) funded numerous relief centers and transient camps which were administered by the states. Author John Steinbeck lived for several weeks at a transient camp in California, imbibing the atmosphere and recording details for his book about migrants. In his *Grapes of Wrath,* the Joad family's stay in a government transient camp stands out as the one happy episode in an otherwise consistently grim tale. The camp has good facilities, is well run, and encourages resident participation. To the Joads, it is paradise; but after a few weeks they reluctantly leave, because they cannot find work on the surrounding farms.

The Federal Transient Service was discontinued at the height of its effectiveness (and after substantial amounts of time and money had been spent to build it up); its critics thought it was an un-American endeavor that coddled freeloaders.

Housing for Young Tourists in the City: A Foreign Concept

The idea of providing special housing for young-adult travelers in our cities—whether migrants or tourists—is so foreign to Americans that no general term exists to describe such facilities. To most Americans the word "hostel" means Youth Hostels, the international private organization that provides supervised lodging for vacationing youths who are hiking or bicycling. But in Britain the word has a broader meaning. This book will use the word "hostel" in the British sense, because the American language needs such a term; without it we will be groping in a sea of linguistic misunderstanding when we discuss America's need for hostels.

A hostel in Britain is any kind of organized group housing for a specific category of people, such as students or the elderly. What Americans call dormitories (organized housing on campus for college students) the British call hostels. But student hostels in Britain may also be off campus, and they may be privately run; what Americans might describe as a rooming house catering to students, the British would call a student hostel. The term "hostel" implies rooms, rather than apartments, but rooms in an organized living unit; if you rent a room from a family, you are not living in a hostel.

In the area of housing for young tourists, the word "hostel" is widely used in Britain. The YMCA is a hostel, and so is a small rooming house or hotel that has low-cost facilities for perhaps fifteen young people. There is usually a supervisor—the "warden"—who sets up the house rules and oversees its operation; if the hostel is a commercial enterprise, the owner or manager may also function as warden.

A number of nonprofit and religious organizations run hostels for young travelers in the cities, and the government's Department of Health and Social Services runs an emergency shelter for homeless young people in London's Soho district.

Until the late 1950s, young Americans who wanted to travel around on their own, especially young optionaires with money, generally skipped the United States and went instead to Europe. The large European cities offered a wide range of safe, low-cost hostels for the student traveler, while in the United States, except for commercial hotels, there was only the YMCA (usually higher in price than student-type hostels because its facilities were not as spartan). When Youth Hostels began operating in the United States, they were situated mainly in the mountains or near the seashore as overnight shelter for young outdoors enthusiasts. Since there were no similar shelters in the cities, young people did not visit American cities as tourists; they visited London or Paris.

The rise of the "beat generation" and the publication in 1957 of *On the Road,* a book by beat hero Jack Kerouac, initiated a change in the travel patterns of young Americans. The beats, who surfaced in San Francisco during the 1950s, rejected traditional cultural norms and adopted a way of life that was at odds with those norms. Many young Americans, feeling more affinity for the beats' beliefs than those of their parents, began to travel back and forth across the United States, trying to emulate the frenetic life-style described in *On the Road.*

These young travelers evoked a negative reaction from the general public, a reaction that was to be further aroused in the next decade by the hippie migration. Any youth on the road who had long hair, jeans, and a backpack was classified as a beatnik or bum—later as a hippie.

San Francisco and Amsterdam: Two Approaches to Youth

Americans' hatred for traveling youth reached its climax in 1967 when San Francisco experienced a mass convergence of "flower children" on its Haight-Ashbury district, a period that was known as "The Summer of Love."[2] Comparing San Francisco's response with that of Amsterdam, Holland, which had a similar influx of youth three summers later, shows the two countries' contrasting attitudes toward youth on the move.

When it became apparent that great numbers of young people would converge on San Francisco in the summer of 1967, the mayor asked the board of supervisors to pass a resolution warning hippies to stay away. Another prominent citizen suggested posting signs reading "Hippies Not Welcome Here" on the bridge approaches to the city. These extremes were not carried out, but the city began eliminating existing facilities where the young visitors might sleep. The Parks and Recreation Department issued a regulation that people could not sleep in Golden Gate Park—the spacious park within walking distance of the Haight-Ashbury district—and the Health Department began a house-to-house inspection of dwellings in the Haight, looking for code violations. That project was not fruitful; the inspectors found only 39 code violations in the 690 premises inspected, and most violations occurred not in hippie communes but in apartments rented by local working-class families, who were largely black.

The Diggers, a utopian organization of young people that operated a soup kitchen and several large communes in Haight-Ashbury, had visited city officials in the spring of 1967. They had been the ones who first apprised officials of the anticipated summer crowds and they had asked for help in providing food, housing, and medical help for them. Instead, the city sent inspectors around to the Diggers' facilities and closed some of its crash pads, saying that they did not meet the required health standards.

San Francisco did not close traditional temporary housing facilities for youths—it didn't have to, because there weren't any.

The YMCA did have a downtown hotel, but, because of the city's paucity of clean, safe accommodations in a low price range, it was equally popular with tourist families and visiting senior citizens. A handful of small missions and hostels, run by religious groups, operated in slum areas such as the Tenderloin, but they were usually set up to help elderly alcoholic men. There was a one-to-four-night limit for their few beds in most places, and attendance at a religious service or prayer meeting was sometimes required. A sprinkling of other small facilities existed in the city, but you needed contacts with the sponsoring church or organization to even know of their existence; they were not listed in any guides to the city. At that time American Youth Hostels, Inc., had no housing facility in San Francisco or surrounding cities. The nearest hostel was at Point Reyes Seashore.

The city's only move to increase resources for the summer of 1967 was an order by the chief of police: He sent more men to Park Station, the police station that serves the Haight-Ashbury district. San Francisco waged an undeclared war against the flower children. If these intruders did not have a place to stay, the city fathers reasoned, they would turn around and go home.

When summer came, the flower children arrived as predicted. Estimates of their numbers run as high as 100,000, and most of them did, indeed, have no place to stay. But they did not turn around and go home. They slept crowded together on the floors of small apartments, their sleeping bags overlapping. They slept in doorways, on shop floors, and in recesses of Golden Gate Park where trees and plants hid them from view. Some people eliminated the need for sleep—at least temporarily—by staying continuously high on psychedelic drugs.

The result was chaos. Physical and mental suffering became widespread, drug use intensified, and property in the Haight deteriorated overnight. By the fall of 1967 the Haight-Ashbury district was in shambles. The authors of *Love Needs Care*—a book about the Haight-Ashbury Free Medical Clinic, which opened that summer—have compared the ravages of 1967 with San Francisco's 1906 earthquake and fire. They point out that the 1967 disaster was man-made and could have been mitigated if the city had stepped in to help instead of fanning the flames of destruction.

*   *   *

Amsterdam reacted differently.[3] By 1970 the center of hippie-dom had shifted to that European city. Young people from England, the United States, France, Germany, Australia, Scandinavia, and numerous other countries, along with Dutch youths from other parts of Holland, poured into Amsterdam as though entering the promised land. Long a holiday center that catered to the low-budget student as well as the affluent tourist, Amsterdam already had numerous low-cost hostels and hotels for youths, both privately owned and sponsored by youth organizations. Young visitors traditionally had a choice of safe, clean accommodations ranging in price from $2 to $6 a night. In addition, there were four campgrounds on the outskirts of the city.

When it became apparent that a mass youth migration similar to San Francisco's summer of '67 was about to hit Amsterdam, the city did not move to close any of its facilities. Instead it augmented them. Realizing that its existing housing facilities would not be enough and that many visitors would arrive without $2 to $6 a night for lodgings, the city opened two low-cost dormitories and later set aside free crashing facilities in a local park.

Not every citizen of Amsterdam welcomed the new transients; some were as opposed to masses of young people converging on their city as their San Francisco counterparts had been. But a youth coalition had gained enough support to insure a protransient policy.

As early as 1966 a youth movement called the Provos had emerged in Holland. It was a reform group, organized by students, which worked against Establishment values and sought to narrow the gulf between students and workers. But unlike youth groups in other countries at that time, which rejected their governments entirely, the Provos decided to get their own people into office. By 1970, when they had evolved into another group called the Kabouters (dwarfs), they ran a slate of their members for the Gemeende Raad—the Amsterdam City Council. Enough older citizens supported their aims for several Kabouters to be elected. Among them was Roel van Duyn, an organizer of the Provos who had become the leader of the Kabouters.

It was this newly elected council that met the need for transient housing by setting up two large dormitories—sleep-inns—in downtown Amsterdam during the summer months. They had 550 and 850 beds respectively and charged around $1.25 a night.

Some young visitors preferred sleeping on the streets in sum-mer. They congregated around Dam Square in downtown Amster-dam, sitting on the steps of a memorial to those who died in World War II, and rolling out their sleeping bags at night. One evening, however, a group of young Dutch soldiers in training, who felt their war monument was being desecrated, arrived at Dam Square on their own initiative and physically removed all visitors from the monument steps. When citizens reacted strongly in favor of the soldiers, the Gemeende Raad bowed to public opin-ion and prohibited visitors from sleeping in Dam Square or in surrounding streets. But it also set up a free sleeping facility in a city park.

The Vondel Park, located in a pleasant middle-class section of Amsterdam a few miles from the center of town, is a fraction of the size of San Francisco's Golden Gate Park. Nevertheless, one section of the park was set aside as a free crashing area during the summers of 1971–1974. Portable toilets and washing facilities were erected, ample trash cans were strategically placed, a luggage depot where packs and sleeping bags could be stored during the day was set up, and many citizens volunteered to help run the facility.

In addition, beginning in 1970 the Dutch government funded a youth advisory center, the Jongern Advises, or JAC, with offices in all major cities. By the mid-1970s the JAC was serving a predominantly Dutch clientele, but its services remained open to young people from any country.

Amsterdam emerged from its period of intense youth migration with increased facilities for young people, while San Francisco's Haight-Ashbury was decimated in three months, leaving behind a legacy of bitterness.

At Last: Hostels for Young Tourists

One outgrowth of the beat and hippie movements was a gradual acceptance of young Americans traveling around in their own country. When the cherished sons and daughters of optionaires began taking off for Denver, Seattle, and San Francisco in the summertime, their parents and grandparents could no longer declare that only bums traveled the highways with packs on their backs.

During the 1970s low-cost accommodations for student-type

tourists began to appear in American cities. In San Francisco, American Youth Hostels opened a downtown facility in 1974. That same year the YMCA opened its Embarcadero facility in San Francisco to the public.* The Embarcadero "Y," built as an army-navy YMCA in 1926, had remained closed to all transients except servicemen throughout the hippie period. In 1974 its 300-bed facility was averaging thirty-eight guests a night, and there was talk of closing it down. Its new director, Ron Cole, turned it into a coed facility for people of all ages, with rooms from $5 to $6.50 a night. He took the top floors of the hotel, which had been closed for years, and turned them into a youth hostel, with rooms renting for $3 a night.

"The hostel went bananas," Cole recalls. "It was packed all summer. By noon all hostel rooms would be rented for the next night." Sometimes so many young tourists showed up at night with nowhere else to go that Cole would open up one of the recreation rooms and let people roll out their sleeping bags on the floor.

In 1976 plans were under way to remodel the Embarcadero "Y," leaving the top floors as a hostel. Seattle had recently spent $200,000 upgrading its downtown "Y," Cole said. All over the country, facilities for summer youth tourists were beginning to emerge. Some colleges, for example, were opening their dormitories to tourists, as European countries had been doing for decades.

By the mid-1970s, young Americans in need of moderately priced accommodations had separated into two major streams: the student tourist who had decided to see America, and the new migrant in search of a job and better life. For the student tourist, facilities keep growing, although they are still scant. By the mid-1980s, the young American optionaire tourist, along with an ever-growing number of young travelers from abroad, may be able to "do" America as well as Europe on a minimum budget, finding simple but adequate accommodations for a few days in most major cities. For people without that kind of money, and for those who need longer-term accommodations, the housing situation remains grim.

Cole took note of the two streams of youth in 1976. A year

* Information about the Embarcadero "Y" throughout this section drawn from author's interview with Ron Cole, Director, Embarcadero YMCA, San Francisco.

earlier he had applied to the United Way for funds to hire a counselor who would work with people looking for jobs or having special problems. The request was turned down, and the "Y" did not consider such a position in its budget. Now Cole was concentrating on providing low-cost housing for tourists and large youth groups from other countries, who were responding to the YMCA's ads in European magazines. "We could never house the down-and-outs here," he said.

The receptionist at the front desk was busy registering guests. When asked what she did when young people showed up with no money, she said brightly, "We refer them to the Haight-Ashbury Switchboard. They run a free crash-housing program."

Still Lacking: Hostels for the New Migrants

At the Haight-Ashbury Switchboard, the free-housing program had reached a new low by 1976. The atmosphere of brotherhood that had once inspired people to open their homes to strangers was as obsolete as the buttonhook. Their 1976 *Survival Manual* stated, "There are no 'crash pads' anymore; most emergency housing is taken by 8:00 P.M. Sleeping in the park is risky and illegal. However, late at night there are very few alternatives for those without money. If you're not prepared to deal with this, perhaps you ought to consider either altering your life-style or returning whence you came."[4]

This stern advice from the cradle of the counterculture reflected the changes of the past decade. The Switchboard could no longer afford to coddle the latter-day hippie who came to feed his soul, expecting his bodily needs to be met by a loving community. Too many people desperately needed beds.

The *Survival Manual*'s listing of free emergency shelters gave the picture: Survival House was for gays; and Raphael House, for women and children, had a three-night limit. Some religious-sponsored facilities required prayer-meeting attendance in return for a bed: At the San Francisco Gospel Mission, "those who sit in the first three rows of pews during religious services get beds; be there by 5 P.M.," while Shiloh House, which housed men and women for one night, was "o.k., if you're into Jesus."

The single, young male who was neither gay nor "into Jesus" was the person most likely to end up sleeping on the streets. But even people who fit the criteria of organizations that ran emergency hostels—women, children, gays, people potentially receptive to religious conversion—could not be assured of a bed in the hostels that catered to them, because there were not enough beds to go around. People who were taken into a shelter could rarely stay for more than two or three nights at best; then they had to leave in order to give others a turn at a free bed.

The situation in San Francisco has grown progressively worse since 1976, as each year more hostels cut back on services or close down altogether for lack of funds. One small hostel that operated for several years during the 1970s can serve as an illustration of the kind of housing that new migrants need.

Aquarius House

Back in 1947, in the study *Transient Youth in California,* social workers and sheriffs alike had stressed the need for temporary housing that would offer counseling and other social services as well for young migrants. Their recommendations were ignored, but the need remained constant. The traditional Youth Hostel with a one-to-three-night limit is well suited to the young tourist visiting a city, but it does not meet the needs of the new migrant, who hopes to find a job and settle in a new area. It may take weeks to find a job and make the transition to a new city. During that period, a safe place to stay, and one that also includes help from a person knowledgeable about the job market and other resources in the city, may make a crucial difference in the young person's life at the crossroads.

In the early 1970s Marjorie Montelius began looking for a way to provide such housing and support for her clients. Time and again she and her staff at Travelers Aid saw new migrants who could never find work and settle down, because wherever they went, they had no place to stay. Often these young people lacked the skills that both the street-smart hustler and the sophisticated optionaire may have for surviving without money in a large city. The crash pads in the Haight-Ashbury overwhelmed these innocents (in the years when such housing existed), but there was no other inexpensive place in the city to house them while they looked for work.

Aquarius House became the answer for a few such transients.*

---

* Information on Aquarius House throughout this section was drawn from author's interview with Louise McCoy, former director.

Initiated by Travelers Aid, funded precariously year to year by grants until it closed in 1978, Aquarius House was a small house for transients, in a residential section of San Francisco. It had beds for eight men, four women, and one family. The residents, 18 to 31 years old, came there through referrals from social agencies and most stayed about a week. Residents were charged $2 a night. If they couldn't pay, they were given a bill when they left and were asked to send the money later. Many people did repay the house months or years later, after they found work.

In order to stay at Aquarius House, a young person first had to negotiate a three-day contract with one of the counselors. In the contract he or she set down goals to work toward during that period. This might include looking for work, applying for welfare, or taking care of other needs—such as seeing a doctor about a recurrent illness or consulting a lawyer to straighten out a legal problem left dangling in some other city. If residents wanted to stay longer, they talked with their counselor every three days and renegotiated the contract. During the day, residents were expected to be out of the house, working on their lives. People who did not fulfill their contracts or who broke house rules (no drugs, alcohol, or physical violence) were asked to leave.

The structured format of Aquarius House did not suit everyone, but it worked successfully for more than half, says Louise McCoy, former director of Aquarius House. Often it acted as a turning point in their lives. "A lot of people who came to us were crying for some structure in their lives," she explains. The house rules and contractual responsibilities, along with friendly, concerned counseling, provided support and security.

"Most everyone who came to us was in a stressful place," says McCoy. "Our basic orientation was to do as solid a piece of anxiety reduction as possible." She viewed Aquarius House as a safe, supportive environment for young people, which encouraged them to take responsibility for their own lives. Freed momentarily from the constant hassles of finding a place to stay, they could sit back, take stock of their lives, and formulate goals for their futures. Trained residential counselors, aided by a half-time psychologist as supervisor, were there to help.

Aquarius House provided a comfortable community to return to after a day in the city that might have included rejection by several would-be employers, or thinly veiled hostility from welfare workers who had been ordered to cut back on General Assistance to migrants. Residents ate dinner and spent the evening together, comparing notes and getting feedback from one another as well as from the counselors.

The residents were a cross section of American youth, but they were a group different from those in Berkeley or the Haight, McCoy believes. On the whole, they were "straighter." "We saw an incredible variety of problems, from the very healthy who arrived in the city expecting to find jobs immediately, to those with long-standing family or drug-related problems."

A small fraction of their residents, perhaps 10 to 15 percent, had serious mental-health problems, she says, and were either coming out of or headed for a mental institution. Occasionally people used Aquarius House as an interim residence until a bed was available for them in a halfway house or a board-and-care facility. But most residents were not seriously disturbed. Lack of money, rather than poor mental health, was their stumbling block. One young man, the eldest of a large family, came west because "there was just no more room in my house; my family told me it was time to go."

Employment was a major emphasis of the program at Aquarius House. "Often the best thing we could do for a person's mental health was to help him find a job," says McCoy. The house received a windfall in 1975 when Robert Martin, one of the two outreach workers from San Francisco's Department of Employment, moved his office from the Haight-Ashbury Switchboard to the basement of Aquarius; if a job came in that seemed suitable for a resident, he or she was likely to get first crack at it.

On Sunday nights the house ran a job-information session after dinner. Attendance was not required, but everyone usually came. Counselors examined the work experience and skills of residents and made suggestions about where to look for jobs. They also explained how to fill out applications, write résumés, and respond to employers' questions during job interviews. Around 40 to 50 percent of the residents were able to find jobs during their stay at Aquarius House. (Young people should be given realistic information about the job situation in the West, says McCoy.)

If residents had not found jobs after two weeks, and no prospects were in sight, staff members encouraged them to apply for welfare assistance, so they could rent a room in a Tenderloin hotel while they continued job-hunting and make space at Aquarius for the newly arrived. McCoy was surprised at the strong resistance young people had to going on the welfare rolls even as an interim measure. They showed a corresponding reluctance to ask their families for help, no matter how desperate their situation.

There is a breakdown of family support in the United States, McCoy believes. Often children are expected to achieve financial independence at an early age, regardless of their circumstances; everyone is supposed to be able to make it on his or her own. As a result, young people are embarrassed to ask their families for help, even when the children are in dire straits and the parents are well off. McCoy spoke of the lack of parental responsibility she had encountered in her work. There were two brothers, 18 and 19, who arrived at Aquarius House frightened and penniless. Their American parents, who had raised their sons in Europe, brought them on a trip to the States and left the boys in Yosemite on their own, with $40 between them. Their father thought the experience would make men out of them.

Aquarius House only took people aged 18 and over because of the legal complexities in housing minors. (Juveniles are considered the responsibility—and property—of their parents, so it is illegal to house juveniles without parental consent.) But many residents of Aquarius House had, in fact, been on their own for years. Statistics compiled during 1975–76 showed that 51 percent of the 392 residents during that period had left home permanently during their midteens.[5]

There is a need for places like Aquarius House all over the country, McCoy said in 1976. But in the years that followed, facilities for new migrants decreased. The experience of Aquarius House is typical: After its initial grant from a private foundation ran out, the house tried unsuccessfully to become part of the United Way's community funding; then it tried other sources of funding, including the city, but to no avail, and finally, after closing and reopening sporadically, Aquarius House shut down permanently in 1978.

Housing new migrants remains an unpopular cause in American cities. The people who allocate money for city social services, or give out grant money, would rather encourage the homeless to move on instead—to move anywhere else, so long as it's out of their bailiwick. As in the 1930s, the vain hope is that if the new migrants are refused help and forced to leave city after city, somewhere along the route they will disappear.

Permanent Housing for the New Migrants: Who Can Afford It?

A number of new migrants do find full-time jobs eventually in new cities. Others, who are clearly unemployable, may qualify for a federal disability pension (SSI) and have a small but regular income. They are ready to settle in and attempt to put down roots, but when they look for permanent housing, a shock awaits them. They face the same problem that confronts all low-income people in the United States: Moderately priced housing is hard to find; cheap housing is virtually unobtainable except in slum areas.

Some new migrants remain alone, but a large number live with a partner or spouse. Often they begin a family. When their babies begin to walk, even the staunchest enemy of private property may decide that a house of his own with a backyard where the children can play isn't such a bad idea. That is, after all, an integral part of the American dream. But that part of the dream, too, is becoming obsolete for large segments of the population. As Robert Lindsay wrote in *The New York Times:* "The single-family home, which since frontier days has been regarded as a part of the American birthright, is becoming increasingly unattainable to millions of middle-income families."[6] For the new migrants, who will never approach middle-income levels, buying a house of their own in or around any major American city is out of the question.

Once the new migrants relinquish the dream of buying their own homes and turn to the rental market, another shock awaits them: On their incomes they can't afford most apartments and houses available in the cities. Even if they do find a place they can pay for (by cutting down on food or other necessities), the move-in costs will usually prevent them from getting it. First and last months' rent is usually required in advance, along with cleaning and security deposits. A renter may need $700 in order to move into a $275-a-month apartment.

In western European countries, the housing situation is much worse than in the United States, but the government generally plays a substantial role in providing housing for low-income citizens through federally subsidized projects. Although the United States does have some federally subsidized housing, the government's role in housing is negligible. Many an American optionaire still regards government entry into the housing field as a Communist plot—unless he can make a profit from it.

Single people face a similar dilemma when they look for permanent housing. Those lucky enough to find full-time jobs are unlikely to receive more than the minimum wage. "Even if our residents found jobs, there's no way they could pay first and last months' rent on an apartment alone," said McCoy of Aquarius House. "Either they teamed up with other people in an apartment, or else they rented a cheap hotel room."

In some cities there have been moves to enact ordinances making it illegal for several unrelated individuals to share the same dwelling. Designed to discourage hippie communes and promote the family, such proposals overlook the economic reasons that cause people to share housing. They also overlook the fact that most adult Americans want their own places; they share only if they have to.

Housing in the Former Hippie Enclaves

The urban hippie commune is becoming obsolete—at least in areas such as Haight-Ashbury. In 1976 Peter Field, an employee of the Haight-Ashbury Free Medical Clinic, went house-hunting in the Haight. As a single man earning $8000 a year, he envisioned sharing a comfortable apartment with two or three other compatible people.

"I checked out more than a hundred places that were for rent, and I only found three apartments where people were sharing," he said. "Four years ago it was more than half." At that time (1976) Field could not find a place in the Haight that he could afford to rent.[7]

At the close of the 1960s, real-estate prophets of doom predicted that the former hippie enclaves would degenerate into permanent slums, unable to attract buyers with money. The opposite happened. San Francisco's Haight-Ashbury, New York City's East Village, Cambridge's Brattle Street and environs, and most of Berkeley are among the areas that have become the rage with optionaires who are interested in the counterculture or who prefer to live in a politically liberal community. By the late 1970s, buyers were vying for the privilege of paying $125,000 and up for desirable housing in these areas.* In some cases a young

* By 1980, prices were pushing toward the $200,000 mark.

couple had rich parents who subsidized their purchase or had left their children sizable trust funds; in others, both partners were professionals in high-paying fields (doctors, lawyers, psychiatrists) or they owned businesses or were executives in large corporations.

Fashionable areas surrounding the former hippie enclaves have become too expensive for middle-income optionaires such as schoolteachers, social workers, librarians, or college professors. These optionaires can still move into a number of other residential areas in most cities, however, while new migrants earning the minimum wage are relegated to slum areas. Even some slums may be out of their reach if the landlord demands first and last months' rent plus a cleaning deposit in advance.

Children Living in the Tenderloin?

Families as well as single people are beginning to live permanently in the run-down hotels of Skid Row areas in our central cities. There is no place else where they can afford to live.

In the mid-1970s, Travelers Aid in San Francisco became concerned about the number of young children living in the Tenderloin. Some lived there permanently, often with a single parent; others were members of transient families that had come west in hopes of bettering themselves financially. But there were no facilities for children in the Tenderloin. Parents looking for work had no place to leave their preschool children during job interviews, and tensions mounted when small children were cooped up all day in hotel rooms with parents who were already frustrated over their lack of success in job hunting.

The indefatigable Marjorie Montelius and her staff decided to initiate a drop-in child-care center in the Tenderloin. But when they approached foundations for funding, the response was amazement. Some people could not believe that small children actually lived in the Tenderloin, an area known for its hookers, hustlers, and alcoholics. Others felt that the Tenderloin was no place for a child to grow up: Efforts should be made to relocate families with children instead of setting up a child-care facility that would encourage families to stay there, well-meaning optionaires advised. Finally, a local foundation gave Travelers Aid a preliminary grant to study the problem and find out if there really were many children in the area. When the study showed that hundreds of children lived in the Tenderloin, and that their parents could not afford to live anywhere else in the city on their incomes, the foundation agreed to fund the child-care center.[8]

The center opened in 1976 in the auditorium of the downtown YMCA. But although the staff had envisioned an informal drop-in facility, so many parents showed up with small children, said director Irene Kudarauskas, that they had to limit attendance to three half-day sessions per week. Advance sign-ups were started, with spaces left for parents in emergency situations. The children, mainly preschoolers, have included white, black, Spanish-speaking, Native American, and Vietnamese youngsters. Statistics for the first six months showed that of the 112 families served, 54 lived permanently in the Tenderloin and 58 were transients. Single-parent families were common among the permanent families, but the bulk of transient families were two-parent, usually in their twenties.[9]

Although the number of families living in our central-city slums is increasing, single people are still the main permanent residents of the squalid hotels in these areas. The young poor are joining the elderly poor there. Young people who cannot find work, who are unemployable because of a physical or mental handicap, or whose earning capacity is limited to occasional jobs at the minimum wage, cannot afford to live anywhere else. Their road to the American dream dead-ends at a shabby hotel.

CHAPTER EIGHT

Reaching the Unemployable

Americans remain unconcerned about the job and housing problems of the new migrants partly because most citizens are not aware that such people or problems exist. There has been virtually no publicity about new migrants in search of jobs. But a small, specialized group of new migrants are receiving some publicity these days. They are the fraction of the street people who are unemployable because of mental illness. If they are also alcoholics or heavy drug users, they may rate a feature story.

Focusing attention on mentally ill or alcoholic street people has the advantage of keeping the myth of the American dream intact. It eliminates the need to consider economic factors or the lack of survival services for new migrants in our cities. Everything can be blamed on a damaged psyche. Thus one can say that of course those unfortunate people can't find jobs or get off the streets, because they have deep-seated psychological problems. If we could just hire enough psychiatrists to straighten out all their heads—or if we could only cure them of alcoholism and drug addiction—then they would have no trouble finding good jobs and leading satisfying lives.

Mentally ill street people receive publicity for another reason as well—the universal fascination with aberrant behavior. The more bizarre an individual's life-style and opinions, the greater the public interest in hearing the details. It is easy to collect such material about street people. The journalist in search of a feature story need only head for the closest Skid Row or former hippie enclave, where he can speedily fill his notebook with statements from defiant alcoholics or flamboyant schizophrenics. They are delighted at the opportunity to lash out at the Establishment with pronouncements on the degeneracy of the government, and to expand on the joys of being freed from an uptight existence, even if it means living on the streets in poverty. With a few connecting lines from the journalist to the effect that these people are leftover hippies whose main concern is their life-style, he has a story that will please editor and readers.

It is against such a background of sensationalism that social agencies, especially alternative agencies, are working these days with street people who are mentally ill or have other problems that make them unemployable. The goals of these agencies are neither public entertainment nor miracle cures. Instead, they seek to reach the unemployable in order to help them get enough to eat and a bed to sleep in, to relieve their feelings of social isolation, and, when possible, to help them lead fuller lives.

The Unexpected Clients of Alternative Agencies

When alternative agencies opened at the height of the hippie movement, they expected to dispense counterculture information to hip optionaires who had chosen to drop out of the system. Staff members were unprepared to deal with young people who were seriously disturbed—people whom psychiatrists would describe as schizophrenic, psychotic, or chronically disoriented. The range and intensity of difficulties varied, but those who had such problems shared an inability to hold a steady job. Some people could not handle their own money—when they had any—or establish any kind of sustained relationship with another person. They were totally isolated.

If disturbed street people went anywhere for help, it was likely to be to an alternative agency. They feared that if they went to a traditional agency they might be labeled crazy and sent to a mental hospital. (This may have happened to them earlier along their route, in another state.) But they did not think they were crazy; they saw themselves as travelers in need of food, a place to stay, and money to live on. So a switchboard run by nonjudgmental hippies seemed the place to go.

The percentage of street people who were seriously disturbed was perhaps 20 to 25 percent, depending on one's definition of abnormal behavior and on the agency's location (in the hippie enclaves it was significantly higher), but their numbers seemed greater. While other new migrants and street people came in for help a few times before settling in or moving on, disturbed street people sometimes came around regularly for years. Finding sympathetic people at last, who did not reject them if they "flipped out" from time to time and started screaming at everyone, or if they continuously lost their money and their identification, many disturbed street people used alternative agencies as day centers, and their staffs as surrogate parents.

At first, switchboard volunteers operated on the hippie principle that all you need is love. Filled with goodwill toward every young person at odds with parents or society, they made themselves available day and night to deeply disturbed people, rescuing them from recurrent crises, trying to reverse a lifetime of isolation and mistrust by administering strong doses of acceptance and love. The result was a widespread occurrence of the "burnout" phenomenon among staff workers. After a year or so of intense involvement, staff found themselves so exhausted physically and mentally that they could no longer continue. There was a high turnover in such agencies throughout the country, as workers dropped out to salvage their own neglected personal lives, or just to regain their own physical and mental health.

Not too many years elapsed before personnel in alternative agencies began to establish working relationships with community agencies and hospitals that cared for the mentally ill. But this liaison was no panacea. The problem was not conflicting values, for the two systems came to rely on each other for certain services —the problem was a lack of adequate facilities in either system.

During the same years that the mass migration of youth occurred in the United States, methods of caring for the mentally ill were undergoing radical changes. The Establishment system of mental-health care was not only in transition during this period, it was often in turmoil. In California, the state that attracted the most new migrants—as well as a disproportionate number of disturbed people—the turmoil was notable.

There had long been a movement in the United States to get patients out of mental hospitals and into community-based facilities whenever possible. California was in the forefront of such reform. In the late 1960s it passed legislation mandating programs of aftercare and rehabilitation for mental patients in their own communities instead of incarcerating them in hospitals far from home.[1] The money saved by closing mental hospitals was supposed to help create new community facilities.

California quickly closed three of its mental hospitals (and later closed more);[2] but in the ensuing bureaucratic shuffle, only a small part of the millions saved found its way into community mental-health programs. In addition, there was local resistance to community programs: Although most people agreed in principle with the concept of treating the mentally ill near home, few citizens wanted a board-and-care home in *their* neighborhood.

With funding low and facilities limited, the former mental-hospital patients who did get absorbed into the community-based system were likely to be docile, introverted people who would not cause trouble.[3] The most disruptive people—especially those who came from other parts of the country and had no relatives nearby to insist on residential care—often ended up living on the streets.

Falling Through the Cracks

An article entitled "Falling Through the Cracks" discusses the problem of disturbed street people's inevitable return to the streets, and describes how this process works in practice.[4] The authors—Steven Segal, associate professor of social welfare at the University of California, and social workers Jim Baumohl and Elsie Johnson—concentrate on the most disturbed street population in Berkeley, a group comprising perhaps a third of the street people.

The authors describe disturbed street people (DSP's) as people who lack "social margin," which they define as "the set of resources *and* relationships on which an individual can draw either to advance or survive in society. Social margin consists of family relations, friendships, possessions, skills, and personal attributes that can be morgaged, used, sold, or bartered in return for necessary assistance."[5]

Young people from all over the country who lack social margin and feel rejected by their families and communities may move to former hippie enclaves, hoping to be accepted into a community of hippies, whom they have heard are also at odds with society. But DSP's find themselves shunned here, too, labeled "space cases" by the more stable street people. For small-time

drug dealers on the street, the unpredictable and sometimes de-
lusionary behavior of "space cases" can be bad for business, while
other street people find the vagaries of forming friendships with
DSP's not worth the trouble.

Ultimately, DSP's find themselves alone once again. They are
vulnerable as victims of crime, especially by heroin addicts, but
rarely report crimes against themselves to the police. They are
afraid of being detained and getting shipped off to a mental
hospital.

In one sense the DSP's are a legacy of the American dream:
They are rugged individuals who have retained a fierce desire for
autonomy, a quality that has always been highly prized in the
United States. But for those who do not succeed financially and
who also lack any vestige of social margin, rugged individualism
may be a detriment, because it keeps people from accepting help
when they need it. As the authors of "Falling Through the Cracks"
explain it: "The high value street people, and thus DSP's, place
on self-sufficiency and autonomy cannot be overemphasized; combined with their powerless state it creates an abiding hostility
to psychiatric and social service institutions."[6]

When DSP's are committed to mental hospitals for observation, they use their wits to get out as soon as possible. Back on
the streets, they are uncooperative with any community after-
care workers they may see. These social workers, who carry heavy
case loads and have limited funds for working with former mental-hospital patients, tend to "cream off" the patients who are receptive to help and work with them, and drop the hostile DSP's.
Thus the most disturbed people in town slip through the cracks
of the social-service system and return to the streets on their own,
often without money to live on. (Segal and Baumohl are now
working on a book that will suggest ways to reach this population.)

Drug Abuse and Alcoholism

So much was heard about drug abuse during the hippie period
that some may wonder why the effects of drugs are not a major
focus of this chapter. The reason is that drug abuse, and its com-
panion of the 1970s, alcoholism, are secondary issues here. Although some new migrants and many street people do have
problems with drugs or alcohol (as does a sizable percentage of

the nation's population) , it is rarely their major problem, nor is it the cause of their difficulties.

The results of the Pittel-Miller study bear out this assertion.[7] In the late 1960s Dr. Stephen Pittel, a psychologist, and Henry Miller, professor of social welfare at the University of California, studied 250 hippies in San Francisco's Haight-Ashbury district who were heavy users of psychedelic drugs. When the researchers did follow-ups on their subjects during 1971 and 1972, they found personal isolation—lack of social margin—to be the major cause of continued drug use.

Pittel and Miller classified subjects into three groups, according to their degree of reentry into the mainstream of society— reentry, semi-reentry, and non-reentry; they found that the extent of a person's past drug use or degree of immersion in the hippie culture had little effect on his or her reentry potential. The crucial correlation was with the person's mental health at the beginning of the study.

"They turned out pretty much the way they started," said Pittel. "Those kids who were reasonably intact to begin with remained intact at the end of the study. Those who came from very disturbed backgrounds had become even more disturbed and they remained disturbed."[8]

Among the reentry and semi-reentry groups, drug use had decreased dramatically or stopped altogether; in the non-reentry group, it had escalated. Pittel described this last group as the outcasts of society, the losers and loners, who had no place to go when the hippie movement collapsed. "They were either overtly psychotic or controlled their psychosis with drugs. The portrait we get of their families is one of overt hostility, brutality, no indication of communication, no vestige of affection for the kids."[9]

The practice of isolating heavy drug or alcohol use as the cause of chronically disturbed people's troubles and trying to cure them by reforming their drug or alcohol habit has usually proved ineffective. Those who work with severely disturbed street people now see drug addiction and alcoholism as symptoms rather than causes. They see that permanent cures are more difficult to achieve than was once supposed.

During the 1970s, federal agencies concerned with drug abuse and alcoholism began to emphasize prevention rather than cures, and made funds available to local communities and groups that set up programs to improve mental health among teen-agers. This is a realistic direction for reducing the incidence of drug abuse and alcoholism—as well as other serious mental-health problems—among tomorrow's adults.

A Practical Approach to Mental Illness

Agencies that work with disturbed street people come to agree with their clients that what the street people need most is food, shelter, and other basic amenities. In the past, what their clients often received was therapy only. Workers in several agencies spoke bitterly about expensive programs of rehabilitation and therapy (especially earlier programs for drug addicts) that neglected to provide the recipient with dinner or a bed to sleep in. As social worker Elsie Johnson put it: "Our clients feel, If my stomach is empty and I only slept a couple of hours last night in a doorway, I'm not going to be very receptive to therapy." Another social worker suggested that the major benefit of rehabilitation treatment programs was to create jobs for unemployed psychotherapists.

Elaborate therapy programs are on the decline now because they're so expensive and have such low success rates. Instead, street people in the former hippie enclaves who are unemployable because of mental illness are being directed onto the Supplementary Security Income program (SSI). This is a monthly pension for people who are unable to work because of a physical or mental disability. To qualify, applicants claiming mental disability must be examined by a licensed psychiatrist who finds that the person is unable to hold a job during the coming year because of a mental disability.

The SSI program, an outgrowth of the old Aid to the Totally Disabled (ATD), is now administered by the Social Security Administration, but its funds for the disabled come from the state and the federal government, not from the retirement payments that workers and employers pay into Social Security. (The exception would be if a person had already earned enough quarters to qualify for regular Social Security, but this is rare among mentally disabled street people, who are unemployable.) SSI pays enough to rent a room and eat regularly; for example, in California in 1978 an SSI recipient received $329 a month if he had to eat out, and $296 if his room had cooking facilities.

Staff workers in alternative agencies view SSI as a practical way to help disturbed street people get enough money to live on. Not only is SSI considerably cheaper than hospitalization and board-and-care homes (or prisons), but it works out better for their clients. The problem with SSI in many cases is that street people, who, as noted earlier, are often ruggedly individualistic, do not want to accept money from the government.

Alternative agencies in former hippie enclaves, along with welfare-counseling agencies in large cities, have become major facilitators of SSI applications on grounds of mental disability. Disturbed street people are more likely to trust alternative-agency personnel than social workers in government agencies. In 1978 Wayne Kwitny, who worked with SSI applicants at Berkeley Support Services, estimated that there were a few hundred people sleeping in the Berkeley Hills or on the streets who were eligible for and in need of SSI. Many were afraid to apply, because they thought if they proved mental disability (admitted they were "crazy") the examining psychiatrist might ship them off to a mental hospital. Part of Kwitny's job was gaining their confidence and explaining that even if they wanted to reside permanently in a mental hospital, they would have difficulty doing so in California under current laws. He worked through contacts with other street people, who certified him and the office as "safe" and brought in people who needed help.

The clients of Berkeley Support Services came from all over the country. If they retained any contact with their families, it was usually tenuous and painful. One mother phoned the office from New York to talk about her 24-year-old son. "Please do whatever you can to help my son," she said, "so he'll stay in California. We simply can't handle him when he comes home."

Parents are not the only people who have difficulties handling disturbed street people. Employees in Social Security and county welfare offices often have problems relating to hostile or disoriented people whose claims they are trying to process. These employees were not trained to work with the mentally ill; they are eligibility specialists who suddenly find they need the skills of a trained therapist in order to process an application. Not surprisingly, employees in such government offices may welcome the existence of agencies like Berkeley Support Services, whose staff members they can phone for help when a client they can't handle comes in to apply for SSI. Not only can these agencies help guide difficult clients through the SSI or GA application process, they may also be able to provide interim survival services such as housing.

HOUSING

Emergency Shelters

As we saw in the preceding chapter, America has few emergency shelter facilities for adults. But during the period when a person's application for relief is being processed, he or she may be in sore need of a place to stay. Even if a welfare worker can find emergency funds to house an applicant at a fleabag hotel for this interim period, the hotel manager may refuse to keep someone who proves to be a difficult guest. Berkeley Support Services runs a hostel that has wider limits of tolerance, as well as cheaper prices.

In 1975 the Berkeley youth hostel, which was started during the hippie period (it has no connection with American Youth Hostels, Inc.), was about to close down for lack of interest. Berkeley Support Services took over the hostel, expecting to house young travelers for a few nights in the typical hostel pattern, but the staff soon found that the hostel's major function was as an emergency shelter for homeless people. Up to 40 percent of their guests were on GA or SSI or had applications for these programs in process. As unemployment among black teen-agers rose, the number of young blacks and other Third World people increased accordingly.

The hostel discontinued its three-night limit, and some guests stayed for a month or longer.* Usually some of the guests were families with small children. By 1978 the hostel was turning away several people a night because its small staff could not handle more. Invariably a few guests were disturbed street people, and looking after them required far more of the staff than collecting the fee and handing out clean sheets.

The need for more emergency shelters for the homeless in the United States is pressing, a subject we will return to in Chapter 19.

---

* By this time San Francisco had both a Youth Hostel and a hostel section in the Embarcadero "Y" to house young travelers who needed a bed for a few nights.

The Hotel Project Experiment

After the large-scale closures of state mental hospitals, permanent housing for the mentally ill became a problem in many communities. There was often a shortage of board-and-care homes; but in the case of disturbed street people, this arrangement did not work out anyway.

In Berkeley, groups working with the street population decided to try another alternative that might be more feasible as well as less expensive: They would bring social services into "welfare hotels," the small downtown hotels that became crowded with young people during the 1970s because they had the cheapest rates in town. In places like Berkeley, these hotels housed a number of disturbed people who had a little money through GA, SSI, or, occasionally, from jobs or family.

In 1976, Berkeley's Departments of Public Health and Mental Health started a hotel project, working cooperatively with staff from Berkeley Support Services. Getting into the hotels proved a problem, because most managers did not want to admit that they housed "crazies" who needed special services. But the manager and part-owner of one hotel, the Pacific, welcomed the Hotel Project. One day a week it brought a public-health nurse, a psychiatric social worker, and an eligibility specialist (for GA and SSI) into his hotel. This meant that when a crisis occurred at night, the manager, whom we'll call Ted, could phone the Project workers instead of the police.

The Project staff began coming in every Friday for a few hours. They made coffee and sat in the lobby, ready to talk and give help, be it for a cut foot, an argument with the management, or a welfare check that failed to arrive. It took a month or so before residents began to trust the Project staff, but gradually some residents came to look forward to Fridays as a social event, while others came down when they had a specific problem.

Frank, a resident of the Pacific Hotel, was in the lobby when the author visited the Hotel Project one Friday. "Welcome to the nuthouse," he said genially, stating at the outset what he assumed would be a stranger's evaluation of the hotel's residents. Frank, from Philadelphia, was 28, but he looked younger; he had the pudgy fat and acne of an adolescent and wore a wool cap pulled down over his ears although it was August. He did not have a job and was receiving SSI because of recurrent depressions as well as a leg injury, but (staff explained later) he helped out with other residents. He played with Lisa, age 3, who lived at the hotel with her mother, Catherine. Catherine considered the other residents beneath her and kept aloof, but she had periodic attacks when she lost control and lashed out hysterically against everyone within earshot. Frank also watched over Elena, who was too disoriented to relate to others. If he found Elena walking through the hotel corridors naked, he would admonish her and lead her back to her room to put some clothes on.

Frank spoke of his renewed interest in Christianity, but he did not seem upset when another resident, who called himself Jesus, swung down over the railing into the lobby from the floor above and began laughing and joking with the Project staff. Jesus, who was 41, bore a remarkable resemblance to his namesake; he was tall, painfully thin, with a reddish beard and shoulder-length hair, which he kept in place with a headband. Until recently Jesus had lived in the hills. Now, with an SSI pension, he lived in the sheltered environment of the Pacific Hotel.

On another day, Phyllis Hunt, the young public-health nurse who worked at the Project on Fridays, talked about the hotel and its residents. The residents had formed a loosely structured community, she said, giving some support to one another. There was an unwritten code of moral behavior: Hard-drug dealing was taboo, and while "you're allowed to freak out at will," there were limits to the degree of "craziness" that residents would tolerate in their neighbors. The Pacific was considered the *pièce de résistance* of the Berkeley welfare hotels, she said; other hotels were centers of drug pushing or had residents who were beyond interaction.

Not everyone there was on GA or SSI, Hunt pointed out; a few residents had part-time jobs, or were trying to find them. Nor was everyone severely disturbed. What they all shared, said Hunt, was a low self-image.

"So many are totally convinced that they have nothing to give. They've been taught that people must be self-sufficient, which makes it all the harder for them to accept help when they need it." The American belief that if you don't earn ten to twenty thousand a year you're no good gets to them, Hunt explained, along with the other tenets of the success myth, such as the idea that one should postpone gratification on the way up. "But, for them, the gratification never arrives."

Many residents sat in their hotel rooms day after day with no place to go. "I'd love to get hold of a van and take some of these people on an outing," Hunt said impulsively. "Just up to Tilden Park on a picnic for a few hours."[10]

But the outing never took place. After a fire in a San Francisco welfare hotel was publicized, Berkeley fire officials came around and said the Pacific was not up to code. Ted, who was overextended financially, did not have the money for repairs. Local members of the American Schizophrenic Association, who took an interest in the Hotel Project, offered to work with city officials to get an emergency grant from city funds for repairs. Meetings were held, but six months later nothing had come through.

"When I went to a meeting of city people, I thought they were going to talk about repairs," said Ted, "but they kept talking about the bugs and the crazy people who lived there. I told them the bugs are brought in by people who don't wash. I think the city just doesn't want these people living in downtown Berkeley."

In the months that followed, two fires started by residents further damaged the hotel. Ted stopped paying the utility bills, the gas-and-electricity company threatened to cut off services, and a resident went to the local Tenants' Union, which helped him organize a rent strike. Then Ted left, and the hotel closed down. Some residents were relocated in other hotels, a few had to be hospitalized because of the trauma, and Jesus went back to the hills. Later the hotel was sold and remodeled into hotel apartments for students at the nearby university.

The Hotel Project at the Pacific ended as a fiasco. "What we accomplished was to give the residents enough confidence to organize a rent strike," the psychiatric social worker for the Project commented wryly. But in retrospect the staff felt that they had been able to bring needed social services to a population that is difficult to reach and thus is generally ignored. They still thought it was a good idea. A few years later, similar projects were started at two other small hotels in Berkeley.

Again it must be emphasized that the disturbed street people who were the subject of this chapter are only a small perecntage of the new migrants. It is necessary to understand their problems and provide services for them; but an overemphasis on the plight of the unemployable 15 to 20 percent may lessen the possibility that the potentially employable 80 percent will receive some notice in the future.

Street people may remain in the same place year after year, but most new migrants keep moving if they don't find jobs. In the late 1970s and early 1980s a new route was emerging. It led to the Sunbelt states.

CHAPTER NINE

Changing Patterns of Migration

Word is finally out—at least to some people east of the Rocky Mountains—that the Far West is no longer a bonanza. Even the luster of California is tarnishing as tales of high prices, tight housing, and unemployment make their way across the continent and reach the Atlantic shores. As a result, the new migrants, like increasing numbers of other Americans on the move, are changing directions.

If Americans are beginning to lose faith in the Far West, this does not mean that the nation has relinquished its belief in a vast frontier swelling with limitless opportunity. It has simply switched the location of El Dorado. The Sunbelt states have become the new land of milk and honey.

In 1970 most Americans had never heard of the "Sunbelt"; but by the close of the decade, use of the term was widespread. The Sunbelt refers to the lower arc of the United States that stretches from southern California to the Carolinas. (Los Angeles County is generally excluded from the arc because its size and congestion are features from which Americans are fleeing.)

By 1976, for the first time in the nation's history, most Americans lived in the western and southern states. Arizona, in the heart of the Southwest, had the largest growth, with a population increase of 25.3 percent in six years.[1] A handful of states above the Sunbelt arc, clearly western but not far-western states—Nevada, Idaho, Utah, Wyoming, and Colorado—had population gains of 12 to 14 percent or more, while every state in the Sunbelt arc had grown, ranging from a 4.1-percent increase in Louisiana to a 23-percent increase in Florida. The five inland western states listed above are usually included in the general use of the term "Sunbelt," although they are above the arc and have cold winters. The popularity of these inland western states suggests that space —with its implications of opportunity and small-town living— rather than sunshine, is the prime attraction of the Sunbelt.

From 1970 to 1976, when the populations of the Sunbelt states were growing, population losses were noticeable in the large cities of the northeast and north-central states. Chicago, New York, Philadelphia, Detroit, St. Louis, Pittsburgh, and Boston all lost population. The exodus to the Sunbelt states has been chronicled as a mass migration from the Northeast, a flight from high crime rates, overcrowding, pollution, and noise, to a safer, simpler, and more satisfying existence. The picture is true as far as it goes, but it does not tell the whole story. First, a look at the story that has already unfolded.

Middle-class Americans—the affluent as well as skilled, experienced workers at the top of the nonaffluent society—are moving to the Sunbelt in great numbers these days; thus far they have found jobs and social acceptance for the most part in the small towns and cities whose numbers they are swelling. When *Time* magazine ran a cover story, "Americans on the Move," in 1967, it described several Americans who had made the change smoothly. Among them were a lawyer, a clinical social worker, a carpenter's apprentice, a manager of an auto-supply center, and a dental-lab-technician instructor. These people came out with their families and with enough savings to see them through the transition; they were welcome in the towns where they settled, because, with their skills and capital, old-timers saw them as positive additions to the community.[2]

The next year the women's magazine *Family Circle* devoted an entire issue to the Sunbelt states. In one article, "The Glorious Sunbelt Comes into Its Own," southern writer Willie Morris spoke of the southerner's new acceptance of migrating Yankees. He described a party in a "Deep Southern city" and some of the migrants from the North who attended: "A scientist and his wife from Vermont, a businessman and his family from Massachusetts, a woman from Iowa who was teaching school, a newspaperman from Illinois, an art designer from New York City, an engineer from New Jersey, a librarian from Michigan. The atmosphere was one of conviviality and belonging."[3]

These recipients of southern hospitality were all optionaires with training and experience in their fields. They are the people for whom the Welcome Wagon goes out in the Sunbelt states today, and who will continue to be welcome—until their increasing numbers visibly alter the complexion of the towns and cities into which they are moving.

Already there are movements in places like Petaluma, California, and Scottsdale, Arizona, to limit growth and keep more newcomers from entering. The most ardent fighters for growth control may be last generation's migrants, such as the mayor of Scottsdale, who said in 1976: "Let's let the town remain the same as it was when I came here."[4]

Little has been said about people migrating for economic reasons; to the contrary, reportage has stressed that Americans who move to the Sunbelt care more about life-style than money. Again true as far as it goes, because the migrants whose moves have been chronicled are people who left one economically viable situation for another. They could make it in both places, so economic considerations were not paramount; for them the quality of life mattered most. But they are not the only people who are heading for the Sunbelt.

People are also migrating to the Sunbelt in hopes of bettering themselves economically. People short on money, skills, and job experience—the new migrants as well as older people who never made it back home. If they fail to make it in the Sunbelt, they may eke out a marginal existence and wait for a better day, move further west, or return home. But whatever their experience, it has gone unnoticed. Nor have the migrants heading *east* toward the Sunbelt received much notice as yet.

Who's Crazy Enough to Leave All This?

In April 1977, a panoramic view of San Francisco appeared in that city's local Sunday paper, with the caption: "Who's crazy enough to leave all this?" Below the picture it reads as follows:

> Surprising as it sounds, the U.S. Census Bureau reported in the past week that an estimated 51,154 seemingly insane city dwellers left San Francisco in the first half of this de-

cade—that's an exodus of 10,000 a year. But the federal statis-
ticians couldn't answer the important question—why? Why
would they leave a city that comes out looking so beautiful
through the fisheye lens of a camera perched atop the Fair-
mont Hotel? And why would they be fleeing in great numbers to the so-called Sunbelt in the South and Southwest
when there's so much sunshine right here in San Francisco?[5]

Why indeed? What about the possibility that these "seemingly
insane" people left San Francisco (and other parts of the Far
West) because they could not make a living there? Or because
they could not find a job that fulfilled their expectations? Such
possibilities were apparently outside the frame of reference of
some employed journalists in the 1970s, a decade when the media
gave heavy coverage to "modern" developments—inner-awareness
symposiums, back-to-the-land movements, religious cults. It was a
time when a concern about making enough money to live on was
considered an anachronism that only fuddy-duddies left over
from the ancient 1930s clung to because they were unable to
readjust their mental set to the age of affluence.

In fact, two streams of migrants are currently leaving the Far
West—especially California—for the Sunbelt: those who grew up
in the Far West, and those who came west as adults in search of
opportunity but failed to find it.

In Chapter 3 we talked about families and individuals who
migrated to California in large numbers earlier in the century:
during the Great Depression of the 1930s, during World War II
when there was a shortage of workers in western airplane and
shipbuilding plants, and in that quarter of a century after World
War II when the state's population doubled. What about the
children and grandchildren of these earlier migrants? Did growing up in California mean that they made it into affluence?

Tracing the lives of the migrants' descendants is tricky, because
these people do not fall into a category for which special statistics
were collected; but chance events may yield a glimpse into some
of their lives. The 1976 school-bus kidnapping case in the small
agricultural town of Chowchilla, California, gave the world an
unexpected look at some descendants of the dust-bowl migrants;
it revealed people who were just making it in working-class occupations. The fabled opulence of California living had not touched
the lives of Chowchilla's citizens.

That same year another incident, in Santa Clara, California, gave us another glimpse of the economic situation that many children of yesterday's migrants are facing. In 1976 the Marriott Corporation was preparing to open its new amusement center— Great America Park—in time to receive the anticipated Bicentennial tourists. Santa Clara is thirty-five miles south of San Francisco, in the midst of an area booming with new industry, commerce, and housing developments. In January, Marriott ran ads announcing the need for 2200 workers at the park—as ride operators, waiters, waitresses, clerks, cashiers, ticket takers, sweepers, gardeners, and guides. It was a veritable treasure-house of job openings for the unskilled and the semiskilled.

The night before the park began accepting job applications, some people camped near the entrance, so they would be first in the job line. When the personnel office opened up at 7:00 A.M., so many cars swarmed toward Great America Park that on the Bayshore Freeway (Highway 101, the main thoroughfare to San Francisco in one direction and San Jose in the other) "traffic stood still for more than three hours and backed up for more than two miles in both directions of the six-lane freeway," the *San Francisco Chronicle* reported.[6] People on their way to work in San Francisco or San Jose could not get through, which made the incident worthy of a story on page 1.

By 10:15 A.M., the personnel staff had handed out the 14,000 application blanks they had on hand and closed their doors. Police on the scene estimated that another 20,000 people on the way to apply didn't get there in time.

The jobs paid $2.25 an hour, which adds up to $90 a week, or under $5000 a year. But since the park would only operate eight months a year, the annual salary would be less.

The spectacle of so many people vying for these minimum-wage jobs in California is sobering. Some young people may have been attracted by the glamour of working in an amusement park (a mini-Disneyland, so to speak), but that could hardly account for the more than 30,000 applicants who showed up. Nor could the new migrants described earlier have been in the job line in significant numbers. The Santa Clara/San Jose area developed around the automobile; to apply for a job at the park that day, you needed a car, or you had to live close by. Sizable numbers of those who flocked into Great America Park that morning in search of jobs must have been descendants of earlier migrants, young people living in apartments and small tract houses with parents who worked at blue-collar and clerical jobs—families like those in Chowchilla, whom California affluence had bypassed.

What happened to the young people who didn't get hired at Great America Park in 1976, and who also failed to find jobs in local stores, offices, or gas stations? The American way is to migrate to a large city in search of a job—in this case, San Francisco or Los Angeles. For those who failed to find jobs in those cities, the next move may have been to a city in the Sunbelt—the section of the country to which opportunity had been transferred, according to most reports. Add to these young people their counterparts who grew up in San Francisco or Los Angeles and experienced similar difficulties locating the jobs they had grown up expecting to fill, and the current exodus from California to the Sunbelt states is not surprising. It helps explain why Los Angeles and San Francisco both had population losses during the 1970s.

East to West—And On to the Sunbelt

Finally, there are the new migrants who left homes in the eastern half of the country for California, Oregon, or Washington, expecting to settle permanently in the Far West. For them the route to the Sunbelt may be an afterthought. Often they have been living in the West for a few years, traveling up and down the coast periodically in search of opportunity. When it fails to come—and they read and hear about the jobs and good living in the Sunbelt—they pack up their knapsacks one day and head for the Southwest.

Gary, the son of a factory worker in Ohio, had high hopes of making it in the South. After an early marriage failed, Gary told us, he came west and worked at a series of jobs in the Los Angeles and San Francisco areas. Although he was a skilled worker (roofing was his specialty), he never found a job out west that paid as much as his father earned back in Ohio. The good jobs in California were unionized, and he was outside of that orbit. Then he heard about a big construction project in North Carolina; he could count on a good job, friends assured him, if he got there in time.

The day before he left, Gary fell into a one-day window-washing job in a house in Berkeley when the young man who had signed up for it got sick. "This is great," Gary exclaimed as he washed the windows with gusto. "Now I'll be able to buy food for the bus trip." Early the next morning Gary left for North Carolina, confident that a steady career in construction work awaited him there.

In the decades ahead, more new migrants are likely to head for the Sunbelt states as well as the Far West. And if employment opportunities continue to diminish in large cities, increasing numbers of Third World youth will also become new migrants, as other avenues for making a living are closed off to them.

CHAPTER TEN

Down-and-Out in Britain

The new migrants may seem like an American phenomenon, inextricably linked to our national history, geography, and expectations. But they are not unique to the United States. There are new migrants throughout western Europe and beyond; most industrialized nations that allow their citizens to move about freely are experiencing the same migration of young people who leave home in search of opportunity. The same machines and technological innovations that displaced American workers have eliminated the need for much of the unskilled labor by which generations of Europeans earned their bread. And in Europe, as in the United States, the publicity that accompanied the hippie movement precipitated an upsurge of migration among working-class youth.

In this chapter, a look at Britain's new migrants will show the similarity of these young people to their American counterparts. We will also point out some differences between the new migrants in the two countries—and in the national responses to their existence and needs.

The new migrants of Britain reflect the American pattern. By 1968, central London was crowded with hippies who came from all parts of Great Britain and from several other countries as well; then a recession in the early 1970s caused the hippie mode of life to fade there, too, as young optionaires moved back into the mainstream seeking jobs and money.

Working-class youth suffered a different fate from the hippies: They found themselves stranded in London with no prospects for the future. It was nothing new for impoverished youngsters to come to London; for centuries that city has been the favorite destination of penniless youths who leave home to seek their fortunes. The differences were in the increased numbers who came, and in their expectations. The media blitz of the hippie period had pictured London, especially "the Dilly" (the downtown area near Piccadilly Circus), as paradise; the life described there exceeded the wildest fantasies of youngsters facing futures in shops and factories at best. And reports of hippies thriving in the Dilly on little or no money made the possibility of moving to London a sudden reality: All you needed was a one-way ticket and a couple of quid to tide you over until you moved into a commune or took a job and rented your own place.

In retrospect we can pinpoint economics as the underlying factor motivating the rash of impecunious young migrants who arrived on the heels of the hippies. These new migrants came largely from working-class homes and had little education or marketable skills. They left areas of high unemployment in Scotland, Ireland, and the Midlands. Some of their parents and relatives were already facing redundancies (layoffs). But economics was not on the minds of 16- and 17-year-olds as they boarded trains for London in the mid-1960s. The phonograph records they heard, the magazines and newspapers they picked up, told of an exciting new life-style for youth.

In London they found that the Dilly had all the glamour that their hometowns lacked. In addition to elegant shopping areas and the theater district, it included Soho, the cosmopolitan district that has absorbed immigrants for more than 400 years. Soho's foreign restaurants did not interest the new migrants, but its amusement palaces crammed with slot machines were a prime attraction. Best of all were the disco clubs, coffee bars, and small nightclubs where you could spend the evening listening to music and feel at home in the company of your peers. The Tiles, a popular disco on Oxford Street, attracted up to 1200 young people on weekends in the late 1960s, but most hangouts of the new migrants were small places tucked into the side streets of Soho.

Paradise, however, had another side. The assumption that jobs and housing were abundant in London proved fallacious, while the high prices there made a few pounds' transition money disappear quickly. The idea of joining a hippie commune faded as class distinction reared its head in hippieland: If you couldn't discuss the triumph of crass technology over spiritual values with the adroitness of an Oxford undergraduate, you were no brother to the hippies. Besides, the hippies weren't living in the Dilly anymore; they were moving into flats and "squats" all over London (especially Notting Hill), and they were not inviting many sons and daughters of butchers or postal clerks to join them.

Some of the more enterprising new migrants managed to find jobs, usually live-in jobs, as dishwashers, busboys, or chambermaids in hotels. Or they tried selling food or trinkets on street corners. A few young women and men turned to prostitution, but most managed to barely survive on social-security money.

As the numbers of young people without resources in London increased, a network of alternative agencies similar to that in America developed there to help them. Centrepoint, a free overnight shelter for newly arrived British youth, opened in Soho in the late 1960s as a three-month experiment.* It is still going, serving more than 7000 young people a year. The Reverend Bill Fitzpatrick, who directed Centrepoint until 1975, told us when we interviewed him that he had never seen a youngster with professional or semiprofessional training come there. He saw Centrepoint as the sphere of working-class youth who had no contacts or other resources in London. At least half of the people they saw had no special problems, Fitzpatrick said; they were normal youngsters who simply needed help making the transition from home to the big city.

At Centrepoint the migrants got a safe bed and free food, along with a chance to talk with staff volunteers who told them what services were available in the area. A social worker from the nearby Soho Project stopped by each evening to invite people to use their services, so many migrants went—and still go—from Centrepoint to the Soho Project.

When the Soho Project opened in 1968, it operated mainly in the evenings out of small discos and coffee bars. Carol Bohnsack, the American social worker mentioned in Chapter 6, was with the Project in its first years and recalls sitting at tables night after

* Centrepoint night shelter in Soho should not be confused with the large office building in Tottenham Court Road of the same name.

night, drinking endless cups of tea, until she gained the confidence of young patrons and they began asking for help. She went to court as a character witness; helped teen-aged girls who got pregnant; found emergency shelter for the penniless; and led others to agencies that might help them find jobs and permanent accommodations.

After the clubs closed down in the early 1970s, the Soho Project switched its major operation to its present third-floor office on Charing Cross Road near Oxford Street. For many young newcomers, the Project is their community. They cling to its dilapidated chairs and couches, and to each other, making it their home away from home.

"Most of our kids are ordinary people. The majority have a working-class background," a staff report said of its clients. "They are not dropouts; they were never allowed in. . . . Their problem is survival, and they have no time to organize themselves into that controversial abstract, the alternative society. They are not political creatures."[1]

The young people at the Soho Project in 1975 fit that description. They lacked the fierce hostility toward the Establishment that was sometimes seen among clients at American alternative agencies; making it financially and building a circle of friends to replace the community back home took precedence over political concerns. They described their adventures selling hot dogs on Oxford Street without a license and dodging the police, but there were no tirades against the government. The regulars at the Soho Project noticed everyone who walked in and greeted one another warmly. What happened to Joe yesterday at the employment office, where Sandy and Doreen were going that night, and whether or not Mick got arrested were the topics that interested them.

Mary, aged 25, was several years older than most of the regulars. She spoke with such authority as she described living and working conditions in detail that at first she appeared to be a staff member, but gradually it became clear that Mary was a client. She had come out of "care"—institutions run by the government for children whose parents do not look after them—and had been on her own since she was 16. Mary described the daily schedule at Holloway Women's Prison (where she had been sent more than once) and she told us how difficult it was to live on a chambermaid's wages, but she expressed no interest in changing the government or the system. Her concern was today's survival; her dream to find a man who would give her the love she had never received.

Gordon's most important possession was a three-piece suit, which he had bought with money earned from a live-in hotel job. "The police don't hassle me since I've been wearing this suit," he told us with pride. Gordon, in his early twenties, had migrated from Wales a few years before, hoping to make it big in London. Now his aim was to return home to Wales for good as soon as he could pay off a fine he owed the London courts. Although he railed against the regimen at the government-sponsored Reception Centre on Dean Street where he was staying, Gordon expressed no interest in changing it; he just wanted to get out and go home. The previous night he had not slept much, he said, because he had a job interview first thing in the morning and didn't want to wrinkle his suit. Because of his arrest record, he didn't get the job.

New Horizons, another alternative agency in the Dilly, opened the same year as the Soho Project to help young people involved with drugs. But by 1970, when the agency moved into larger quarters near Covent Garden, drug addiction had become secondary to housing and employment problems among young people in the Dilly. (The drug culture shifted to a different part of London, as we will see later.) New Horizons became a multi-service day center for people 15 to 25 years old, working closely with the "regulars," those who had been on the streets of central London for several years. "Our main concern is the people at the bottom," said staff at New Horizons.

Part of their job was interpreting the system. They translated government instruction booklets into understandable English, explained what resources were available, and supported clients in their efforts to find jobs, services, and housing. Their aim was to encourage people to take responsibility for their own lives instead of remaining dependent on social workers.

"Some people come here with the idea that we're an agency where a worker sits behind a desk, tells you what to do, and performs a few miracles. None of which we do." Young people coming out of "care" were the most dependent, they said, because they had never been allowed to make decisions for themselves.

Workers at New Horizons wanted to see more community-action projects where people could learn to help each other and to have more control over their own lives and environments. They also spoke of the need for social changes that get at the root causes of unemployment and homelessness.[2]

THE HOUSING SHORTAGE AND UNEMPLOYMENT

The term "homelessness" has different meanings to various people, but, to those experiencing the situation, being homeless means having no place to live. In Britain, homelessness is a serious problem because of the housing shortage; and the housing shortage is interrelated with unemployment to a degree that many Americans may find incomprehensible. Low-paying jobs, such as those on the Underground (subway), may go begging in London, because the people willing to take them at that salary cannot afford to live in London. Skeptics may point out that people *do* work for the Underground in London and support families as well; if they can do it, why can't unencumbered youth manage? It is precisely because they are single that young, unskilled workers cannot afford to live in London or other industrial cities.

Britain has subsidized-housing programs throughout the country. The local authority (council or borough) builds blocks of flats or buys existing ones and rents them to qualified citizens for a fraction of what they would pay on the open market. But council housing is in such short supply that many people who qualify must wait years for a low-cost flat; in some London boroughs there are 10,000 or more families on the waiting list. One's place on the list is determined by a point system, and the points rise with each dependent. Without children it is virtually impossible to obtain most council housing. Young single people cannot even get their names on most lists.

Some privately owned housing is covered by rent control. Although such housing costs more than council flats, it is within the means of the working person; but it is so scarce that it is mainly obtained through contacts—you have to know someone. The new migrant without family or other contacts in London finds rent-controlled housing as far out of his reach as council flats. Housing on the open market is prohibitive in price; the rent per week for a "luxury flat" may be two to three times the salary of an unskilled worker.

The Squatters

The tight housing situation has led to "squatting"—that is, taking possession of an empty house or flat and living there rent-free. No one knows how many squatters there are in London, but estimates run from ten to twenty thousand. Squatting is so widespread in London that the squatters have formed associations. The 1974 *Squatters' Handbook* listed twenty squatters' associations in greater London.[3]

Who are the squatters? They are people who need housing and they are usually under 40; but they are not the poorest people in the city. It takes self-confidence and skills to enter an empty flat successfully and set up housekeeping. In addition, it takes legal know-how and good verbal skills to cope with potentially hostile neighbors and with landlords who may take you to court. The former hippie, the newcomer with a background similar to the hippies', and the British equivalent of America's borderliners are the mainstays of the squatters' movement. Along with their need for housing they may also be politically motivated, seeing squatting as a protest against the system. "By squatting you are challenging fundamental values about property and the rights of owners," says the *Squatters' Handbook*.

Squatting rarely provides a solution to the housing problems of the new migrants. They do not know people in squats who will invite them in, and they are unlikely to possess enough self-confidence to venture into this illegal method of housing on their own. Other flats—whether council-owned, rent-controlled, or on the open market—are also out of their reach. Even furnished rooms may cost more than they can afford to pay. For many young migrants the only way to stay in London is through a live-in job in a hotel or other tourist facility.

Live-in Jobs

As one of the world's great tourist centers, London offers numerous low-paying jobs in what the British call the "catering trade"—as chambermaids, busboys, bellhops, and dishwashers. Cathy Coyne, who runs a small employment agency in London, does catering placements. The nearby Soho Project refers their clients to her agency. "There are fewer live-in jobs than daily ones, but the live-in jobs are more sought-after, because people need places to live," says Coyne. For every live-in listing she gets, there are fifty or more people who want it; the job is usually taken in half an hour. The most persistent people, those who check back serveral times a day, are the ones who get these jobs. "There's not a lot of work for the unskilled in London. Catering is not that well paid, so it attracts people who can't get any other job," Coyne says.[4]

Housing in the Private Sector

New migrants who cannot find a live-in job or who want their own place, but lack the skills for squatting, must hunt for a room in the private sector. Such a search can be a nightmare. In recent years the demand for rooms has escalated, while their availability continues to shrink. Between 1965 and 1972 Britain lost 6000 beds in private rooming houses and hostels.[5] The developer's bulldozer hit numerous districts filled with old hotels whose rooms the poor could afford. Southwark, a borough along the docks south of the Thames, lost 1500 low-cost beds when that area was redeveloped into a flourishing commercial center.[6] Little or no effort was made to relocate the people who had once lived permanently in the demolished hotels.

Other changes added to the loss of beds. Low-cost rooming houses that once filled whole sections of central London have been converted into bed-and-breakfast places for tourists, with appropriate rises in prices. In addition, many Georgian and Victorian houses that were turned into rooming houses a few generations ago are now being remodeled back into private residences, often for affluent young professional couples who prefer central London to the suburbs, and can afford urban living because they have two good incomes.

The refurbished Victorian houses are a delight to those concerned with historical preservation and architectural beauty; the increased facilities for tourists bring in foreign currency that is good for the economy; and the commercial centers rising on the ruins of old rooming-house districts are good for business. But to the young migrant from Glasgow or Wigan who needs inexpensive housing, these improvements may mean personal disaster. Expecting to join the work force of London and settle in permanently, he instead finds himself joining the ranks of the homeless.

CHAR: A LOBBY FOR THE SINGLE HOMELESS

Homelessness is not a new problem in Britain. A report published in 1891 showed that 938 persons, including women and children, slept in refuges and casual wards in London on a typical winter night.[7] Those sleeping on the street were not included in this number. In Victorian times, as earlier, the homeless individual was regarded either as a hopeless derelict or as a rogue who lived by criminal activity. Moral failure was considered the problem, and it could only be resolved by influencing the person to give up his bad ways. This attitude toward the homeless has survived with regard to homeless single people, but has softened somewhat with regard to families.

In the 1960s, thousands of families in London and other cities had no place to live. An organization called Shelter worked intensively with them, and a television special, "Cathy, Come Home," dramatized the problem, touching off a media campaign about the effects of homelessness on families. Public opinion began to change as people realized that families might be homeless not due to moral failure or adjustment problems but because of the housing shortage: They simply could not find a place to live. Since homelessness made it difficult, if not impossible, for the parents to find steady employment, the government was encouraged to increase its efforts to house families and to provide interim accommodations, such as rooms in bed-and-breakfast hotels, until flats were available.

This new concern for the homeless did not extend to single people; they could and should manage on their own, most people thought, while families with small children could not. But every day in overnight shelters and alternative agencies, workers saw single people whose main problem was no place to live. Their homelessness kept them from jobs and a settled existence.

Single people with low incomes are the group hardest hit by Britain's housing shortage, because the housing laws overlook them for the most part. Fragmented geographically, often on the move, and powerless, the single homeless are not likely to organize themselves into an effective lobby to pressure the government to help them. Nor are any of the agencies that work with the single homeless in a position to lobby for them. So in 1972, thirteen agencies serving this population formed an umbrella organization to fight for the rights of single homeless people. They called themselves CHAR—the Campaign for the Homeless and Rootless.[8] By 1975 CHAR had nearly a hundred member organizations, including all the alternative agencies mentioned earlier. (Later CHAR changed its name to Campaign for the Single Homeless, to get away from the pejorative connotations of "rootless," but kept the original acronym.)

CHAR does not work directly with homeless people; instead, it is the political and public-relations arm of agencies that do provide such services; it campaigns to urge the government to take a larger part in providing housing and services for single homeless people. CHAR works with a few sympathetic members of Parliament who have formed a parliamentary lobby for the single homeless—perhaps the first lobby in history, in any country, ever to address itself to the needs of this powerless group.

David Brandon of Christian Aid, a member group of CHAR, is doing research on the young homeless. Brandon, a longtime crusader for homeless people of all ages, and his staff interviewed 120 Britons under 26 who had been in London for less than two months, and did follow-ups a year or so later. One purpose of the reasearch is to see if the short-term homeless are forced into the mold of permanent homelessness by lack of options.[9] Some of Brandon's working hypotheses are that young people come to London not for its glamour but to get away from an unpleasant home situation; that a high proportion of the migrants have already been "institutionally processed" in such settings as children's homes, child guidance clinics, the courts, and penal and psychiatric settings; that many migrants fall into permanent homelessness involuntarily because of the lack of jobs, accommodations, and social services when they arrive; and that these homeless people come to regard themselves as victims.[10]

The work of CHAR is nationwide in scope. It campaigns to show that all single homeless people do not come to London: Cities throughout England are attracting migrants in search of opportunity, which means more facilities for the homeless are needed all over Britain. We interviewed June Lightfoot, former field secretary for CHAR, who traveled a lot as a consultant.

When a group in Manchester wanted to set up a night shelter for homeless people, they were opposed by local citizens who claimed there was no need for such a facility: "We have no homeless people in Manchester," they insisted. The shelter finally opened and has been serving an average of 200 people per night. Now Manchester is trying to set up more facilities for the homeless, Lightfoot told us. Liverpool receives substantial numbers of young migrants from Ireland and North Wales, while many Liverpudlians migrate to Birmingham or London in hopes of bettering themselves there. But the new migrants are unwelcome in most cities.

"Most Local Authorities are unwilling to provide facilities for fear of 'importing problems' into their area," says CHAR's charter. "Most people know little of the acute poverty of these men and women and want to push them out of their neighborhood."[11]

One CHAR study explained:

These young people who leave home and are unsuccessful in finding employment and accommodation are not attributed with the characteristic of initiative often attributed to young people who are successful in the transition from one area to another. They are sometimes resented by people who feel they are a burden on the local authority in whose area they become homeless where in fact they may be the young people who have the initiative to leave unsatisfactory conditions at home in search of employment. Rather than remain unemployed in their home areas, they have decided to make a move in hope of finding a better life elsewhere. Just because they are unsuccessful or unprepared, they should not necessarily be considered as "dropouts."[12]

Despite CHAR's lobbying efforts and its many publications, its campaign for the single homeless attracted little notice in Britain until a television special called "Johnny Go Home" highlighted the problems of homeless youngsters. The film, screened by Yorkshire Television on the BBC in July 1975, followed two actual teen-aged migrants during their first days in London and showed footage of a Mr. Gleaves, dressed in a clergyman's outfit, meeting trains at Euston Station and inviting young men to stay at his hostels. The second part of the special gave the details of

"The Gleaves Case," a recent scandal involving homosexual pro-
curement and murder. Young men who came to Gleaves's hostels
had been encouraged to participate in homosexual activity; a
16-year-old Scotsman who balked and joined an anti-Gleaves
faction had been killed.*

"Johnny Go Home" caused a sensation in Britain and led to
a sudden nationwide interest in the plight of homeless youth.
The film was shown twice in the House of Commons, M.P.s made
speeches, and a working party (committee) was set up to study
the problem and make a report to Parliament with recommendations for action. Lightfoot of CHAR, who was a member of the
working party, said her organization was besieged by reporters
and other interested people who wanted to know what could be
done. She expected real changes.

The working party's report recommended setting up more
hostels and services for young homeless in cities throughout the
country. Providing help closer to home, it reasoned, would discourage mass migration to London. It also recommended putting
information booths for young migrants in Euston railway and
Victoria bus stations, so newcomers could be referred to the
services available to them in London.[13] But by the time the report,
"Working Group on Homeless Young People," appeared in August 1976, public interest in the subject had faded. The report,
like the California study on transient youth in 1947, was filed and
forgotten. The most substantial result of "Johnny Go Home" was
the distribution nationally of 6000 posters and 70,000 leaflets by
a London organization, advising young people not to come to
London because of the housing and employment difficulties there.
Stay home! was the message. But no alternatives were suggested
for young people who could not find work at home or were otherwise unhappy there.

None of the working party's recommendations was followed.
Even the plans for a booth in Euston Station fell through when
railway officials opposed it. "They were afraid it would cause
young people to mill about Euston, but it would have done just
the opposite," commented Lightfoot, who was much discouraged
by the turn of events. "I guess nothing more will be done for the
single homeless until we have another murder."

---

* Gleaves, who was not implicated in the murder, was convicted of sodomy
and assault in May 1975.

BRITAIN AND THE UNITED STATES: A COMPARATIVE VIEW

In 1978 June Lightfoot of CHAR came to America to do a comparative study of single homeless people and the social services which the two countries provided for them. One of the first differences she noted, to her surprise, was the sharp age cutoff on services for migrant youth in America.

In Britain, hostels for homeless youth are generally open to anyone 16 years old and over, but in America, Lightfoot found, most free shelters for youth were available only to people under 18. The few scattered housing facilities for those over 18, such as San Francisco's Aquarius House, were small, grass-roots-type projects operating on a shoestring and usually in danger of closing down for lack of funds. Why the disinterest in the over-18 homeless? she wondered. The answer was that funds to provide facilities for migrant youth under 18 (known as "runaways") had been available only for a few years and were still scarce; before that, few shelters existed for homeless youth in either age group.

It had taken a sensational crime that had much in common with Britain's Gleaves case to get Washington to give some help to migrant youth under 18. Late in 1971 Senator Birch Bayh had introduced the runaway-youth bill, which would provide shelters and counseling for runaways. The bill passed the Senate in 1972, but could not get through the House; some legislators felt that the existence of such facilities might encourage children to run away.

Then, in August 1973, 17-year-old E. W. Henley turned himself in to the police in Houston, Texas, with a grisly tale. Henley said he had just killed Dean Corll, who had been murdering teen-aged boys regularly for the past three years, after homosexually molesting and torturing them first. Police investigated, and dug up the bodies of twenty-seven teen-aged boys.[14] When many of the victims were identified as runaways, a wave of outrage and concern for the safety of runaways swept the nation. The Runaway Youth Act was passed: Under its provisions a national toll-free telephone "hot line" for runaways was set up, and federal funding was made available for community-based shelters and counseling for runaways.

"That's the difference between our countries," Lightfoot commented after hearing about the Houston murders. "In America it took twenty-seven murders to rouse the public; in Britain it only took one."

Another surprise awaited Lightfoot in America. When she visited projects that did house migrants temporarily and told staff members she was studying homelessness, she drew a blank. They didn't know what she meant, although they were working with homeless youth themselves. The confusion was more than a semantic one. The concept of homelessness does not exist in America, even though many citizens, young and old, are homeless. There are not supposed to be any homeless people in the land of opportunity; if people lack a place to stay, it is attributed to individual adjustment problems that keep them from settling down. This may explain why Britain, with the more serious housing shortage of the two countries, provides far more temporary housing for homeless people in the form of shelters and hostels than America does.

One of Lightfoot's working hypotheses was that America has a therapeutic approach to homelessness and tries to "cure" everyone who is wandering around, while Britain is more concerned with providing basic amenities for the homeless, such as food, housing, and medical care. America, she said, saw itself as an endless reservoir of open spaces, natural resources, and money, where there was room for everyone to fit comfortably into the mainstream if their heads could be straightened out; while Britain took a more pragmatic view.

"Americans think 'There's always more,' but we think 'You'd better be careful; there may not be any more left where that came from,' " said Lightfoot.

Doing More on Less

Although some Britons disagree with parts of Lightfoot's analysis (as we will see later), observation of agencies serving the young homeless in the two countries bears out much of what she said. In London there was more cooperation among social-service agencies than in American cities such as New York City and San Francisco. This does not mean that the British have conquered the differences of opinion and the individual drives for power that make cooperation difficult in America and most countries in any area of endeavor; it means they have been able to overcome or sublimate such differences to the point where they can work together, because they realize that existing resources will go further if they are pooled and coordinated. Thus the alternative agencies serving young homeless in central London—Centrepoint, the Soho Project, New Horizon, and Kingsway Day Centre —have combined into the West End Coordinated Voluntary Services for purposes of funding and coordinating their services.

A larger project encompassing far more than young homeless also points up this type of cooperation. In Britain, staff members from umbrella organizations in several areas of social services work together each year to produce an annual *Directory of Projects,* which lists every known project in England and Wales that has facilities for helping single homeless people, alcoholics, drug users, adult offenders (former prisoners) and their families, and the mentally ill.[15] (Services for children have a separate network.) The *Directory* is compiled cooperatively by CHAR, SCODA (Standing Conference on Drug Abuse), CCA (Camberwell Council on Alcoholism), Cyrenians, NACRO (National Association for the Care and Resettlement of Offenders), and National Association of Mental Health.

The *Directory of Projects* is a practical tool designed for easy referral use. Facilities are listed regardless of their sponsorship or political orientation: For example, in the section on emergency housing, Centrepoint and the Salvation Army shelters are listed along with the reception centers run by the government's Department of Health and Social Services; in the section on national organizations, Radical Alternatives to Prison (RAP), which seeks to abolish prisons, is listed along with the Howard League for Penal Reform, which works for changes within the penal system.

The *Directory* also acknowledges the interrelationship of problems that various social agencies deal with and the services they provide—for example, that paroled prisoners and ex-mental patients are unlikely to hold steady jobs and make it back into society if they cannot find a decent place to live because no one who knows their background will rent to them.

David Carrington, field worker for NACRO, stressed the practical needs of ex-offenders. He did not agree with Lightfoot's view that the therapeutic approach is uniquely American, because he had encountered plenty of that attitude at home. In Britain's typical after-care hostels, he said, the staff assumes that ex-offenders have emotional problems first and practical ones last.

"Many social workers are so imbued with the treatment ideology that they ignore survival needs. But when people get out of prison, they need a place to live and a job first. Then they can worry about their emotional problems. Otherwise they get in a revolving door that leads from prison to mental hospitals to homelessness and back to prison again."[16]

Social workers who follow the treatment ideology tend to categorize people in terms of their weaknesses instead of their strengths, said Carrington, and to completely overlook the self-help tradition. He would like to see more grass-roots community programs run by local people, which would encourage active participation of ex-offenders.

The Homeless and the Hippies: Separate Spheres

British agencies that work with homeless youth have escaped the burden of their clients' misidentification with the counter-culture, a problem that plagues equivalent American agencies. The organizations that work with the new migrants in Britain have remained separate, for the most part, from those that cater to voluntary dropouts of the middle classes. The two spheres have their own networks of organizations and publications.

BIT Free Information Service is the agency of the counter-culture in London. It dispenses a variety of information, from the locations of crash pads and squats to advice on foreign travel, enjoying brisk sales of its own books, *Overland to India and Australia* and *Overland Through Africa,* which tell how to travel cheaply and avoid drug busts.

Alternative London is the guidebook to the counterculture in London, with extensive information on squatting, Eastern religions, political movements, and other topics of interest to its readers; its 1974 edition had eleven pages on drugs, ten on sex, three on work, and two and a half on community involvement, including information about the homeless, community services, and conservation. *Time Out,* which appears every Thursday with a listing of weekend events, is the magazine of the "trendy liberals" and other affluent young Britons who want to know what's happening in London. One reviewer described the magazine as "a unique blend of left-wing politics and show business."

Drugs: The Overlapping Entity

Time Out and the *Directory of Projects* are geared to the needs of populations so different that they might have come from separate planets. But in one area the counterculture has had a marked effect on the lives of some of the nation's poorest young people. That area is drugs. What started as an adventure for the intellectually curious ended up as a broken crutch for the downtrodden.

In the late 1960s the Dilly was London's center of both the hippie movement and drug traffic, but that was soon to change. The counterculture movement gradually shifted its focal point to Notting Hill, a residential area a few miles west of the Dilly and encompassing the districts of Ladbroke Grove, Westbourne Park, and Notting Hill Gate. When sociologist Richard Mills studied the hippies in 1970, he found the heavy drug scene still in the Dilly, while the intellectuals had moved on to Notting Hill.[17] Mills spent evenings in the Notting Hill flats of dropouts who had left universities and comfortable futures to embrace the hippie life. Although they were still involved with drugs (some supported themselves as dealers), these hippies were not passive "acid heads" but rather philosophers seeking the meaning of life. In their nightly discussions the Notting Hill hippies rejected the West in favor of the East.

"To have 'made the East,' or at least summered in Morocco, has replaced the Grand Tour of European cities as the entree to the great world," Mills wrote in *Young Outsiders*. "It reflects a current motif of the contemporary mutiny of youth: rejection of their own advanced industrialized society in favour of those African and Asian cultures that their fathers not long ago regarded as 'primitive' and 'simple.' "[18]

Five years later Notting Hill—particularly Ladbroke Grove—had become the center of heavy drug addiction among youth in London. The streets where the addicts lived had turned into slums with high crime rates and other signs of urban blight. A sprinkling of optionaire hippies still lived there, but most of the intellectuals had moved on to comfortable futures elsewhere. Their places had been taken by Britain's most disaffected working-class youth.

Virtually all the clients at the Blenheim Project, an alternative agency in Ladbroke Grove, came from working-class backgrounds. But they were a more alienated group than their counterparts who had clustered around the bright lights of the Dilly a few years earlier.

"There's a big disillusionment among young people who were given goals they can never achieve," said Bob Blyth, director of the Blenheim Project. "They were failures from the beginning. They've been given the idea that the main thing in life is to get as much money as possible. At home they think they'll find fantastic jobs in London."

The main concern of Blyth and his staff was drug addiction. Thirteen of their clients had died from overdoses in 1974, they said, principally from barbiturates or barbiturates in combination with alcohol. If a client had a long history of heavy drug use, the staff tried to get him out of London, hopefully into a retreat in the country. "If he stays here, he'll be dead," said Blyth.[19]

In the United States the combination of alcohol and barbiturates was equally popular—and equally lethal—during the 1970s. Psychedelics went out of style. As a drug specialist in San Francisco's Haight-Ashbury district explained it, "People don't crave highs these days; they want downers to help blot out reality."

In both countries the high expectations with which the new migrants leave home, followed by the grim reality of the job and housing situations they encounter in the cities, create a continuous stream of young people who are disillusioned and defeated before they turn 21.

Class Distinctions and Impossible Promises

Part of the hippie movement's initial appeal to Britain's new migrants was its promise to eradicate class distinctions. The new migrants there soon realized the emptiness of that promise: Social classes are an integral part of British life, and the privileges accorded those in the middle and upper strata are unlikely to disappear in the foreseeable future.

In the United States the issue of class differences is trickier, because part of our national mythology is that we are a classless society. The difficulty is further complicated by the fallacy of equating class with skin color, which can lead to such absurdities as the assumption that if a corporation president and a truck driver are both white, their children will have the same educational advantages and career opportunities. Class differences are increasing in the United States, and their major basis is an economic one.

In Part Two we will explore the affluent and nonaffluent societies in the United States, noting the advantages that children raised in affluence enjoy, and the growing tensions between the two societies. We will discuss the anger of blue-collar workers who find that they can never achieve the financial success that the American dream promised them—and the unwitting role that the counterculture movement has played in exacerbating the frustrations of workers in the nonaffluent society.

Part Two

TWO SOCIETIES

CHAPTER ELEVEN

The Advantages of Being an Optionaire

The United States is dividing into two societies—the affluent and the nonaffluent. The gap between the two—in terms of income, education, standard of living, life-style, and outlook—is widening, and so is their distrust of each other's values. We still have the super-rich at the top and the very poor at the bottom, but most citizens fall between these extremes. The egalitarian ethos of the United States pushes people toward the middle-income ranges, with the dividing line between affluence and nonaffluence a movable one. Roughly one-third of Americans belong to the affluent society. Two-thirds are excluded.

Money is not the only factor that separates the affluent from the nonaffluent, but in a country grounded in making money, it is a convenient divider. The U.S. Bureau of Labor Statistics provides guidelines. Each year the BLS takes a hypothetical urban family of four and computes budgets for that family at lower, intermediate, and higher levels. The BLS higher budget is the standard used here to define affluence. These are, of course, American standards. In many parts of the world, people would consider themselves affluent on the lower budget; but Americans measure their standards of living against others in their own country, not those in Upper Volta.

In 1978 an urban family of four needed $27,420 to maintain a higher, or affluent, standard of living. That same year a family needed $18,622 for the intermediate standard, and $11,546 for the lower standard.[1] Each budget had categories for food, housing, transportation, clothing, personal care, medical care, taxes, and miscellaneous expenses such as recreation at home, vacations, church and other memberships, and charitable contributions. None of the budgets included a category for savings.

The affluent budget allowed around $480 a month for food. That may seem high if you think only in terms of weekly supermarket totals; but if you include downtown lunches for the father, school lunches for the children, milk delivery, fast foods picked up at the local pizzeria or fried-chicken outlet, some dinners at restaurants, liquor, and the extra costs of inviting friends or relatives over for meals, then the amount does not seem out of line for a city family of four earning $25,000–$30,000 a year.

How many Americans can afford to eat and drink at that level? Less than 25 percent. In 1977, 22.4 percent of all American households earned $25,000 a year and upward, while 45.9 percent earned less than $15,000 (27.5 percent of these earned less than $10,000). Of the families in between, 17.7 percent earned $15,000–$19,999 and 13.9 percent earned $20,000–$24,999.[2]

These in-between groups form the "gray" areas, where factors besides money may determine whether a family belongs to the affluent society. Lower-echelon professionals—schoolteachers, social workers, health technicians, librarians, and the like—may earn less than $25,000 a year and yet be part of the affluent society. They cannot afford to spend money as freely as a doctor or lawyer, but their life-styles have marked similarities to those in wealthier professions: They may read the same general periodicals and listen to the same type of music, their children are also likely to graduate from college and enter a profession, and the parents themselves may achieve financial affluence in their forties by moving up into administrative positions. Conversely, the plumber, electrician, or small businessman who earns $40,000 a year may retain the earmarks of the nonaffluent and continue to identify with that world.

But money remains the crucial divider. More than half of American wives now work outside the home,[3] but the combined salaries of husband and wife did not add up to $20,000 a year in most households in 1977. In that year the median income for all *families* was $16,010. Adjusting for the gray areas where there may be people who belong to the affluent society although their incomes are below par, and some who don't join even though they make enough money to qualify, we arrive at our statement that one-third of our citizens belong to the affluent society, while two-thirds do not.

Affluent and Middle-Class: Some Notes on Definitions

The term "affluent society" as used here differs in scope from John Kenneth Galbraith's use of the term in his book *The Affluent Society,* published in 1958. Galbraith's meaning—that Americans in general were affluent except for a few stubborn pockets of poverty—reflected the widespread belief of the 1950s that poverty had been conquered in the United States and was on its way out as a major world problem. That optimistic view received its first setback in 1962 when Michael Harrington published *The Other America,* which documented that a third of America's citizens still lived in poverty. Since then a continuous rash of troubles—inflation, unemployment, racial tensions, and political unrest or rebellion throughout the world—have mitigated the postwar optimism of most people, including Galbraith himself.

The Affluent Society is not primarily about affluence; it is a scholarly economic treatise arguing that increased production should no longer reign supreme as the answer to the nation's economic ills. Although the validity of Galbraith's thesis has increased since 1958 (see Chapter 20 of this book for more on his thesis) , thus far the title of *The Affluent Society* has attracted more notice than its message.

In a country that prides itself on being classless, definitions of class are hard to formulate, because there are no standards to relate to. Affluence was chosen here over the term "middle class," because the meaning of "middle class" differs so greatly among people that it has little use as an indicator of social class or income. An auto worker and his wife who together earn $18,000 a year and own a small house and a car may consider themselves middle class, but so may a businessman who earns $300,000 and owns a large house, two cars, a summer cottage, and an apartment building. To the businessman, "upper class" means du Ponts and Rockefellers.

The terms "affluent" and "nonaffluent" avoid the ubiquitous middle-class label and help us place Americans in socioeconomic perspective. Under this division, the new migrants fall into the nonaffluent society. We will return to the new migrants at the end of Part Three when we fit them into the larger context of job seekers in the nonaffluent society. Now we need to explore the world of optionaires from the affluent society to understand their sphere of privilege and see how it contradicts the myth of equal opportunity.

SOME PEOPLE ALWAYS MAKE IT

"Optionaires," as we said earlier, is a new word to describe people who grew up in the affluent society. The word derives from "options," because the upbringing and education that people in the affluent society receive gives them a wider range of career choices and life-styles than those who grew up in the nonaffluent society are likely to have.

A third of all Americans—more than seventy million people—are optionaires, a higher percentage of affluent citizens than any other large nation has produced. Indeed, so numerous are they in America, and so firmly in charge of running the nation and virtually everything else, that the impact of their presence blocks out our awareness of people who have not become affluent.

There is some recognition among optionaires that the country has minority groups of nonwhite citizens who are excluded from the affluent society because of racial prejudice; a handful of people from these groups is admitted into affluence and their membership is touted as evidence of America's inherent equality of opportunity. But the vast majority of people in the non-affluent society—more than 140 million Americans—are generally ignored. (An exception is just before election time, when option-aires running for office remember the existence, and voting rights, of the nonaffluent until all the ballots are in.)

When optionaires think of "today's youth" or the problems of today's youth, they think of their children or their relatives' and neighbors' children; if they are young, they think of them-selves or their friends. The sons and daughters of two-thirds of the population are overlooked. A newspaper article about ap-plicants for a job in San Francisco illustrates the point.

In 1976 a new restaurant in San Francisco needed more help. It ran the following ad in the newspaper: "Host or hostess. Full-time position available. Monday through Friday, daytime. Experience helpful but not necessary."[4] The job paid $90 a week, the minimum wage at that time.

The restaurant managers were amazed when upward of 400 people applied for the job—and they were even more stunned to find that more than half the applicants had college degrees.

These applicants with degrees were optionaires who a decade earlier would have had a range of jobs to choose from after graduation. Now, after frustrating attempts to secure "professional" positions in San Francisco, they were ready to take whatever they could get, at least temporarily, to keep themselves going until something better turned up. A hosting job in an elegant restaurant would be more prestigious and interesting than waiting on tables or delivering the mail (although it would pay less), and the contacts with rich customers might lead to a better position in time.

Both the restaurant management and the newspaper reporting the incident empathized with the predicament of these college-educated young people who could not find suitable jobs. "It's sad, terrible," said the restaurant's assistant manager. "And what a waste of brains. Over half of them have college degrees. They're desperate enough to take anything." The article's sub-head read: "The Anguish of College Grads Who Are Forced to Grab Any Work."

There was no mention of the anguish of college dropouts who cannot find work. Nor the anguish of high-school graduates who are being pushed out of the unskilled jobs they traditionally have held, by educated optionaires. In fact, there was no mention at all of the more than 200 people without college degrees who had also applied for the job.

The restaurant picked "Catherine," aged 23, as the daytime hostess and "Elliot," a man of 29, for the evening shift. Catherine was a Phi Beta Kappa from Boston, with degrees in sociology and psychology, who had already been accepted by a California law school and wanted a job until the term started in the fall. Her father owned a Cadillac dealership, and her mother sat on a hospital board of directors. Elliot was a lawyer from Philadelphia who had quit his job and headed for California after his marriage broke up. For several months he had hunted unsuccessfully for a position in a San Francisco law office. He'd finally taken a job as waiter, but was laid off a month later.

Catherine had spent a "heartbreaking year" in San Francisco

looking for a job until law school started. When she and the girl friend with whom she shared a flat on lower Nob Hill ran short of cash, "We'd be so poor we'd play little tricks, like if one of us was going out for a lunch interview, the other would pretend to walk casually by the table so we could both get our lunches free."

Clearly Catherine knew how to work the system. She did not need to visit the Haight-Ashbury Switchboard in search of one-day cleaning jobs or eat at the Food Project. Employed or not, Catherine belonged to the world of optionaires, and she would stay there.

Elliot said, "If I were getting out of high school now, I wouldn't bother going to college. You might as well plan on becoming a bartender, waitress, or whatever."

Elliot's advice was well meant, but it overlooked the facts. He, with his law degree and optionaire polish, was chosen over a few hundred applicants with lesser qualifications. The entrance of optionaires like Elliot into the job market for waiters and hosts increases the probability that those who don't go beyond high school may have difficulty finding any job at all.

Contacts and Confidence: The Unbeatable Duo

Education counts when you go job hunting, and so does individual initiative; but these may not be the crucial factors that determine whether you are hired. Whom you know, or whom your parents know, and what you think of yourself may supersede education and initiative. If you have contacts (also known as "connections") with the people who give out the jobs, and if you have a high opinion of yourself and your abilities—regardless of the factual basis for such belief—you are more likely to succeed than people without such assets; in some cases you may win out over people who are better qualified by education and ability to hold a particular job than you are.

People from the nonaffluent society may enjoy contacts on a small scale. The young man who gains admittance to a union because his father is a member has contacts; so does the teen-ager who gets a job as a garage mechanic because his uncle knows the manager, and the young woman who gets a job at the beauty shop near her home because her mother's best friend owns the shop. Such contacts are generally local and they rarely extend to the professional sphere or to jobs that pay on a scale that allows one to enter the affluent society. The young man or woman from the nonaffluent society who aspires to go up the socioeconomic ladder will need a superabundance of self-confidence and drive to compensate for a lack of contacts.

Although some people in the nonaffluent society have self-confidence, this quality is far more common among optionaires; the higher up one goes on the social scale, the greater the chances for self-confidence.

Professor G. William Domhoff, a sociologist at the University of California in Santa Cruz who specializes in studying the upper class, has isolated confidence as the chief characteristic of upper-class people. Confidence begins in early childhood, says Domhoff, when rich youngsters are singled out for special attention, and it continues as they attend a series of exclusive schools. Living in a special world where they and their parents are constantly deferred to because of their wealth, they grow up believing they are special people. They expect doors to open for them everywhere, and doors usually do open for them, which reinforces their high opinion of themselves. As Arlene Daniels, another sociologist who studies the upper class, puts it: "They have this confidence even if they are boobies."[5]

Only a few percent of Americans are members of the upper class, so their world would not interest us here if it did not illustrate in pristine form how privilege and contacts operate. (These families also wield significant power in business, foreign affairs, and domestic policies, including programs for the unemployed and the poor. In *Who Rules America?* and *The Higher Circles,* Domhoff argues that the upper class is also the ruling class.)

The upper-class network of contacts is national—even international—in scope, formed through attendance and membership in exclusive schools, clubs, and summer resorts, through intermarriages, and through business, professional, and social connections of the very rich. If Elizabeth, an upper-class daughter in New York City, wants to work in San Francisco, she will not have to apply for a job as a restaurant hostess or visit the state employment office. Before she leaves home, her father can arrange a suitable job for her in San Francisco while her mother arranges for her to stay with friends on arrival who will sponsor her entrance into upper-class social circles on the West Coast.

The line separating the "upper class" from the "upper middle class"—like all class distinctions in America—is difficult to draw. Here (using 1979 prices) we will define "upper middle class" families as those with incomes of roughly $70,000–$300,000 a year, as well as plenty of college degrees and social connections.

The book *Passages,* by Gail Sheehy, provides case histories of upper-middle-class youths and their sphere of privilege. There is "Donald Babcock,"[6] whose father graduated from Hotchkiss and Yale before entering business. The son, Donald, after finishing Hotchkiss and a year at Yale, decided to leave home and strike out on his own in California, but on the way he was seriously injured in an automobile accident.

"The accident was a setback for me in a lot of ways," he told Sheehy. "I couldn't take the job that was waiting for me in California."

How did a young man with one year of college and no work experience have a job waiting for him on the other side of the country? Presumably he had contacts, through the father whose life-style he was fleeing.

After the accident Donald found himself at home in a back brace, but his disability did not stop him from finding a job. "My father came through with a job for me as a security guard on a museum estate. As a Republican committeeman, he has a lot of jobs to give out."[7] On the estate, Donald fell in love; he married, returned to Yale, and followed his father into business.

In *Passages,* whose subtitle is "Predictable Crises of Adult Life," Donald was presented as "an example of how the Merger Self can overwhelm before the Seeker Self has a chance to kick up its heels." But in the context of this book, Donald is an example of someone so firmly ensconced in the world of optionaire privilege that he would come out on top no matter which Self emerged.

Moving down the social scale we come to the group that includes most optionaires, the people at the base of the affluent society, who traditionally were called the middle class. They come from families with incomes of $20,000–$70,000, with the bottom end open for those in the gray areas. Contacts are less pervasive here than at the higher levels, but they still operate to a marked degree. When optionaires from this group seek admission to college, professional jobs, and entrance into other areas of privilege, contacts may be their most important resource. But confidence ranks as a close second. Those without contacts may still be able to make it if they have a high enough opinion of themselves and are sufficiently adept at working the system. A traditional optionaire upbringing builds its members in both these areas.

If optionaire children do not go to private schools, they are likely to attend up-to-date public schools in pleasant suburbs or well-preserved sections of the city. Their formal schooling is supplemented with music lessons, books from the library, help with homework, trips to zoos and museums, summer camps, and travel. Verbal and written fluency develop as naturally as learning to walk. Each child has a separate bedroom or shares one with a sibling of the same sex. The parents (whether a couple or alone) may have their problems, but chronic financial worries are not paramount in their lives. In this milieu, discipline is achieved more often through talks than beatings.

Confidence begins to grow at an early age. To see how this happens, let's look at Michael, a hypothetical young man from an optionaire background.

When Michael comes home from nursery school at age 3 with a few blotches of color on a sheet of newsprint and his mother exclaims, "What a beautiful picture you painted, Michael!" as she tapes it on the wall for father (an accountant) to admire later, Michael's self-esteem zooms upward. It continues going up as Michael does well in school, becomes a pitcher in Little League, and is elected president of his senior class in high school, while his parents and relatives form a chorus of admiration in the background.

Michael comes to adulthood with an unshakable sense of self-worth. He expects to make it. He feels he deserves to make it. A college education and a career of his choice are options that he takes for granted.

Michael decides to be a lawyer and goes to law school. Graduating in the mid-1970s, he encounters job problems he never expected, because numerous other well-educated, confident young men and women from optionaire backgrounds have also become lawyers and are looking for jobs with good futures in prestigious law firms. This may be a setback for Michael, but it will not stop him. Michael is one of those people who will always make it.

If 300 people apply for the same job and 220 have the necessary qualifications, of whom 60 also have the personality and charisma the employer is seeking, Michael will be among the 10 finalists.

He may even be the one selected. If not, he will probably make it the next time. Or the next. Michael will not give up. Nor does he need to. He is sure to make it.

If Michael runs out of money while job-hunting, his family will come through with funds to keep him going. If for some reason he doesn't get family help (he isn't speaking to his parents that year or his father just quit his job and ran off to California to become a guru), Michael has other options: Friends or relatives will let him occupy the spare bedroom for several months and eat at their table; he will move into the apartment of a young woman who has a job, and become her "old man" until he finds the right job; or he will become part of a commune for a while and live off other members' salaries.

If necessary, Michael may take a nonprofessional job temporarily (he generally comes out on top in such competitions). If he doesn't want to tie up his job-hunting hours with work, Michael knows enough about working the system to get himself onto some form of welfare. He will never have to sleep in the street or skip dinner while he looks for a job.

Michael may spend a year looking for the right job, but he will eventually find it. And then he will make lots of money. Twenty years later, after he has been a partner in the firm and is appointed a federal judge, Michael may view all unemployed people as wastrels and those on welfare as cheats. He will speak from the heart—and from direct personal experience—when he says with feeling, "Anyone can make it in this country if he tries hard enough."

Obviously not every optionaire has Michael's confidence. He is of interest here for two reasons. First, the example of his success serves those who want to disprove the theories of Domhoff and others who claim that the United States is ruled by an upper-class elite; which brings us to the second reason: Michael is the kind of person who succeeds in politics. He has charisma and drive, and he is not shy about pushing himself ahead. It is the Michaels of this country, along with the children of the upper-class elite, who make the laws and regulations that govern employment, welfare, health insurance, and other social services for the masses.

If confidence like Michael's could be ordered through the Sears catalog, then equality of opportunity would be more widespread —and people like Michael would lose the advantage they now enjoy.

Optionaires with Problems

What about optionaires at the opposite end of the confidence spectrum—the people who grew up in the affluent society but are unsure of themselves, or those who have severe emotional problems that may hinder their education and careers? Mental illness may occur at any level of society; it does not respect class distinctions. But parents in the affluent society can better afford professional help—doctors, psychiatrists, special schools—for children with serious problems, and in their milieu it is socially more acceptable to seek such help than in many sectors of the non-affluent society. This help is not always effective, but often it is. The disturbed adolescent whose parents spend $200,000 in hospital and psychiatric fees may emerge from a few years of treatment as a functioning adult, able to hold a job and marry, while his or her counterpart in the nonaffluent society who receives no help is more likely to end up permanently incarcerated in an institution.

As for shy, insecure optionaires, they may be buttressed by contacts and money, or they may be guided into careers that suit their temperaments. Without such help, the shy optionaire may not make it, for the meek have a low priority in a country built on aggressive individualism.

Finally, the neuroses of optionaires may not impede their ability to make a good living. Alexander Portnoy, the hero—or antihero—of Philip Roth's novel *Portnoy's Complaint,* is a case in point.[8] He is a neurotic, self-pitying man who has difficulties achieving intimacy with other people, but in school and on the job he has nothing but success. Part of the book's satire derives from the contrast between Portnoy's public success and private hell; but the former is impressive.

Portnoy graduates from a top law school and serves as commissioner of human opportunity for New York City. He functions effectively on the job (the job itself lacks substance, not Portnoy's performance), he makes a high enough salary to eliminate financial worries and allow him to travel abroad in style, and he enjoys respect and status because of his high position. Although Portnoy rails incessantly against his mother, blaming her for all the obnoxious personality traits he displays as an adult, his optionaire upbringing has given him enough skills and self-confidence to make it handsomely in the Establishment. Many a workingman might be glad to take on Portnoy's troubles if he could also have his salary and his status.

Variations on the Optionaires Theme

People who grow up as optionaires and then drop out of the Establishment—to go back to the land and live a natural life, to pursue their art even if it means living below the poverty level while they try to sell their handcrafted jewelry on the street— are often thought of as being wholly outside the optionaire framework. In fact, they are variations on the optimistic theme. Such people may see themselves as outsiders, but they drop out with all the advantages of their optionaire upbringing intact.

When optionaires pursue an occupation outside the main-stream, they bring to it all the skills and confidence they learned at home. Although they may not use their Establishment con-tacts in their new pursuits, they will quickly build up contacts within the counterculture framework. As surely as their fathers back home knew who ran city hall, they will learn who are "the right people" to know in their special world and who are the dregs to avoid. The business acumen they imbibed from their successful parents will stand them in good stead when they refuse to join the system. Yesterday's bohemians fit this pattern. Today's street craftsmen are a current example.

In any area where the counterculture flourishes, you will find young people selling their crafts on the streets. It could be the Embarcadero Plaza in San Francisco, the Spanish Steps in Rome, the East Village in New York, or Telegraph Avenue in Berkeley. They sell leather goods, jewelry, woven belts, candles, knitted caps, wooden bowls, stained-glass objects, photographs, and paint-ings, to name but a sampling. Whatever is the rage among buyers that season you will find in abundance, be it tie-dyed T-shirts or terrariums. For the purpose of street selling is to make money.

It would seem natural to call these craftspeople "street people," since they sell their wares on the streets. But they bear scant re-semblance to the down-and-out young people described earlier in this book. The street craftspeople are not street people, nor are they new migrants; they are either optionaires or border-liners. Most new migrants would not have enough capital to buy the equipment and materials needed to set up shop; even if they did find the money by a fluke, they would be hard put to keep up with the knowledgeable competition they would face from other street vendors.

In the early 1970s, when the recession had not yet touched their lives, young street vendors often spoke of their work in terms reminiscent of hippie philosophy. "Shelley," who sold her handmade silver pendants on Telegraph Avenue, sounded that way. She was a graduate of Northwestern University who had previously worked as a schoolteacher and then as a secretary. "I was making five hundred and fifty dollars a month in my last job. I could get that tomorrow if I wanted to do that kind of work again," she said when we interviewed her in 1973.

Shelley's face went blank when she was asked about new migrants in Berkeley. "I've never met anyone like that," she said. "Lots of the people who sell on the street here have Ph.D.s. They could easily get other jobs, but they prefer the freedom of this life to the hassle of a large university or big business."

While Shelley talked, people kept walking by her street stall. Some of them were new migrants, but they could have been 3000 miles away as far as Shelley was concerned. They simply did not penetrate her awareness. She did not meet such people at the parties she attended after work; she never talked to such people: Therefore, they did not exist.

Three years later, street craftspeople in Berkeley were more aware of the poverty that surrounded them, and of their own tenuous positions. Some of their friends with master's and doctoral degrees were delivering mail or working for the new subway system, not by choice but because they could not find jobs in the academic world. The street craftspeople of 1976 knew that making it in the Establishment was not easy—at least not in California.

"Richard," a leather craftsman from a nearby suburb, felt that his business was "too good to last"; but while it did, he was making a comfortable living and enjoying his trade. "I'm lucky I got here while the licenses were still for sale," Richard told us. "It gives me a hell of an opportunity. You learn so much when you start from roots like this. How to manage money. How to budget yourself. You learn about different personalities and how to use tact; you have to, or else you miss a lot of sales."

The romantic concept of street vendors as rebels against modern technology and the Establishment does not hold up in Berkeley. Many craftspeople take credit cards these days. A conflict over which vendors should get the most desirable locations along Telegraph Avenue was resolved by means of a computer. Now every morning a city employee arrives with a computer print-out of the day's spaces; if licensed craftsmen do not claim their spaces by 10:00 A.M., the choice empty spots are reassigned by a lottery. This procedure has operated in Berkeley for several years. Modern technology and city hall have helped the street vendors survive in Berkeley, and most of them are all for it. If street vendors complain about city hall, it is because officials do not enforce the regulations strictly enough.

The major conflict among street vendors is over handcrafted items versus manufactured goods. The city issues inexpensive licenses to street vendors, with the stipulation that they sell only items which they have handcrafted themselves. But a few entrepreneurs have imported manufactured "craft" items from Mexico or Europe in bulk and sold them on the streets as "handmade" at considerable profit.

This practice angered the merchants with stores along Telegraph. As one businessman explained: "We're glad to give young people a chance to sell their own handcrafted work on the streets; but some of these people are setting up three and four stalls with cheap junk from Mexico and paying streets kids less than the minimum wage to sell for them. I pay my employees a decent wage and lots of other benefits as well. It isn't fair to let some unscrupulous entrepreneurs come in and make a killing. They don't even have to pay rent or property tax."[9]

Two sides developed in the conflict, but the sides were not street craftspeople versus the business establishment. Instead, street sellers who wanted to keep manufactured goods off the Avenue formed a coalition with some store owners; together they went to the city council and demanded that the city enforce the regulation forbidding the sale of manufactured items at street stalls.

The craftspeople who teamed up with the store owners could relate to one another because they spoke the same language; the businessmen were similar to the fathers and uncles the craftspeople had grown up with. It would be hard to imagine street people or new migrants forming an alliance with store owners— or expecting help from city hall. But you will not find new migrants selling crafts on Telegraph Avenue, unless they work for some entrepreneur for a pittance. The craftspeople are a contemporary variation of the optionaire theme.

In every circumstance, it pays to be an optionaire.

CHAPTER TWELVE

"They Don't Want to Work Anymore"

The real job problem today, many an optionaire believes, is that people don't want to work anymore; they would rather get handouts from the government or be paid a salary for merely putting in an appearance at their jobs.

Are there people who don't want to work? Listen to any discussion on this subject among businessmen or administrators who do a lot of hiring and you will learn that there are. Who are these people who don't want to work? There are different types.

Perhaps the largest number of work-shy people suffer from a temporary malady known as youth. Immaturity may be a symptom, but it often masks a deeper cause. Young people have just emerged from childhood, a period when they went to school full time and otherwise did what adults in charge of their lives told them they had to do. Now approaching adulthood, they feel the urge to be free—to explore the world and themselves, to do what *they* want to do for a while.

Psychoanalyst Erik Erikson has postulated a "psychosocial moratorium" for youth, a period between adolescence and adulthood when a young person may not be ready to accept the responsibilities of adulthood.[1] Erikson believes this postponement of adult commitments can be a positive period in human development, leading to more integrated and productive adults.

But, he says, this moratorium depends on a "selective permissiveness on the part of society."[2]

In the United States, as in most societies, the only youths to whom we grant moratoriums are optionaires. The businessman who foots the bill (however reluctantly) for his son's and daughter's urge to roam around Europe for a year or two "finding" themselves is unlikely to recognize a similar urge among young people who apply for jobs in which their main interest is the paycheck. These reluctant workers may also be yearning to be free for a while, but the accident of their birth sentences them to seek full-time work as soon as they finish high school—or drop out—regardless of their readiness.

Youth is a condition that time alone will cure. People who shy away from a job at 19 may plunge into work with gusto a few years later, especially if they have had an interlude of freedom in which to finish growing up.

Some young people who were nurtured on the American dream may revolt against work when they grow up and realize that they are excluded from the dream. Their $8000-a-year job is not a temporary step up the ladder to affluence, as they were led to believe, but a permanent slot. They can go no higher, while they see sons and daughters from optionaire homes entering careers that will start at $20,000 and double in salary by the time they are 40. The need for some money, as opposed to having no money, usually triumphs in such cases eventually, and the open revolt ends. But the disillusioned people who are relegated to dead-end jobs may harbor a deep resentment against those who made it because they were born into the right family and had education, money, and contacts.

A different situation arises with people who don't want to work because they feel defeated by life and want to withdraw from the whole discouraging business. Many of the street people we saw in Chapter 8 fall into this group. It would be futile to argue whether such people should be forced to work—or whether there is any way to motivate them to want to work—when they generally are unemployable in today's labor market and when we already have more people who want to work than we have jobs for them. A way to survive with dignity is what this small segment of the population needs.

Stereotypes and Ambivalences about Work

The gamut of human behavior exists within every class. At each level of society there are ambitious people who strive to get ahead, and there are easygoing people who take life as it comes; there are altruists who are ready to help others, and there are opportunists who care only about themselves. But if you only move within one class, it is easy to categorize the other classes by means of stereotypes. Thus the poor may view all rich people as evil, while the rich may view the unemployed poor as morally inferior loafers who don't want to work.

In the nineteenth century this view of the unemployed poor was so widespread that labels such as "the dangerous class" and "the criminal classes" were used as factual descriptions of the poor, even by those who wanted to help them. Marx and Engels, in their 1848 *Communist Manifesto,* referred to the poorest people as "the 'dangerous class,' the social scum." The authors thought a few of that class might be swept into the proletarian revolution, but "its conditions of life, however, prepare it far more for the part of a bribed tool of reactionary intrigue."[3] In other words, scum are likely to be finks, so forget about them when planning a revolution; stick to people with jobs.

Current opinion among optionaires who influence legislation on welfare and employment sometimes reflects a similar negative evaluation of poor people, although it is expressed more circuitously. No American official today would dare to describe poor people as "social scum," but they may imply as much. When legislators argue at length about the need to tighten welfare regulations to keep cheaters off the rolls, the underlying assumption is that most people who apply for welfare have no backbone and will only work if forced to do so in order to eat.

The optionaire's view of the unemployed may be complicated further by an ambivalence about devoting one's life to hard work, a conflict that only surfaces occasionally but may be triggered by the sight or mention of people who don't work. William Hamilton captured the essence of this ambivalence in a cartoon in his series "The Now Society." Two middle-aged men in suits and ties are drinking their preprandial martinis in a first-class restaurant. One says to the other, "Steel, of course, has been my life. But sometimes I wish my life had been sitting with a pretty girl in a sunny café in Provence, drinking Beaujolais."[4]

In his *Cannery Row* John Steinbeck went a step further with the theme that people who live on the fringes of society lead more satisfying lives than the rest of us. In *Cannery Row* five men who come from what we now call "disadvantaged" homes and who are virtually unemployable live a makeshift existence in an old warehouse in Monterey, California. But they are a happy crew. Steinbeck describes them as "a little group of men who had in common no families, no money, and no ambitions beyond food, drink, and contentment. But whereas most men in their search for contentment destroy themselves and fall wearily short of their target, Mack and his friends approached contentment casually, quietly, and absorbed it gently."[5]

Try as they may, these men can't do anything right. But they have a series of rollicking misadventures and lead fun-filled, carefree lives. Having no money and no responsibilities makes life a great lark.

The story of Mack and his friends may delight a tired senator after a frustrating day in committee meetings, when he curls up in bed for a quiet read. But how will he react the next morning when asked to support a bill creating jobs for the unemployed?

What? Give handouts to poor people when they already have more fun than the rest of us and do little to help themselves? Nothing doing. Better to spend our tax money on national defense.

A romanticized view of the poor may increase the employed person's antipathy for programs designed to create jobs, but it is a minor cause of these feelings; the major factor that leads to such antipathy is the assumption that opportunity exists for all who are ready to take it. Optionaires who have made it may believe that the road to riches is equally open to all Americans. They may also believe that people go on welfare because they don't want to work. The social circles of such optionaires do not include anyone on welfare. Nor have their lives brought them into contact with people raised in homes where defeat was absorbed along with mother's milk, homes devoid of the characteristics which build the confidence that is the optionaire's mainstay. The optionaire of conservative bent may in good conscience fight every government move to create jobs for the unemployed, serene in the assurance that "those people" could have made it if they'd tried.

People do exist who don't want to work, aren't ready to work, or are unemployable. But their sum total dwindles into insignificance when compared with the numbers of people, young and older, who want to work but cannot find jobs.

More numerous are Americans from the nonaffluent society who work, but not at the level they expected to reach—people who set out to climb the ladder of success, only to find themselves trapped for life on one of the lower rungs of employment. Their disenchantment, or alienation, has received scant notice from optionaires. But a different kind of alienation sent shock waves across the optionaire network in the 1960s, because it challenged the dream itself.

CHAPTER THIRTEEN

Two Alienations

The 1960s was the decade of alienation. In the spate of books written to explain the upheavals of those years, alienation became the hallmark of distinction. "Alienated" was the word used to describe sensitive young optionaires who, although stuffed with material goods, found that they were starving. The possibility that other Americans, greater in numbers than the optionaires, suffered from a different kind of alienation was not considered.

In fact, two kinds of alienation were rampant throughout the decade. The first was caused by having too much of a material nature; the second was the result of not having enough.

ALIENATION IN THE AFFLUENT SOCIETY

The media seized on the first type of alienation and featured it as a main symptom of the youth revolt. But many adults in the affluent society were manifesting the same alienation; this portion of the adult population responded to the youth revolt with enthusiasm, because young people were verbalizing the anger and misgivings these older Americans had long felt about their government and its values. Indeed, most books about alienated youth were written not by dissenting youths but by older admirers. A few writers were so delighted to find young people publicly protesting against situations they themselves had long deplored that they endowed the new generation with messianic powers:

Today's youths, freed from the hang-ups that had held back the older generation, would transform the nation.

Historian Theodore Roszak expressed this view in *The Making of a Counter Culture* (1969). "The alienated young are giving shape to something that looks like the saving vision of our endangered civilization," he wrote.[1] Now that young people could take economic security for granted, Roszak argued, they could turn their attention from material and political concerns to the realm of the spirit: "They see, and many who follow them find the vision attractive, that building the good society is not primarily a social, but a psychic task."[2] Roszak saw technology as the wrecker of civilization and looked to the young to overpower "The Technocratic Society," his name for the Establishment.

The Making of a Counter Culture popularized the term "counter-culture," replacing the less dignified "hippie movement," a name that was already tarnished by its close association with psychedelic drugs. "Counterculture" was an apt term, because it expressed the movement's belief that American civilization was in such a sorry state that trying to change it directly was a waste of time; instead, alienated youths must set up an alternative or counter culture. As Roszak concluded: "This, so I have argued, is the primary task of our counter culture: to proclaim a new heaven and earth so vast, so marvellous that the inordinate aims of technical expertise must of necessity withdraw in the presence of such splendor to a subordinate status in the lives of men."[3]

A year later another book urging an alternative culture appeared. *The Greening of America,* by Charles A. Reich, had a somewhat different perspective from *The Making of a Counter Culture:* Liberal reform replaced technology as the archenemy in Reich's book, and the development of individual consciousness was heralded as the solution to the nation's woes. The easy-to-read style of *The Greening of America* expanded its potential readership, while its hedonistic message struck a chord of response among liberals of all ages who were worn out from a decade of activism that apparently produced no results.

During the 1960s, Americans of liberal persuasion had marched against the war in Vietnam, worked in organizations that promoted civil rights and equal opportunities for all citizens, written letters to their congressmen urging changes, and sent money to numerous causes. But in the end such activities seemed futile. When the 1970s rolled around, America was still heavily involved in Vietnam, while at home, poverty and lack of opportunity remained prevalent in our inner cities. In addition, those who had contributed to causes found they were being sneered at by the very people to whom they had sent money—they were called "liberal" as though that were a dirty word.

It was a depressing and confusing time. Then along came *The Greening of America* with a refreshing perspective. Reich offered a solution that was balm to weary activists young and old, to people suffering from battle fatigue yet driven by a sense of moral responsibility to help set the world right.

Political action could not save the nation, said Reich; significant changes would only come through the development of individual consciousness. Forget politics and reform, drop out of the Corporate State (Reich's term for the Establishment), and concentrate on doing your own thing. Listen to rock music (or Bach if you prefer), cultivate a garden, bake bread, go surfing, and you would hasten the "green" revolution.[4]

Reich's thesis grew from his interpretation of American history as a series of "three consciousnesses," which he labeled Consciousness I, II, and III.

Consciousness I was essentially the Horatio Alger view of life, embodying the belief that "the American Dream is still possible and that success is determined by character, morality, hard work, and self-denial." It led, said Reich, to competitiveness, suspicion of others, unbridled self-interest, and corruption of American life. Out of touch with reality, it refused to acknowledge that individuals are not competing against each other but against a giant system. "The beliefs of Consciousness I are drastically at variance with reality. But they are held in a stubborn, belligerent, opinionated way against all contrary evidence."[5]

Reich did not like the Consciousness I mentality, but his greatest wrath was reserved for Consciousness II, the thinking of liberal reformers. Reich showed that reformers of the 1930s did not solve all the country's problems and turn the United States into paradise; therefore, he rejected reform. He criticized leaders of the New Deal for concentrating on economic problems during the Great Depression. "None of the great modern problems, such as loss of meaning, loss of community and self, dehumanization of environment, were in any way approached, except to encourage the trends toward making them worse," he said.[6]

"Consciousness II," said Reich, "believes that the present

American crisis can be solved by greater commitment of individuals to the public interest, more social responsibility by private business, and above all, more affirmative government action—regulation, planning, more of a welfare state, better and more rational administration and management."[7] All of which was rubbish in his view, not for failing to go far enough (Reich scorned revolutionaries as well as reformers, though in gentler terms) but for failing to ignore the primacy of Consciousness III.

Consciousness III, the state of heightened individual consciousness, was the way to green America, said Reich. Unlike past revolutions, the green one would involve no bloodshed, no organizing, and no effort other than dropping out of the Corporate State and developing your consciousness. The example of your satisfying existence would encourage friends and relatives to follow suit. The anti-Establishment pattern would snowball as more and more people refused to participate in the Corporate State. Eventually there would be no one left to run the great machine; it would self-destruct for lack of support, the country would be greened, and the milliennium would arrive.

The youth culture would be the model for adults seeking to achieve Consciousness III: The simple acts of attending a rock concert, wearing jeans instead of a suit, or smoking a joint could be the catalysts that released the powers of Consciousness III within one.

Prepublication excerpts of *Greening* in *The New Yorker* left its affluent readers panting for more. When the book appeared in late 1970, it was a runaway best-seller. Here was a book by an authority—a professor of law at Yale University—who said you were not copping out if you turned your back on the social and political struggles of the day. Instead, you were helping to save the nation by ignoring it and concentrating on your own development and pleasure. You could relax. A course in transcendental meditation might do more for the cause than organizing a protest meeting. Reading *The Greening of America* in 1970 was like discovering a calorie-free banana split.

The "Me" Decade

The 1970s became the decade of self-awareness. The human-potential movement flourished along with Oriental religions, whose teachings of frugality and moderation were devoured by eager devotees. A few members of the New Left were captivated by the consciousness route, but the major thrust of the new consciousness came from people who had been attracted earlier by the hippie movement. Leaders and followers made the transition from drugs to Eastern religions and inner awareness as smoothly as a woman of fashion changes from maxiskirts to peasant dresses.

Thus Richard Alpert, who in the 1960s had been transformed from a Harvard professor of psychology into an LSD proselytizer working with Timothy Leary, went to India for study and was transformed once again in the 1970s—this time emerging as guru Ram Dass. Officials at the University of California must have heaved a sigh of relief when he came to the campus in 1975 not as a drug advocate but as a spiritual leader. The alumni magazine described his triumphant appearance:

> Ram Dass returns to Berkeley, fills Pauley Ballroom. 1200 young spiritual devotees flock to his presence. There is chanting and singing. Ram Dass discourses eloquently on the yogic path of enlightenment, leads us in meditation, gives mantra. . . . After four hours people are loath to leave. Hundreds linger until, in a stroke of inspiration, he throws them flowers from the stage, one by one, in a sweet, slow blessing.[8]

As the drive toward inner peace mushroomed—and the state of peace outside oneself became secondary, if not irrelevant— thousands rushed to join movements that would heighten their consciousness. The new converts shared one characteristic: They came from the affluent society. Occasionally a black was seen, or the son or daughter of an Anglo factory worker came around; but in the main, the consciousness movement was composed of optionaires. It attracted people of many ages and occupations, but they were people who took economic security for granted.

The rising unemployment rate of the early 1970s, which intruded even into the professions, affected some of these people —but not drastically. They did not move into Synanon, the Moonies' Creative Community, Esalen, or a Hare Krishna temple in order to get free room and board. They attended *est* seminars, or studied Rolfing, bioenergetics, or biofeedback, not because they expected that this training would impress personnel managers at job interviews but because they sought psychic or spiritual salvation. If they embraced poverty or asceticism, they embraced it by choice, knowing that whenever it suited them they could leave frugality for the world of microwave ovens and ski condominiums.

The popularity of inner awareness produced a new industry that sold consciousness like potato chips. *Newsweek* reported that Erhard Seminars Training (*est*) grossed $9.5 million in 1975 and expected a higher take in 1976. The consciousness movement, said *Newsweek,* had led to "a lucrative market for packaged programs in enlightenment such as Silva Mind Control, Transcendental Meditation (TM), and est, which have blossomed into multi-million-dollar organizations by promising a 'new you' to anyone who can pay for it."[9]

Its followers had the money to pay. But, unlike potato chips, there was a limit to the number of spiritual "new yous" the educated optionaire had appetite for. Seminars in mind expansion began to have competition from courses in a different realm: the body.

Physical fitness became the new rage. In 1978 two books on running were national best-sellers. Jogging, eating "natural" foods, and following principles of holistic medicine were embraced as sacraments that would lead to salvation. Concentration on oneself remained all-absorbing.

But while people who took vigorous runs before breakfast were feeling satisfied with life as they ate their granola, some other citizens were not satisfied. These were people whose economic concerns overshadowed their interest in self-awareness or physical fitness. In the late 1970s this group included not only sizable numbers of optionaires but most people in the nonaffluent society.

ALIENATION IN THE NONAFFLUENT SOCIETY

After *The Greening of America* appeared, two sociologists published an article called "The Blueing of America." In it, Peter L. Berger and Brigitte Berger hailed the greening of America as an unparalleled opportunity for upward mobility among children of the working class. The abdication of Ivy League students from the Establishment would not cause the country to fall apart, they said; if the young elite refused positions in business and government, children of blue-collar workers would rush in to fill them. "If Yale should become hopelessly greened, Wall Street will get used to recruits from Fordham or Wichita State. Italians will have no trouble running the RAND Corporation, Baptists the space program. Political personnel will change in the wake of social mobility."[10]

Yale was never hopelessly greened, nor was any other American university. The deteriorating economic situation of the 1970s sent more young optionaires than ever scurrying to prestigious universities. The new crop of students wore bell-bottom blue jeans, and perhaps they spread old-fashioned peanut butter on their bread, but their career goals remained unchanged: They were training for jobs that would start at $15,000 to $20,000 a year and lead upward. A sprinkling of people, young and old, were permanently greened, but their defection caused neither Wall Street nor the RAND Corporation to organize search parties at Wichita State. There were always more qualified people from the upper strata ready to take high-paying, prestigious jobs than there were jobs available for them.

Instead of moving upward, children of nonaffluent workers found themselves hard-pressed to keep up with their parents' standard of living. And with rising inflation their parents, in turn, found it difficult to maintain that standard of living on the wages of a factory worker or a shop clerk. Among this segment of Americans the second kind of alienation predominated, an alienation caused by not enough affluence rather than a surfeit of its delights. Workers became despondent when they found themselves systematically excluded from the promised American dream.

It was not a new feeling. Back in the late 1940s sociologist Eli Chinoy had noticed a conflict between the reality of workers' lives and the promises of the American dream when he studied workers at a major auto plant. "The tradition of opportunity and success has long been a folk gospel deeply imbedded in American life," said Chinoy in *Auto Workers and the American Dream*.[11]

Belief in that gospel, he said, caused frustration among workers who were locked into a structure that gave them little chance for advancement. Neither unskilled nor semiskilled workers could achieve substantial wage increases by transferring from one job to another within the plant, and the higher-paid foremen jobs were generally closed to them. They had gone as far as they could go.

Younger workers expressed a strong desire to leave the plant and go into a small business or farming, but they could rarely save up the needed capital on their wages. The examples of fellow workers who had tried that route and failed was a further deterrent.

These workers of the late 1940s would not give up the dream. Regarding themselves as personal failures for not getting ahead, they maintained their belief in success by projecting it onto their children: Their sons and daughters would move up and start their own businesses or enter professions, they believed, thus fulfilling the tenets of the American dream.

A study of meat packers in East St. Louis and Kansas City in 1953 by Theodore Purcell found workers more satisfied with their jobs than were the assembly-line workers in Chinoy's study, but the "great majority" of the meat packers did not want their children to work in the plant when they grew up.[12] One man who had been at the plant since he was 19 said it was "a wonderful place to work" but he had other plans for his children. He refused to let his children even tour the plant, because it might arouse their interest in working there one day. Workers felt that manual labor was held in such low esteem in America that their children must do other work in order to be somebody. As Purcell put it, "The community's frequent lower evaluation of factory workers . . . is probably the major influence over the aspirations these people have for their children."[13]

Parents' dreams of upward mobility for their children were not always realized; in fact, generational mobility could as easily be downward. In a study of job mobility published in 1955, Herman Miller found fathers ahead of their sons in job status. Miller studied 835 male workers in three job categories—semiskilled, service, and laborer—who lived in six different cities. He compared their occupational status with that of their fathers. In all three categories more than half of the sons had jobs that ranked lower than those of their fathers. Among laborers, 70 percent of the fathers held better jobs than their sons, while 68 percent of service workers and 61 percent of semiskilled workers were behind their fathers in job rank.[14]

Of course they earned more. Workers' wages rose steadily in the 1950s and 1960s—but so did prices, often canceling the benefits of larger paychecks. Television commercials meanwhile deluged workers and their families with a stream of products advertised as indispensable to the well-run home. Luxuries became necessities when most of the neighbors had them. While workers caught on the consumption treadmill were finding it increasingly difficult to keep up the payments on house and car, pay taxes and insurance premiums, educate their children, and eat, economists were congratulating America for raising up the workingman into unparalleled affluence.

Behind the Blue-Collar Backlash

Within the nonaffluent society, workers of factory and other manual-labor jobs are called "blue-collar workers." The name contrasts the rough working clothes of manual workers with the starched white shirts and ties worn by office workers, making a class distinction without spelling it out. The division based on collar color is not wholly accurate; for example, it overlooks women workers, ignoring the numerous low-paid clerical and secetarial jobs in offices that are performed primarily by the wives and daughters of blue-collar workers. Despite its limitations, however, the clear visual image of the workman in a blue shirt makes the term useful for describing the working classes within the nonaffluent society, so, with reservations, it is used here.

In the early 1960s, interest in the blue-collar worker waned. Researchers shifted their attention to the poor, a forgotten segment of the population that Michael Harrington brought to public attention in *The Other America*. In the antipoverty programs that followed, poverty came to be equated with a dark skin color; if prejudice and discrimination could be wiped out, said the prevailing wisdom, then every American could enjoy a high standard of living.

Blue-collar workers crept back into the news a few years later, when some of them manifested a reaction that was called the "white backlash." Young intellectuals of the New Left, who had dreamed of a coalition of workers and students against the capitalist Establishment, turned away in disgust at the actions of "hard-hats" (a name deriving from the protective helmets worn by construction workers) who resisted the antipoverty programs, supported the war in Vietnam, and hated college students. The activists viewed hard-hats as dense racists who had betrayed the class struggle by refusing Third World people the benefits the hard-hats themselves had derived from a hundred years of labor struggles.

Tension lessened in the Seventies, but the 1960s image of the blue-collar worker has persisted among optionaires. Archie Bunker, the dim-witted, bigoted buffoon of television fame, and his brainless wife have become symbols of the blue-collar family and its mentality.

Defending the Blue-Collar Worker

Against this tableau of derision for the blue-collar worker, several writers who had close ties with labor countered the attack with books and articles explaining the white backlash and defending the workers. These publications appeared largely in the 1968–72 period when everyone was explaining the 1960s, but they were little noticed. It is worth taking a look now at what the blue-collar defenders had to say, for their message may have relevance for the 1980s and 1990s.

These writers pointed out, first of all, that blue-collar workers, contrary to popular myth, had not achieved affluence; they were struggling to make it in boring jobs that offered them little or no chance of advancement. Secondly, workers believed that the emphasis on helping the poor (which they equated with helping inner-city blacks) was an edict handed down by wealthy people who would not personally feel the effects of their policies.

Gus Tyler, assistant president of the International Ladies Garment Workers Union, explained:

As they [the workers] hear it, this is what the rich are saying: "We must fight poverty and discrimination to the last drop of *your* blood. Share *your* job; share *your* neighborhood; pay *your* taxes." These moral exhortations come from the high and mighty ensconced in tax havens far from the maddening [sic] crowd. . . . Since our worker does not know how to deal with the system, he tries to do the next best thing: to act within the system to protect his own skin. And in our torn and turbulent cities, it is too often his "skin" that determines his mood.

This mood is generally called "backlash," a reawakening of ancient prejudice directed against blacks because they have dared to raise their heads and voices. But to explain the growing tension simply as "backlash" is once more to create a mischievous myth out of partial truth. To deny that prejudice exists is naive; to ascribe rising racial clash to a simple proliferation of prejudice, equally naive. The white worker feels economically threatened, personally imperiled, politically suckered. His anxieties make him meaner than he means to be. Racial suspicion turns into tribal war when people—no matter what their color—are oppressed by their circumstances. Maldistribution of income and people must multiply strife. This strife, ironically, tends not to change but to continue the system that produced the conflict. So long as black battles white and poor battle not-so-poor, the establishment can continue to "divide and rule."[15]

In *Blue Collars and Hard Hats,* Patricia and Brendan Sexton also debunked the myth of worker affluence. At that time, 1971, an urban family of four needed $14,000 a year to reach the lower limits of affluence. Auto workers, the nation's highest-paid industrial workers, were earning $7280 a year without layoffs, and the median income of all American families was $8632. Although 29.6 million Americans lived in families that earned $15,000 a year or more, another 118.6 million people lived in families whose total earnings fell between $5000 and $15,000. The Sextons called this larger group "middle America." "The great mass of middle Americans outnumber the affluent by four to one," they said.[16]

Workers did not show their discontent as openly as youth and the poor, said the Sextons, but they were equally alienated. A 1968 national survey found "serious political alienation" among the majority of Americans. The lower the income, the higher the level of alienation.

When workers did protest, they were likely to direct their grievances toward people just above or below them on the socio-economic scale, people whose lives were visible to them. They ignored the truly rich and powerful, whose lives and very existences they knew little about. "Not since the Depression have people known or cared much about the holders of great wealth and power," said the Sextons.

Just below the workers were the poor, most visibly the black poor; just above the workers were dissenting college students and hippies from the affluent middle class.

Students who were spearheading the drive against the war in Vietnam became objects of an anger that was often more bitter than that directed against ghetto blacks and other Third World peoples. A major reason for this hatred was the government's draft policy during the Vietnam War: College students could get a deferment; young people who worked could not. Sexton reported conversations with workers which expressed their outrage.

"I've got one son, my youngest, in Vietnam," a worker told her. "He didn't have a chance. He says that all the men are in the same boat. They come from average families just like ours, and a lot of them are bitter as hell about being picked to go over there and get killed. They just don't get the same breaks as college kids.

"Of course my son's willing to do his duty to his country if he has to. And I feel the same way. But we can't understand how those rich kids—the kids with the beads from the fancy suburbs—how they got off when my son has to go over there and maybe get his head shot off."[17]

Another man asked: "How come these privileged kids get away with messing up the colleges we're paying to support? I'd give my right arm to get my son into one of those colleges and all these kids seem to do is parade around and denounce the government."[18]

When protesting workers found themselves labeled as hard-hats, racists, and rednecks, the rift between the rank-and-file worker and the optionaire college student widened. The hippie movement and the counterculture increased the gulf: Workers were personally offended by attacks on the work ethic and statements denigrating the kinds of jobs they were locked into.

In 1970 labor specialist Jerome Rosow analyzed the workers' dilemma in a paper, "The Problem of the Blue-Collar Worker." He pointed out that blue-collar workers were by no means all white. "There are some two million minority-group males who are skilled or semi-skilled blue-collar workers who are full-time members of the work force and who share many of the same problems as whites in their income class. . . . Both these groups have essentially 'working class' economic and social problems." These workers were not making it into affluence, said Rosow, and their children were facing similar restrictions in economic opportunities.

Their children, black and white, were dropping out of high school in greater numbers than disadvantaged ghetto youths (because in America there are far more young people from working-class homes than from poor ones) ; defections from high school ran as high as 30 percent in some working-class districts of large cities. The dropouts often had great difficulty finding work, but these children of blue-collar workers were ineligible for government job-training programs, such as the Neighborhood Youth Corps, because their parents' incomes were above the poverty level.

In areas other than employment—health care, welfare, legal aid, and subsidized housing—blue-collar workers earned just enough money to disqualify them and their families from government help. But they were taxed to help pay for those programs, although "often their wages were only a notch or so above the liberal states' welfare payment," Rosow said. Their resentment at being excluded from the benefits of social programs was exacerbated by their feeling that they had no standing in the community. "According to union leaders," said Rosow, "the blue-collar worker increasingly feels that his work has no 'status' in the eyes of society, the media, or even his own children."[19]

In 1971 Robert Krickus wrote about a segment of the population that was virtually ignored in the 1960s—white working-class youth. He pointed out that one youth agency under Health, Education, and Welfare had a threefold category for youths in those years: black, Mexican-American, and college students. These divisions overlooked the majority of America's young people, said Krickus, since 65.4 percent of high-school students never enter college at all. "By 1985, it is estimated, only 14 percent of America's population will be graduates of four-year colleges." . . .

"Approximately 21 million Americans between the ages of 15 and 29 are out of school and never graduated from a college," said Krickus. "In many industries they are the backbone of the rank and file. Approximately 40 percent of the auto workers are under 35 and in some auto plants 70 percent of the production workers are under 30. . . . These working class youth comprise a subculture in which affluence is not taken for granted."[20]

Krickus found these young workers increasingly dissatisfied with their jobs and with the country. "They will tell you that government, the major parties, union leadership, management, and the media are insensitive to their needs."[21] Like optionaire dropouts, they were often estranged from our mainstream institutions. Yet the bulk of the young workers Krickus studied had no affinity for the counterculture movement or for political activism. A few turned to the far right, but most, like their fathers before them, ignored politics and concentrated on amassing material goods, a pursuit that could never be satisfied on their limited paychecks.

BLUE-COLLAR DROPOUTS IN THE COUNTERCULTURE

Most young blue-collar workers rejected the counterculture, but some did not. Among the potential twenty-one million young people who were not college graduates, there were bound to be workers who identified with the hippies. For the working-class young man or woman with serious family problems, for the "loner" who did not fit in with his peer group at home, for the introspective son or daughter who read widely and was disturbed by worker support for the war, identification with the counterculture seemed to provide a way out of their dilemma. They could escape a boring job and the consumer treadmill by switching their allegiance to the values and work ethic of the hippies.

For alienated children of working-class parents, children who wanted a different life, the arguments of the counterculture were enticing. *The Greening of America* told them, "The new way of life proposes a concept of work in which quality, dedication and excellence are preserved, but work is non-alienated, is the free choice of each person, is integrated into a full and satisfying life, and expresses and affirms each individual being."[22]

If working was not your bag, you could surf full time instead. "In the world that now exists, a life of surfing *is* possible, not as an escape from work, a recreation or a phase, but as a *life*—if one chooses," advised *Greening*.[23] [Reich's italics.]

What the book didn't tell was how to find self-affirming jobs, or how you could surf all day and still pay the rent and buy groceries. Such explanations were unnecessary, because this theory was meant for the nation's elite: You could find a satisfying job, once you put your mind to it, if you had a degree from a top university, a plethora of communication skills, an abundance of self-confidence, and enough money to tide you over until the right job turned up. You could surf full time and manage to survive if grandfather had left you a trust fund, if your parents were able and willing to send monthly contributions, or if you were a talented, self-assured young man or woman who thoroughly understood how to work the system to your advantage. For people without such resources, there were problems.

If the hippie work theory had come with a disclaimer similar to that printed on cigarette wrappers—i.e., "Warning: The Secretary of Labor has determined that following the counterculture work ethic may be hazardous for the job futures of unskilled workers"—perhaps some young people might have proceeded with caution. But there were no warnings. The dictum of "satisfying work or nothing" was hailed as an option for everybody. "There is no class struggle; today there is only one class," wrote Reich. "In Marx's terms we are all the proletariat, and there is no longer any ruling class except the machine itself."[24]

Today there is a residue of unemployed people from poor and working-class backgrounds who dropped out of school or work to join the counterculture. It is difficult to know how many such people there are, because their names appear on few records—they pay no taxes because they have no incomes—but a conservative estimate would be several hundred thousand. Now in their early to mid-thirties and predominantly male and white, their job futures are bleak. Many were heavy drug users during the years when LSD and heroin were fashionable. Some are still heroin addicts or have switched to cheaper drugs; others have become alcoholics. Most dropouts have a blank employment record during their adult years. Even in good times, employers would be loath to hire these casualties of the counterculture, for their appearance does not inspire confidence. In today's job market they don't stand a chance of being hired.

Sixty years earlier these men might have become hobos and and found seasonal work on the frontier to sustain their bodies, and a hobohemian culture in the city to sustain their minds in winter. Now, as former centers of the counterculture turn into fashionable residential areas for optionaires, no place can nourish them. Their problem is similar to that of Vietnam veterans who carry the stigma of a dishonorable discharge, but their response is often different. Veterans have formed organizations and pressure groups to try to force the government to respond to their needs, while many blue-collar converts to the counterculture view all government as the enemy. They want no part of it.

Clyde feels that way. Clyde, a dropout of the 1960s, gets along. A borderliner with good verbal skills, he earns enough from sporadic odd jobs to rent a cheap hotel room. He eats at the Food Project and takes clothes from the free boxes when he needs them. He resents criticism of his life-style. "If a person looks at me from a mainstream attitude, he thinks: There's something wrong with him. But for me it might be a right-on thing."

Clyde is vehemently against the government: "If people were left alone, they would form semitribal groupings and take care of each other," he said when we spoke with him. He opposes government grants to alternative agencies, viewing them as a copout to the system and a loss of autonomy. "If we relied less on the government, it would stimulate more private activity," he says.

Clyde's position ironically coincides with that of the most conservative sector of the business community, a group he hates even more than the government. Both Clyde and large corporations want the government to keep its hands off them.

Clyde gets by, but many of his contemporaries do not. Some dropouts who hate the government are eventually forced to go on some type of welfare in order to stay alive. Others who remain on their own are barely surviving or are dying in hotel rooms. They are caught between the two conflicting ideologies—an alienation stemming from too much and that which comes from not having enough.

Confusion often results. Although some people will tell you that they have no job because they refuse to do meaningless work in a corrupt society, if they woke up in the morning and decided to take any job, they would be no better off in the job market. Their ideology gives them a little self-esteem and the illusion of making a choice. But it does not feed, clothe, or house them, nor does it give them a way of occupying their days. A generation of poor and working-class dropouts now in their thirties have little chance of ever finding full-time work. They were sold down the river by the promises of the counterculture.

Meanwhile, most optionaire dropouts of the 1960s have returned to the mainstream. The hippies studied by Pittel and Miller, all once heavy users of psychedelic drugs, were already moving back into the Establishment as early as 1971 and 1972. Their parents had average incomes of $13,000 to $15,000 in the 1960s, so these young people dropped out with the advantages of an affluent background. Psychologist Stephen Pittel has called the drug involvement of the hippies he studied a "chemically induced moratorium for youth," tying it in with the youth moratorium postulated by Erik Erikson.[25] Many optionaire hippies emerged from their drug moratoriums like hungry bears coming out of hibernation; in short order, they hit the trail to affluence.

Young people from the nonaffluent society are not experiencing affluence whether they migrate or stay home. Nor are their parents becoming affluent, for the most part, no matter how hard they work. Unlike the auto workers Chinoy studied in the postwar years, however, today's nonaffluent workers can no longer project their dream of success onto their children with confidence.

Blue-collar workers have started to rebel against their exclusion from the dream; that rebellion has led to some strange alliances and unlikely enemies.

CHAPTER FOURTEEN

Combat on the Domestic Front

Disenchantment, as we have seen, is increasing among blue-collar workers who find that they can never achieve affluence. Instead of blaming themselves as in earlier eras, the nonaffluent are looking elsewhere for culprits. But the working classes have not turned on the groups that a Marxist might expect them to rise up against—big business in general and the multinational banks and corporations in particular. Instead, growing numbers of people in the nonaffluent society have turned against big government, political idealists, and the entire spectrum of the counterculture.

The battle between the affluent and nonaffluent societies has escalated over the past two decades, but participation is limited. The rich, who might be expected to serve as chief warriors of the affluent, are on the sidelines, or, what seems an anomaly at first, they are occasional allies of the nonaffluent camp. The poor, caught up in a day-to-day struggle for survival, are also absent from the battlefield for the most part. The participants in combat come from the middle-income zones, with blue-collar workers and their affiliates lined up on one side against idealists and counterculturalists from the base of the affluent society.

The 1960s polarized these two camps. During that decade the archenemies of workers were the hippies and the antiwar and civil-rights activists. In the 1970s a new enemy appeared in the shape of the environmentalists. Exploring the sides in that con-

flict delineates the issues at stake in many such battles, and un-
covers some causes beneath the surface.

Environmentalists versus Workers

In 1976, environmentalists opposed the Dow Chemical Company's plans to build a $500-million petrochemical plant in the
delta area of California. When the government held hearings,
workers in the area came in sizable numbers to root for the Dow
plant, which meant jobs for them, and to boo environmentalists
as they spoke of endangered bird species that would face extinc-
tion if the chemical factory, with all its pollutants, went up. Some
workers at the hearings wore hard hats. They had not rushed
from work to the hearings in such haste that they had no time
to change clothes; they wore hard hats as symbols of who they
were and where they stood.

Dow decided not to build that petrochemical plant in California for the present, for reasons that must be complex consider-
ing the financial outlay involved. But in the eyes of the workers,
the environmentalists—college-educated optionaires from the affluent society, who enjoyed salaries and a standard of living the
workers could never hope to achieve—had won; their interest in
bird survival was considered more important than jobs for
workers in the area.

The following year another controversy erupted between workers and environmentalists, this time over a bill to expand Redwood National Park in northern California. Environmentalists
supported the plan, while loggers and other citizens in the areas
affected vigorously opposed park expansion, fearing that pro-
tecting the trees would mean the loss of their jobs. When hearings were held in Eureka, a town in the heart of the redwood
country, thousands of local residents marched to protest the park
expansion. Congressman Phillip Burton, a sponsor of the bill,
was booed, as were members of Friends of the Earth who testified
in favor of park expansion. A child in the audience wore a hard
hat and had a placard over her chest which read: "Burton, why
are you taking my Daddy's job away?"[1]

The next day another hearing was scheduled in San Francisco.
That morning nearly 100 trucks filled with redwood logs arrived
in San Francisco in the midst of the rush hour, their drivers
honking their horns. Other demonstrators arrived in twenty buses

from lumber-mill cities in the north. "No more parks. No more parks," they chanted.[2] David Snodderly, executive director of the Associated California Loggers, told reporters that the loggers planned to drive a five-truck convoy to Washington, D.C. "We want legislation declaring the logger an endangered species," said Snodderly.[3]

A 62-year-old mill mechanic blamed the trouble on "environmentalists, rich bitches, and nature babies," who donate money to save-the-redwoods campaigns. "Poor old sliver-pickers like us don't have money to spend on trees," he said.[4]

To environmentalists, the workers' response was a shock. The environmentalists saw themselves as the good guys who were trying to stop business interests from denuding the land for profit. They knew the history of logging in America, knew that it had been agitation by earlier conservationists (who gained support from politicians such as Theodore Roosevelt) that had led the government to create bureaus and departments whose policies saved America from having no more forests left to cut down by the middle of the twentieth century. They also knew that cutting was so heavy in the redwoods area that workers there would be out of jobs in ten years anyway, when there would be no more mature trees left to cut down. If the government was ready to trade the lumber-company owners other lands away from the edge of the park and to create new jobs for displaced loggers in the area, then why the bitterness?

The dispute went beyond the visible issues. It was a fight to uphold the economic aspirations that shaped the nation. Laborers could identify more easily with their bosses than with environmentalists or officials from Washington. The experts, with their statistics and intellectual arguments, aroused the loggers' suspicion, while their bosses were examples of the American dream brought to fruition: They had achieved what the loggers hoped to achieve one day. But here was the government trying to put limits on these rugged individuals, saying that businessmen could be restricted for the common good. Whose good? the workers wondered. Surely not theirs.

Where did the lumber executives stand in the dispute? At first they seemed to be neutral observers. At the hearings in San Francisco when Congressman Don Clausen, representing a constituency in the redwood country, said, "I'm not here to protect the companies. They're going to be paid off. It's the workers I'm trying to protect," he was cheered by the loggers.[5]

But when reporters sought out lumber management, they found that executives *did* object to having some of their timberlands annexed for a national park. The *San Francisco Chronicle* reported: "So incensed at the park proposal were company executives that they produced a half-hour slide presentation, shown to visitors at the plant, in which the expansion is blamed on 'urban-based' preservationists who seek to turn Humboldt County into 'another Appalachia.' "[6]

In the office of one lumber executive a reporter saw signs that had been used by loggers at the recent trek to San Francisco. The signs read: "I want to work," "What happens to my family?" and "Sierra Club, kiss my axe." The lumber executives said, "The protection bit is a bunch of hokum. I'd use it too if I wanted to pull off a land grab."[7]

To workers, the lumber executives became the good guys, the providers of jobs, while the government and its supporters were the bad guys who wanted to take away jobs in order to save a bunch of trees. In a move that confounds the history of labor, the loggers and their unions formed a coalition with their employers against the park-expansion bill. For lumber executives, the coalition might have been made in heaven. Now they could argue that it was concern for their workers' welfare, not profits, that made them hire lawyers and send lobbyists to Washington to try to block passage of the park bill.

Beyond the immediate issue, the park controversy gave workers an opportunity to express their anger toward their country, which promised them so much but failed to deliver the goods. Postwar America promised workers affluence—told them, in fact, that they already had it. Conservatives said some people were not affluent because they didn't try hard enough; liberals said some people were not affluent because they were victims of racial discrimination; workers told themselves they were not affluent because of a series of circumstances in their individual lives, circumstances that would change for their children. But no one doubted that every citizen could be affluent. It was only a matter of time.

Today, workers are wondering whether they will *ever* make it into the affluent society, and whether their children stand a chance of reaching that goal either. They resent those who grew up with opportunities that assured them a place among the affluent. These days they especially resent idealists who, secure in the advantages of an optionaire upbringing, discount the importance of material goods and sneer at workers whose main interest is making money. The rank-and-file worker can better understand a millionaire pulling off another land grab than a university graduate with two degrees who lives in a log cabin in the woods and grows vegetables.

PERILS OF COUNTERCULTURE?

The counterculture plays an ambiguous role in the battle between the affluent and nonaffluent societies. The back-to-the-land movement stresses a reduction in individual consumption of goods to conserve our natural resources and make what we do have go further. How can a movement that facilitates conservation receive anything but kudos from people like myself who sympathize with its aims?

The problem is that the counterculture has turned its back on the political arena for the most part, opting to set up a separate society that it believes can ultimately serve as an example for the rest of the nation. In doing so, counterculture enthusiasts ignore the basic economic concerns and problems that most citizens face. And they ignore or ridicule the desire for more material goods among people who feel that they have never had their fair share of affluence. At a time of galloping inflation and widespread political discontent, this tendency to ignore the concerns of the nonaffluent—especially nonaffluent youth—can be dangerous politically, as the example of Germany shows.

In Germany a youth movement of optionaires, which preceded the Hitler Youth by a few generations, developed a philosophy that is remarkably similar to that of today's counterculture. Germany's main youth movement in the twentieth century was the Wandervogel (1896–1919) , which after World War I became the Bünde (1919–33) . The Wandervogel, which is translated into English as "ramblers," began in 1896 as a group of young people who went on weekend outings into the countryside to enjoy the beauties of nature. Its members were high-school students from the middle classes—young people who faced no economic worries in the years ahead, but who were dissatisfied with their lives and country. They saw the old order of life collapsing around them, and they chafed under the authoritarian atmosphere of their families. Deeply concerned about the future path they and their nation should take, the Wandervogel chose to ignore politics and concentrate on a return to spiritual values.

Walter Z. Laqueur, a British scholar of German birth, explains it in this way:

> The youth movement wanted above all to be integrated human beings, as one would put it today, and they were critical of a society that was not conducive to the development of such men and women. They felt very strongly what an earlier—and a later—generation of philosophers called "alienation.". . . They wanted a change in human relations and there was no certainty that these could be changed by a new political and social system, however radically different from that under which they lived. The *Wandervogel* chose the other form of protest against society—romanticism. Their return to nature was romantic, as were their attempts to get away from a materialistic civilization, their stress on the simple life. . . .[8]

Turning away from the "wicked" West of industrialism led a part of the Wandervogel toward mysticism and the East. "In 1917 there was another rediscovery of the wisdom of the East. . . . soon everyone was talking about Taoism, Zen Buddhism, and *tat tvam asi,* and the *Siddanta* of the Ramanujas and Vishnu-Narayana were being reprinted. Tagore's gospel of spiritual unity, of 'love, not power,' found enthusiastic disciples," said Laqueur.[9]

Other mysticism had medieval Christian roots and was geared to a less sophisticated audience than those who studied Tagore or the Indian classics. In the early 1920s, Laqueur recounted, a young man, Friedrich Muck-Lamberty, led a popular folk movement:

> With twenty-five young companions he went from town to town in Thuringia, calling the population to contemplation, urging them to wake up to life, to combat the decay of society and to be gay. How was all this to be accomplished? By dancing, singing, and lectures on the revolution in the Soul. His followers, like the early Christians,

shared all their worldly possessions, and were vegetarians
and abstainers. . . . Wherever the barefooted or sandaled
"Neue Schar" made its appearance, thousands joined in its
meetings and dances, there was a triumphant procession
and the clergy had to open the church for Muck's lectures
and community singing. . . . It seemed that the millen-
nium was about to dawn and the New Jerusalem was close
at hand.[10]

Friedrich Heer, a professor of history at the University of
Vienna, says of the Wandervogel: "It was a flight from the town
into the country and its forests. Its center was the campfire, its
form of expression folk-singing and folk-dancing. There were
strong feelings against capitalism and industrialization."[11] As the
movement grew, it developed youth hostels, summer camps, and
some experiments in communal living. "Several of the component
groups sought to grasp the opportunity of putting into practice
their new spirit of fraternity by living, like the early Christians,
in close communities. They set up rural communes, in which
there were no leaders and no followers."[12]

In 1923 an American, Stanley High, published a book called
The Revolt of Youth in which he hailed the German youth
movement as the hope of humanity. "The political interests are
tending to disappear, the great spiritual forces are on the as-
cendancy," said High. The new youth are "the apostles of a
wholly new life for young and old alike. . . . With their spirit,
the old heaven and earth—of suspiciousness and selfishness—will
pass away."[13]

In 1976 John de Graaf, an American writer involved with the
counterculture movement, was stunned when he came across
High's book and noted the similarities between the German
youth movement and the American counterculture. After more
research, de Graaf wrote an insightful article, "Perils of Counterculture," pointing out the parallels and trying to fathom their
message for today's counterculture. De Graaf says of High's book,
"Indeed, this book could well have been entitled *The Greening
of Germany*. Reading it, one is unsure whether this is Germany
of the twenties or America of the sixties that High is describing."[14]

What went wrong, asked de Graaf, that ten years later Hitler
came to power in Germany? De Graaf's conclusions were tenta-
tive, for he believed the subject merited further study, but he

cautioned the counterculture not to ignore political reality. At the same time, however, he cautioned the Left not to ignore the counterculture or "it [the Left] will not appeal to the young."

Who are the young to whom de Graaf referred? They are a small slice of the one-third of the nation's youth who are optionaires. De Graaf's article appeared in the *East-West Journal,* a magazine for the strata of the counterculture that are interested in psychic and spiritual phenomena; it carried ads for Zen Buddhist institutes; courses in shiatsu, yoga and Oriental studies; and for meditation pillows, orgone energy blankets, and pyramid products. The young whom de Graaf and others in the counterculture see as representing all young people are but a fraction of the Americans who fall into that age range at any given time.

In Germany the Wandervogel and then the Bünde, with a social composition similar to that of the American counterculture, also ignored the economic problems—and indeed the very existence— of nonaffluent youth in their own country. During a decade of political and economic chaos (1920–30), when rival political factions were killing their opponents in battles waged in several German cities, when inflation and currency devaluation reached such astronomical proportions that a suitcase full of money could not buy a shirt, members of Germany's youth groups, themselves economically secure, urged spiritual values on an ailing country. Ignoring the political struggles of the day, they studied Eastern religions or withdrew to the country to live natural lives.

Meanwhile Adolf Hitler was building a following among youth below the middle class. He attracted young people from the working class and the peasantry into his own organization, and also recruited sizable numbers from the lower middle class, the children of small shopkeepers and businessmen, a group that was hit particularly hard by the country's galloping inflation. Hitler hated the youth movement of the affluent classes. Once in power, he copied a few of the youth movement's trappings—its organizational structure and its trail greeting of *"Heil"*—then, in June 1933, he outlawed these groups. The entire youth movement collapsed. Some Bünde leaders fled the country, others were imprisoned; some joined the Nazis, but they were never given positions of leadership in the Hitler Youth hierarchy. Their influence on the nation was nil.

The parallels between the youth movements of pre-Hitler Germany and today's counterculture are striking. But it does not follow that the American Nazis may gain a mass following if we don't watch out. The Nazi party of Germany embodied centuries of German traditions and beliefs. The country that voted Hitler into power had long sneered at both democracy and individualism; its history was one of ardent nationalism and a militaristic belief in strict obedience to an all-powerful leader. "Some day a man will come to lead us—a Man who unites German Spirit and German power! Believe me . . . things will be just a little better for us then!" a military leader wrote to his sister before 1920, after Germany's defeat in the Baltic.[15] In the difficult years that followed World War I, the German people were searching for a savior whose every command they could obey.

America has a different past. A strong tradition of personal freedom has always permeated the nation, and democracy has long been cherished. Although racism provides a convenient scapegoat for the discontented, it runs counter to American ideals. The demagogue who would capture a mass following in America must be able to pull more than myths of racial superiority out of his bag of tricks.

But if nazism seems unlikely to gain a foothold in the United States, that does not preclude other right-wing movements, more American in their appeal—i.e., stressing rugged individualism and undiluted laissez-faire economic policies—from attracting wide support among Americans who are deeply dissatisfied with their incomes, and thus with their government. If sizable numbers of the nation's young optionaires ignore the cries of the dissatisfied majority and reject the political arena in favor of religious or environmental fulfillment (or retreat from the mainstream altogether to set up rural mini-utopias), plenty of other people will be ready to step in and take over as leaders of the people. It could be a field day for demagogues. The government policies some leaders would put into effect once in power might not appeal to the dropouts, but, as in Nazi Germany, such policies could ultimately affect everyone.

The first imperative of a democracy is to participate in it. The lesson of Germany's youth movement is that you turn your back on your country's political system at your own peril. If you can't see the people for the trees, there could be trouble ahead.

Part Three

MAKING A LIVING: THE CURRENT IMPERATIVE

CHAPTER FIFTEEN

The Rise and Fall of Meaningful Work

History plays strange tricks. With blue-collar workers and option-aires at loggerheads throughout the 1960s over goals and values, who would have suspected that by 1980 the two groups would share some economic goals, and that many of their values would have merged? This chapter, which charts the rise and fall of meaningful work, tells what happened.

"Meaningful work" was a central theme of the hippie and counterculture movements. Instead of pursuing money and power as prime goals, young people were encouraged to seek work that was personally fulfilling and socially relevant. This switch in career goals was part of the whole new way of life that would lead, as envisioned in *Greening*, to "a liberation of each individual in which he is enabled to grow toward the highest possibilities of the human spirit."[1]

The concept of meaningful work was inspiring. Many option-aires who took up its banner found the idea so appealing that they wanted all people to enjoy its satisfactions. In their enthusiasm over the universal satisfaction that meaningful work would bring to mankind, they did not stop to ask who would assemble the cars or clean the public toilets in a society where everyone only did work that he or she found personally fulfilling.

The theory of meaningful work often included an affirmation

of physical labor as opposed to machine tending or mental work. Young optionaires dropped out of universities or left well-paying office jobs to become farmers, carpenters, and jewelry makers, or to enter other occupations where they would work with their hands. They thought they were on the side of working people, and could not understand why workers reacted so negatively to them and their theories.

The working conditions of the new artisans bore little resemblance to those of most workers in the nonaffluent society. The artisans set up their own conditions: They worked alone and were their own bosses or they became members of small collectives in which every member had an equal say. They rarely worked in factories, stores, or other large buildings and institutions—the places where most wage earners spend their adult lives in order to make a living. Nor were they bound to strict schedules, rules, and regulations.

The sons and daughters of farmers may be unable to go into farming themselves today; land is too expensive and competition from large corporations too difficult to fight. Counterculture farmers, however, bought their own land, separately or collectively, with capital that the average farm youth could never amass. Moreover, the farms of the back-to-the-land optionaires did not need to be in the productive agricultural sections of the country, noted for good soil, because making a living from farming was only one option of the back-to-the-landers. If optionaire farmers didn't have a sizable bank account from a previous professional job, or an independent income, one partner or member could probably find a job in a nearby town teaching school or doing social work. If not, they might earn money for the mortgage by writing books in the evening, explaining how to churn butter and set up your own electric generator, or describing the joys of natural country living. Some fugitives from affluence made a virtue of surviving on income levels that most farmers were trying to rise above.

To working-class men and women whose great dream was to see their children graduate from college and become well-paid, respected professionals, the sight of young people from affluent homes dropping out of universities to become laborers or subsistence farmers was puzzling.

The theory of meaningful work was not new to the working classes; the concept had been used before to downgrade them.

Soon after World War II, sociologists, predominantly from the affluent society, began visiting large factories to study job satisfaction and the quality of working life. Some of these researchers published reports or books showing that manual workers, especially those on the assembly line, turned into alienated robots. Workers thus found themselves twice belittled—first because they had not become affluent in the tradition of the American dream, and second because they were willing to perform the repetitive tasks that produce the goods our society consumes.

The findings of these sociologists are open to interpretation. Was automobile industrialist Henry Ford, wizard of mass-production techniques, correct when he said, "The assembly line is a haven for those who haven't got the brains to do anything else"?[2] Or is it the case that people of normal intelligence turn into programmed automatons after they fit a hubcap onto a car wheel for the ten thousandth time? Scholars may write books in the future to resolve this dilemma, but meanwhile many workers and their champions are questioning the results of factory surveys that show workers as dehumanized by routine jobs.

Auto Work and Its Discontents (1976) contains essays on job satisfaction by scholars, but they are scholars with a difference: Each author had a minimum of three years' experience in an auto plant and served as a union bargaining agent before entering the academic world, and each has retained an interest in industry, unions, and workers. Robert Reiff, director of the Center for the Study of Social Intervention of Albert Einstein College of Medicine, was once a welder in an auto shop. He takes a dim view of sociological studies that show workers as dehumanized. When social scientists study production workers, says Reiff, "they do not see them as human beings, but as mechanized robots, and project their feelings of alienation on them . . . my experience in an auto plant has convinced me that alienation of workers as a personality characteristic is in the eyes of the social science beholder."[3]

Reiff also pointed out that while workers may not derive satisfaction from performing unskilled jobs in an auto plant, they do get social satisfactions from working together with their peers. "The production worker is almost always part of a group. There are many opportunities for social relationships in the work situation, and these are often crucial in providing satisfaction," he said.[4]

Patricia C. Sexton agreed. Sexton, now a professor of sociology at New York University, was an assembly-line worker at the Dodge main plant in the late 1940s. She felt no nostalgia for the work she performed there, but she did miss the camaraderie on the job. "I loved the people, the variety of them, the toughness and honesty of them, their good humor and spontaneity. I very much like working with 'blue-collar' men," said Sexton, who was one of three women on a 500-worker assembly line in those years.[5]

Al Nash of Cornell University's School of Industrial and Labor Relations threw brickbats at the idea that workers are robotized by repetitious jobs. "I have met auto workers with all kinds of personalities, those who were authoritarians, racists or company stooges as well as those who were permissive, tolerant or rebellious. I never met a worker who resembled the Chaplinesque figure in *Modern Times*," says Nash, who formerly worked four years in an aircraft plant and then six years in two auto plants. During his five years as chief steward on the motor line at Chrysler, he relates, there were two walkouts, but neither was caused by assembly-line pressures; one was related to a new worker who refused to join the union and "the other was over the failure of the company to patch up the roof so that rain would not pour down on the workers below."[6]

Workers have two main concerns about their jobs—the working conditions and the size of their paychecks. They do not like rain pouring down on them at work, noxious fumes destroying their health, or overbearing foremen harassing them on the job. But their pay is the most important consideration. Above all else, workers want enough money to live comfortably. (When Professor William H. Form studied auto workers in factories in four countries—Italy, Argentina, India, and the United States—he found that they all shared these same basic concerns.)

For most people in America and elsewhere, a major concern of adult life is to make enough money to live on. It has been that way in the past, it is that way now, and there are no indications that it will be much different in the future. Working full time at interesting, creative, personally satisfying work is a luxury —like caviar and sports cars—for the lucky few. Although some people in every class are fortunate enough to enjoy their work, the search for meaningful work is an option open mainly to people in the affluent society.

What is meaningful work? Is it only the work of alfalfa-sprout farmers, hand-toolers of leather bags, or civil-liberties lawyers? Or is it all the work that keeps a society functioning? If city food stores suddenly shut their doors, if there were no food for sale and people could not get out into the country, the city populations would starve. This point is not an invitation to flee to the countryside, hoard canned goods, or start growing vegetables in pots on the windowsill; it is one illustration of the dependence of our urban industrial societies on the meaningful work that numerous other people perform for them every day. Standing alongside a conveyor belt sorting peaches for canning may be boring work, but it helps bring peaches to people's tables year-round as well as providing a living for the sorter.

What about that least desirable of all work, the "menial" job? It is not the work itself that is so hated; rather, it is the low social status that accompanies the job and, most important, the menial paycheck. Growers import migrant labor from Mexico because, they say, white men in America refuse to do the stoop labor involved in harvesting some crops. It's too menial. If those growers offered $12.50 an hour, and if adequate, affordable living accommodations were available nearby, Americans of every color would be ready to do stoop labor. Likewise, if managers of large office buildings in New York City advertised next week that they would pay women $17.00 an hour to clean toilets and mop floors in rest rooms, their personnel offices would not be able to hold all the applicants. Some men might file sex-discrimination suits to try to get the jobs themselves.

Deifying the search for meaningful work, while sneering at those who remain in routine jobs, degrades the daily work performed by millions in America and billions throughout the world. It is little wonder that the working classes, for the most part, have been singularly unimpressed with the ethic of meaningful work.

THE GET-RICH-QUICK REVIVAL

Workers won't be plagued much longer with talk about meaningful work, because it is going out of style. A new work ethic is sweeping the country. Its message is to make money. Lots of money, all the money you can get your hands on. It is a goal that blue-collar workers can share with optionaires, for it is nothing less than the American dream revitalized.

The get-rich-quick movement is flourishing at all levels of American society today, as we will see, but to follow the continuity of preceding chapters, we will start by looking at the current popularity of moneymaking in one sector of the counterculture.

From Money-Isn't-Important to Get-Rich-Quick

In the days of the hippies, when the message that counted was Love Is All You Need, some skeptics—especially impoverished blacks and Hispanics who were trying to rise above the poverty level—took a jaundiced view of such sentiments. Hippies were only playing at poverty, they said; whenever it suited the hippies, they could go back to the money. Now many former hippies *have* gone back to the money, but under the comforting framework of the human-potential movement; their drive for big money is not considered crass materialism, it is seen as a higher level in fulfilling their human potentials. In some circles the quest for riches is called "The New Practicality."

In 1978 Sherman Chickering, who ran Kanaka Trust, a camp in the Sierras, explained it this way: "The third stage of the growth movement, which seems to be emerging now, applies the principles and practices of encounter and body work to the material world . . . through politics, professions, and possessions." At his camp, Chickering invited seekers "to identify their personal resources, connections, expertise, talents, money and possessions—and to 'put them ito play' to get maximum vitality out of them."[7] Read "profit" for "vitality" and you get the picture of The New Practicality.

The tie-in between the spirit and the bank account was aptly expressed by Tom Robbins, a young writer popular with the counterculture, when he said of his own financial success, "There is a certain Buddhistic calm that comes from having this money in the bank."[8]

People who have completed their inner-awareness and fitness training can move on to seminars that are set up to teach them how to get rich. Bill Schwartz, who runs such seminars as part of his School for Entrepreneurs, views them as a logical step up the growth ladder. "I think of *est* and other things designed to raise consciousness as 'ground schools,' " said Schwartz. "This is a 'flight school.' Okay, so you've got yourself together. Now let's see you fly."

According to Schwartz, the first rule of the entrepreneur is: If you've got the idea and the energy, the money will follow. But some participants in his seminars were troubled by that rule; they wanted specific information on where to get money for their business ventures. A newsman who attended one of Schwartz's seminars reported:

> Several students balked when Schwartz explained that investors rarely put money into a business unless it had been operating for a few months, at least.
>
> "Where do you get the money to do the initial start-up?" someone asked.
>
> "Listen," Schwartz said, "I can't tell you how to get money out of your uncle. But don't worry about it. The money will follow." . . .

Schwartz's assumption that the twenty-five seminar participants all had rich uncles or other wealthy relatives in the background who could be hit for money was not out of line. The cost of the weekend seminar was $350, and the participants came squarely from the affluent society:

> Most of the students were in their 20's or 30's; none was black, Asian, or Latino. Many were veterans of workshops and talked of their experiences with *est,* centering, rolfing and others. . . . A few already had businesses in operation, but most had only schemes and dreams of prosperity, and frantic desires to translate these dreams into cash. . . . One woman was determined to raze an entire city block to erect a "natural foods" mall.[9]

Leaving in limbo the question of how many participants are likely to succeed in business even if they do get money from their uncles, we return to the country at large, where the desire to get rich quick transcends class lines.

From Horatio Alger to Niccolò Machiavelli

The late 1970s and early 1980s bear an uncanny resemblance to the period after the American Civil War (described in Chapter 2) in the amount of success literature that is flooding the market.

Books, magazines, and newsletters galore, along with courses, seminars, and lectures, all claim to tell—for a price—how to get rich quickly. As in the Gilded Age, rugged individualism is celebrated, and unlimited economic opportunity is promised to those who play the money game.

But the rules of the game are different. The ideals of Horatio Alger have been discarded in favor of those of Niccolò Machiavelli, the Renaissance statesman whose name has come to symbolize unscrupulous, deceitful behavior in pursuit of one's goal. Some may argue that ours is a more honest age, because we openly admit how fortunes and power bases are built and maintained; the point here is that today's manuals give a different message to those who seek to get rich quickly.

Two books that made the best-seller lists in 1977 and 1978—*Looking Out for Number One* and *Success! How Every Man and Woman Can Achieve It*—serve as preliminary reading for those about to start playing the money game. These books do not give specifics about moneymaking as the manuals, seminars, and magazines do; instead, they assuage any guilt feelings readers may have about dumping concepts of honesty and social responsibility in favor of making millions.

In *Looking Out for Number One,* author Robert J. Ringer (whose earlier book, *Winning Through Intimidation,* also became a national best seller in the 1970s) views a concern for anyone but yourself as a sign of immaturity; he advocates unbridled self-interest at all times. "Unless someone is poor because you robbed him, no downtrodden individual is your responsibility and shouldn't be a mental blockade in your happiness," advises Ringer. Regarding charity, he says: "The best way to help the poor is by not becoming one of them."[10]

The logic behind that statement is not elucidated; it doesn't have to be, for Ringer's readers want only to hear such soothing reassurances before plunging guiltlessly into the money game. Ringer's philosophy, said one reviewer, "is that if you are selfish, greedy, avaricious, cutthroat, and without morals, you will find true happiness."[11] And make lots of money.

Michael Korda dishes up more of the same in *Success! How Every Man and Woman Can Achieve It:*

If you're going to work at all, and most of us have to, you might just as well become rich, famous, and successful in the process. . . . The people who succeed do not as a rule work all that much harder than the people who fail, and in some cases very much less hard—they have simply mastered the rules of success.

You can too. . . . tell yourself:

It's O.K. to be greedy.

It's O.K. to be ambitious.

It's O.K. to look out for Number One.

It's O.K. to have a good time.

It's O.K. to be Machiavellian (if you can get away with it).

It's O.K. to recognize that honesty is not always the best policy (provided you don't go around saying so).

It's O.K. to be a winner. And it's *always* O.K. to be rich [italics Korda's].[12]

Under the heading "Greed Is Good for You," Korda urges readers to cash in on the inequities of our tax system:

Success gives you the right to be greedy. . . . It is just as well to face it squarely: *the successful get rich and the unsuccessful get poorer.* It is not for nothing that when the House Ways and Means Committee was debating tax cuts it swiftly approved $165 million worth of tax rebates "to wealthy investors who had sizable capital losses . . . in the stock market," while arranging matters so that the only group which did *not* benefit from the projected cuts was "low income families with children." Not surprisingly, a report from the U.S. Senate indicates that 53 percent of the benefits from federal tax loopholes go to the 14.6 percent of taxpayers who make more than $20,000 a year, and that seven persons with incomes in excess of $1,000,000 a year paid no federal income tax at all. Under the circumstances it makes sense to get what you can [italics Korda's].[13]

Once guilt is assuaged, readers can proceed to the specifics of how to make a fortune. The get-rich-quick seminars that are now proliferating throughout the United States generally stress two steps for achieving financial success: (1) Avoid paying income tax on your earnings. You pay the instructor for his expertise in ways to avoid taxes legally or extralegally, so you can get rich and let wage earners support the government; and (2) Use other people's money for your investments.

The second step might not seem like a tip worth paying for, since it is standard procedure in business: Banks exist in large part to lend money to businesses; the banks earn their money when the loan is repaid with interest. But when borrowing money is presented as a top secret of the successful, would-be-entrepreneurs are ready to pay as much as $350 per weekend to hear it.

The most popular topic for get-rich-quick seminars is real-estate speculation, apparently because of its rich possibilities for tax loopholes and quick profits.

Just Plain Folks Who Happened to Get Rich

More prolific than seminars these days are the manuals that tell how to get rich. Available mostly by mail and often self-published, different success manuals are written to appeal to people at various socioeconomic levels—from college-educated optionaires to unskilled workers who may be barely literate. But they all have a similar message: The authors are just plain folks who happened to stumble across the magic formula for making millions; they are not special people or smarter than the average American—anyone can duplicate their financial success by purchasing their book that contains the magic formulas. A sampling of advertisements pitched to different audiences gives the picture:

"Millionaires aren't a lot smarter than you," said "Multi-millionaire Steven West" in a full-page ad in *The New York Times Book Review* in 1977. "They simply learn to master the illusion of luxurious living in a society that depends on credit." West went on to describe his own meteoric rise from rags to riches:

> Many people are amazed to learn that in just five years my net worth has gone from zero to more than five million dollars. But my wife Sheri and I can still remember what it was like to be over our head in debt, living in a tiny, crowded apartment. . . . In desperation I began to read and research lives of successful millionaires like Rockefeller, Dupont [sic], Getty and Mellon. I read book after book, I learned that millionaires were just like me—they were not mental giants—they were people who had learned the for-

mulas for success and wealth. . . . Today I am Chairman of the Board of eleven multinational corporations engaged in manufacturing, wholesaling and retailing with sales of over $100,000,000 a year![14]

West's formulas were available in book form, *Live Like a Millionaire,* which could be ordered from him for $9.95 plus 95 cents for postage and handling.

"Millionaires Are Not 100 Times Smarter Than You, They Just Know the Wealth Formula," said "Millionaire Mark O. Haroldsen" in a full-page ad in the *Saturday Evening Post* which told "How to Achieve Total Financial Freedom in 1978." Haroldsen, pictured with his smiling wife and four small children on the tennis court of their two-and-a-half-acre estate in Utah, explained that by following the formula he had become so rich that he no longer had to work. "I guess I am bragging now, but I did start spending a lot of time in our backyard pool, travelling around the country and doing a lot of loafing. . . . Then one day a friend asked me how he could do what I had done."[15] The result was a book, *Financial Freedom,* available direct from Haroldsen in Utah for $10.

"The secret to making a quick fortune in America has been reduced to a simple 7-step system by an entrepreneur from Canton, Ohio," began a full-page ad that appeared on the back page of the comics section of the Sunday *San Francisco Examiner and Chronicle* in 1978. The ad, written in the form of an interview, described the rise of Ben Swarez, a former frustrated factory worker who discovered the Net Profit Generator System (N.P.G.S.) and became rich overnight. "It was unbelievable," a neighbor recalled. "One day he's driving around in a rusted out '68 Pontiac station wagon, living in an uncarpeted house that didn't even have a color T.V. and struggling to make ends meet like the rest of us. The next day he's driving a brand new Lincoln Mark, a brand new Mercury station wagon, a $35,000 GMC motorhome, his house is fixed up like a palace, and he's traveling all over the country."

The ad gave no clue as to what kind of system the N.P.G.S. was, but it offered readers the opportunity to find out by immediately ordering the book that contained the secret. "I can keep everyone from knowing my secret by only making the book available on a limited, controlled basis." Order instructions were easy enough for a third-grader to follow: "To order (1) Get a blank piece of paper, (2) At the top of the paper print the words '7 Steps to Freedom,' (3) Print your name and address, (4) Mail this along with $10.00 in cash, check, or money order. . . ."

"My system is geared to the working man who is in the same situation I was," said Swarez, "living from pay to pay, no savings or assets, working an 8 hour day for a big company, no experience, no rich relatives, nothing." Who could work his system for big profits? "Just about anyone," said Swarez.[16]

The Last Train to Millionairesville

In America today, what kind of people are likely to make millions of dollars once they put their minds to it? The answer is precious few from any class will earn millions. The would-be entrepreneur who invests in a success manual or a weekend's instruction in real-estate speculation is more likely to enrich the purveyors of such books and seminars than himself; but even the purveyors of success will not become millionaires in most cases. The era of meteoric individual fortunes is coming to an end.

Here cries of protest may emanate from those who can hold up an example or two of men who literally went from rags to riches in their lifetimes, businessmen who are living proof that the American dream machine still operates on schedule, cranking out millionaires. The autobiographies these millionaires write in their old age usually stress the same themes as the success manuals: They were no different from anyone else; if they made it, so can you.

Such men can afford to be self-effacing in print, because their investment portfolios speak for their abilities. Whatever else can be said about such men and their reasons for success, they are not just plain folks who stumbled across a success formula; they are men of outstanding business ability. Just as some people have a natural talent for music or art, the man from the nonaffluent society who makes millions has a rare talent for making money, along with a powerful engine of ambition that keeps churning day and night.

Among his special talents is the ability to convince the super-rich who control the big money that his moneymaking scheme is a sure winner. The successful entrepreneur from the nonaffluent society may later sprinkle hayseed in his hair and cling to his midwestern twang to proclaim his oneness with the common man, but without the approval and cooperation of the super-rich who lend him the money to build his factories or restaurant chains, he will never get near the millions.* And without the help of a bevy of lawyers, tax accountants, and other specialists from the affluent society, he also will not make it. The successful entrepreneur from the nonaffluent society is neither average nor is he a "self-made man."

In 1980 even individuals with outstanding business ability are less likely to amass fortunes and hold on to them than in previous times. As more and more of the nation's capital and business is concentrated in fewer and fewer hands, the individual entrepreneur who tries to compete against a conglomerate is like a sardine fighting a blue whale. The natural-foods store that does a landslide business in 1979 may find that it can scarcely give away its wares in 1986. If, by a fluke, some of its products become staples of the American diet, General Foods and the Kellogg Corporation will be sure to come out with similar products, heavily advertised on television and sold in supermarkets at lower prices.

A number of optionaires now setting up their own businesses may earn enough to support an affluent life-style, but few will make millions. Some will face bankruptcy before 1990, perhaps more than once. Yet many optionaires cling to concepts of rugged individualism and unlimited opportunity; the myth of the American dream, combined with faith in the boundless power of those liberated through inner awareness, causes many a would-be entrepreneur from the affluent society to persist in believing that he or she will make it to the top. If lack of social margin breeds a low self-image, a glut of social margin may cause overconfidence, a tendency to rank oneself a little lower than the angels, with the possibility of advancement.

The new entrepreneurs do not want to believe that the days of building fortunes in the tradition of the nineteenth-century robber barons are coming to an end. The current rush for millions is a grasp at a way of life that is on its way out, a mad dash to catch the last train to Millionairesville. Only a handful will catch

---

* This explains why the word "man" is used here. Unless a woman perfects a sure cure for the common cold, in this century it is unlikely that any bank or other big-money source will lend a woman on her own the capital needed to put a multimillion-dollar business scheme into operation.

the train, and those who do may arrive to find that Millionaires-ville has been sold to a multinational corporation; they can only live on the outskirts of town in modest dwellings, if they are allowed to stay there at all.

If few optionaires can catch the train to Millionairesville, the nonaffluent cannot even buy a ticket. People in the working classes still dream of becoming financially independent by own-ing their own business or farm, but their chances of achieving such independence are minuscule. There may be the occasional promoter from the working classes, that one in ten million who manages to push himself up into the big money and become a celebrated symbol of America's opportunity for all who try hard enough; but such mavericks will become increasingly rare in the decades ahead.

For most young people in the nonaffluent society, quests for meaningful work or individual fortunes are equally irrelevant these days. Their need is for jobs that pay enough to live on, an income they can count on throughout their working lives.

Other Americans from various economic strata are beginning to realize that this, in fact, is their need, too. Many of these peo-ple are optionaires from the base of the affluence pyramid, young people who grew up believing that a college education would assure them a professional job in the affluent society. Suddenly they are learning that this is no longer the case. So many edu-cated optionaires are out looking for professional jobs that the market is glutted. But another option has appeared on their horizon.

CHAPTER SIXTEEN

Optionaires and the Business Route

Nineteenth-century entrepreneurs scorned higher education: The only way to get ahead was to start your own business, they said. But by the turn of the century the belief in unlimited business opportunities for the ambitious was waning. Reality intervened. In 1903 Orison Marden, a writer of success manuals, advised:

> In these days of trusts and monopolies, when everything tends to great centres, when the great fish eat up the little ones, when wealthy men are becoming wealthier and poor men poorer, one should be extremely cautious about advising young men and young women to go into business with their little hard-earned savings. . . . Much may be said in favor of working for a salary, especially at a time when the great majority of those who go into business for themselves ultimately go to the wall.[1]

Amidst such uncertainty in business, a college education that would train one for a professional job emerged as the never-fail method for achieving upward mobility and economic success. Not millions of dollars, but affluence, respect, and economic security. A college degree became the standard admission card to the affluent society. That a professional job awaited everyone who successfully completed the necessary training in a given field was considered as certain as that night follows day. Although the

Great Depression of the 1930s disproved that belief (unemployment was widespread among professionals as well as laborers in that decade of economic doldrums), World War II and the boom period that followed wiped out the memory of bad times.

The Optionaires Encounter Job Problems

Children who grew up in the affluent society from the 1940s through the early 1960s took it for granted that, if they graduated from college, a good job would await them. Likewise, children from borderline homes were instructed early by their parents that a college degree was all they needed to achieve upward mobility and the higher standard of living that came with it. Daughters being primed for the marriage market were often encouraged to get a degree in education as an insurance policy, while they hunted for a husband. "Become a schoolteacher; then if you ever need money, you can always get a job," parents sagely advised at a time when youngsters from the wartime baby boom were reaching school age and communities were hard put to provide enough schools and teachers for them.

At first it came as a shock to young people graduating from college in the early 1970s to find that jobs in their fields were scarce, and that a degree was no guarantee of employment. Teachers were among the hardest hit. Even optionaires from the upper middle class sometimes had difficulties; young people from such homes usually found good jobs eventually, but often it was only through contacts provided by their parents or relatives after a search on their own failed to produce results. Masses of recent college graduates from the base of the affluence pyramid, as well as those situated on the borderline of affluence, encountered prolonged bouts of unemployment when they went out looking for jobs that fit their college training.

By 1976 the situation was no longer surprising, it was commonplace. *Time* magazine reported "Slim Pickings for the Class of '76," citing case after case of degree-laden youths who could not find jobs in their fields: a trained high-school teacher delivering lunch trays in a Seattle hospital; a man with a Ph.D. in medieval history working as an office boy in a real-estate office in Kansas; a psychologist with a Phi Beta Kappa key and a master's degree from UCLA who could not even get a job interview—he sent out fifty résumés and received one reply, which was negative.

"By the end of this academic year [1976], about 1.3 million people will receive bachelor's, master's and doctor's degrees, nearly double the level of ten years ago. During the same period, though, the number of professional, technical, and managerial jobs has grown by barely more than a third," reported *Time*.[2]

Those with higher degrees were hit as hard as holders of bachelor's degrees—sometimes even more so. People who had spent seven to ten years earning the doctoral degrees that would qualify them as college professors found that their services were not needed. At the 1977 convention of the American Historical Association in Washington, D.C., there were 100 to 150 applicants for every job opening; all applicants had doctoral degrees.

"The basic problem is oversupply," reported the *Washington Post*. "The number of students going to graduate school and getting advanced degrees far exceeds the jobs available for them. Yet, despite the bad news on the job front, the number of graduate students has not been going down. . . . According to recent surveys, the oversupply of Ph.D.s is worst in history, English, and foreign languages, and it is getting worse in mathematics and physics and other sciences as well."[3]

In 1979 when Wabash College in central Indiana had an opening for a two-year position teaching philosophy at $13,000 a year, 155 candidates from across the country applied; all had doctorates or were about to receive them. One of the three finalists was a 29-year-old Phi Beta Kappa whom a former professor described as the university's "most talented student"; he had already applied for thirty different jobs, but was unable to find a full-time academic appointment anywhere in the United States. When the job at Wabash College went to another finalist, he expressed his frustration: "I'm back at square one. I knew when I went into graduate school that it wasn't going to be easy to get a job, so it is no surprise. But this is starting to drain me. I'm considering looking for something in business management."[4]

Even the most prestigious professions have become fraught with uncertainty. Architects are vulnerable to business recessions; when construction slows to a snail's pace, so does the need for architects, as hundreds of young architects found out to their consternation in the mid-1970s. And so many people are becoming lawyers these days that unless more citizens initiate lawsuits or commit crimes in order to provide work for lawyers, their job prospects will continue to diminish. Already it is not uncommon for law-school graduates to spend more than a year looking for work; many end up in other fields.

The situation in medicine is a little different because the number of students accepted into medical schools is more carefully limited. One result, however, is cutthroat competition to get into medical school. Merit alone may not be enough: "Payments totalling millions of dollars are being made to these schools by parents and friends of prospective students to assure their acceptance," *The New York Times* reported in 1978. "Bids of as much as $250,000 have been made for one place in the freshman class of a California medical school."[5]

It is not that wealthy parents are trying to slip unqualified children into medical school; their children meet all the entrance requirements. The problem is that so many highly qualified students are applying to medical schools these days that administrators are in a quandary over whom to reject. Some parents who can afford it help administrators decide whom to admit by donating money at a time when even the best-endowed academic institutions are having financial troubles.

No wonder people clamor to get their children into medical school. In the United States, doctors enjoy a series of unbeatable benefits—high social status, veneration in office and hospital, plus the double satisfaction of doing meaningful work (curing sick people) while making lots of money. "Federal officials say that doctors now [1978] have an average income of $75,000, the highest of any occupation, and for some specialists an income of more than $100,000 is the average."

But it is so hard to get into medical school these days, while in many other professions, as we have seen, there is no assurance of employment after graduation. Under these circumstances, many optionaires are looking for other routes to affluence. Business is one of the most popular alternatives.

THE BUSINESS OPTION

Every person has but one life and wants to make the most of it. To optionaires who were raised to take affluence for granted, and to borderliners who expected to move up to affluence through their careers, the prospect of plunging downward on the economic scale is frightening. The possibility of not finding a professional job at all is even scarier. But as the decade of the 1970s ended, many young people faced that possibility.

Increasing numbers of young optionaires and borderliners are turning to business as a way out of their dilemma. Their great resurgence of interest in business careers cannot be attributed wholly to a desire to reach Millionairesville, as described in Chapter 15. Many an optionaire is turning to business because it seems to be the one avenue that is still wide open to making an affluent living. Sometimes the two motives are intertwined.

Within the business option, there are two alternatives: working for someone else, usually in an established company; or going into business on your own. Both options are enjoying widespread popularity these days.

In the days when the counterculture flourished, the idea of working for a large corporation was anathema to idealistic young optionaires. Rejecting money as a prime goal in life, many dreamed of serving others—as librarians bringing books and reference services to the people, as social workers helping the poor get ahead, as college professors awakening the young to the history and wisdom of the past, as scientists doing research that would benefit humanity. Although they expected to earn enough money to live on, their major satisfaction would come from their meaningful work. But, as we have seen, they completed their training to find that often no institution, including the government, at any level, had the funds with which to hire them at even a modest salary; when an opening did occur in their field, numerous other people like themselves rushed to apply for it.

At the same time, business was opening its doors to welcome the optionaires, offering salaries higher than what they would have earned in their respective fields. As money became tighter in the United States, the one place where dollars seemed to be flowing abundantly was in the business sector. Along with livable salaries, businesses even had enough money for operating expenses and sometimes for special programs as well.

When young idealists began applying for jobs at IBM and the Bank of America, it did not mean that they had renounced their former views and adopted the conservative outlook; it meant that they were taking jobs where they could find them. At first some people went to job interviews in secret, trying to keep their friends from learning that they were "selling out" to the Establishment, so to speak. But as their friends followed suit, it became socially acceptable to be both liberal and on the payroll of a multinational bank or corporation. In time the stigma of big business evaporated in all but the most radical circles—and the liberal viewpoint was often diluted by immersion in the business perspective.

Providing the Education That Optionaires Want

As business has become increasingly popular with optionaires, colleges and universities as well as private entrepreneurs have enlarged their curricula to offer more courses that train people for careers in business and industry or teach them how to start their own business. In providing the courses that optionaires want, the academic world has also been helping to keep its own doors open. At a time when college enrollment is dwindling, competition is still keen to enter schools of business administration and other fields, such as engineering, where jobs in industry are said to be abundant. As soon as a field is identified as one that has jobs for trained personnel, enrollment bulges in courses relating to that field.

University Extension, the adult-education division of the University of California, makes a special effort to offer courses that currently interest the public. This policy is mandated in part by financial necessity; state funding for adult education is limited (many legislators and their constituents consider adult education a frill), so the courses must pay for themselves; if enrollment in a course is not large enough to cover the instructor's salary, that course is canceled. Thus Extension's catalog, *Lifelong Learning,* is a barometer of what has interested optionaires over the years. (Extension's courses and seminars are open to all citizens, but they are taken mainly by optionaires for two reasons: They are expensive compared with courses for adults offered through the city school or community college systems; and the level of education among Extension students is high. The high-school graduate who enrolls in an Extension course may find that the student next to him has a master's degree from Stanford, a discovery likely to intimidate all but the most supremely confident individuals.)

Nineteen seventy was one of the last years when college graduates still took good jobs for granted. In the spring 1970 edition of *Lifelong Learning,* Business was one of the smallest divisions in the catalog, with four courses or seminars offered, as compared with thirty listings under Art and Design, and fourteen under Natural Environmental Studies, a new division that reflected the current interest in ecology. Two of the four business listings were under the Psychology Department—"Communication in a Work Setting" and "Leadership in the Changing Organization"—while a seminar sponsored by the Economics Department was distinctly theoretical—"Economic Values of Human Beings," described as "A study of the concept and measurement of human beings as capital, defined as the present value of future economic values that probably will be produced by a human being in his remaining life expectancy." The final business offering was a "secretaries' forum."

Less than five years later, in the fall of 1974, a recession was in full swing and optionaires were facing job problems after graduating from college. University Extension, "recognizing the growing importance of graduate education for careers in business, industry, and government," now offered a master's in business administration (M.B.A.) in conjunction with the university's School of Business Administration. Offerings under Business now included some prerequisite courses for the M.B.A., such as accounting and economics, while one course, "How to Look for a Professional Job," was a forerunner of the practical business emphasis ahead. But Business was still a small division in the 1974 catalog with fifteen offerings as compared with forty-one listings in Art and Design and thirty-seven in Natural Environmental Studies.

By the end of the decade the situation was reversed: Business had become the runaway favorite of the Extension program. The spring 1979 issue of *Lifelong Learning* listed a whopping 114 entries under Business and Management, more than double the number of listings in any other division. Along with the graduate M.B.A. program, the Business and Management division offered six certificate programs—in accounting, contract administration, credit union management, industrial relations, management, and marketing.

The 114 listings covered several areas of business and management, but the emphasis throughout was on the practical. There were three levels of accounting courses, while "Fundamentals of Discounted Cash Flow Analysis" covered "Basic mathematics, net present value, ROI (return on investment), effect of cost of money, loans and savings calculations, and effect of depreciation and taxes." Some courses, such as "Purchasing," "Advertising," "Effective Professional Selling," and "How to Borrow Money," were relevant to people who planned to work for others as well as those who wanted to start their own businesses. Other courses were oriented specifically to the entrepreneur: "Small Business I," for example, would "stimulate entrepreneurship by providing a working knowledge of the practical business and legal tools needed to start a business or expand or negotiate one."

The most popular field for people who wanted to start their own businesses was real estate. Of the 114 listings in the Extension catalog, nearly one-third (thirty-four) dealt with real estate. There were "How to Find, Analyze, and Invest in the Small Apartment House," "Starting Your Building and Development Company," and "Creative Leasing Techniques for Commercial-Industrial Properties." There were also seminars on "Advanced Tax Deferral Techniques," and "Preventing Real Estate Brokerage Malpractice."[6]

THE REAL-ESTATE BOOM

For several years real estate has also been the favorite topic of the get-rich-quick seminars discussed in Chapter 15. Advertisements for weekend courses in real-estate speculation lure students with such statements as: "Two famous multi-millionaires want to teach you the last remaining method of financial security and wealth still open to the average person. It's 1600 times safer than going into business yourself."[7]

The seminar above was geared to the "average person," but many are designed for optionaires. An ad for a "Tycoon Class" appeared in a magazine whose readers are 91 percent college-educated; this weekend seminar in real-estate speculation promised to give "Specific steps to gain a million dollars in assets within one year!" Two of the many topics to be covered were "Legal ways to never again pay a cent in taxes, plus a refund of the taxes you've paid in the last three years," and "Morality and success."[8]

Real estate has become so popular with optionaires that by 1979 there was keen competition even to sell it. A newspaper feature article on the subject began: "The job of selling real estate, a profession that was considered all but loathsome just a decade ago, has become the hottest occupation in California. Now it is perceived as a glamorous and exciting career that almost anyone can have. . . . For a super hustler, the financial rewards can lead to the truly good life of Ferraris, second homes at ocean-front hideways, and quality vacations."9

The stampede of young people into real estate raises some hard questions. Is the popularity of real estate due to the vast economic opportunities it offers, or, conversely, are many turning to real estate because there is so little opportunity in other areas of business? Is so much capital required to start a new business, the overhead so large, the competition so keen, and the market so uncertain that, by contrast, real estate seems like a sure thing?

Real estate, the tax-shelter-seeker's dream, the field that benefits from the universal need for housing and commercial space on the one hand and the finite nature of land on the other, has reaped a windfall from inflation—getting rich from that which it helped to create. But how long will the opportunity to make big profits in real estate last, and how many people will get in on the proceeds?

These questions lead us into other considerations about the current rush of optionaires—and others—into the business world, including its relationship to the future of the American dream.

HOW MANY BUSINESSES? HOW MANY JOBS?

Just as in 1950 people assumed that there was an endless need for schoolteachers, in 1980 those opting for business assume that there is an endless market for products and services; likewise in the job area they assume that the demand for trained executives and other specialists in business and industry is bottomless.

Are there limits, even in business? For example, how many hamburgers and french fries can a nation of 220 million people consume in restaurants in one year? Is there always room for another good hamburger restaurant, or is there a saturation point when a new restaurant featuring hamburgers can only succeed by putting some existing restaurant out of business?

Decades ago American businessmen learned that there *were* limits to how much the people in one country could consume, but the discovery did not pose a major problem. These businesses simply expanded their operations abroad. The rest of the world appeared as a giant void with an infinite capacity and desire to fill itself up with American goods. That picture is changing, however, as we will see in Chapter 20.

What about jobs in business? Are there limits there, too? Take the burgeoning field of computers: Could we even begin to saturate the market for trained programmers, analysts, engineers, and executives in the coming century?

Mention computers in the United States and the eyes of those attuned to business will glisten. Mention that you are interested in the computer field and you will be assured that the career opportunities awaiting you are limitless, that job security at high salary levels is something you will always be able to take for granted. You will be assured this by people who have no knowledge of the industry except for what they pick up through the media; but if you read the literature of the computer industry, you may occasionally hear a different story.

"Despite rosy predictions of unending job opportunities for computer professionals, recent data from the Bureau of Labor Statistics (BLS) and several educators in the field indicates academic institutions may glut the market for computer science graduates as early as 1985," said a lead article in *Computerworld,* "The Newsweekly for the Computer Community," in 1979.[10]

Graduates of two-year schools that trained DPs (data processors) were already facing a saturated market, the article reported; in fact, "Many private two-year DP schools that produced great numbers of graduates in the late '60s went out of business in the '70s because many of the graduates couldn't get jobs."

Four-year graduates could still find jobs, but their futures were not as secure as commonly assumed. The number of students graduating from college in computer science had increased tenfold from 1967 to 1977. "At some point we will saturate the market," said Dr. Bruce Gilchrist, director of computing activities at Columbia University. He advised the computer industry to watch the market for students at the four-year and graduate levels. "We have to avoid the situation that evolved in physics and engineering—attracting too many people into the field and running out of jobs," he said.[11]

The situation in computers is being repeated in other industries: Suddenly managers realize that there is a limit to how many trained people they can absorb. With the growing overload of people trained in the professions, the opportunities ahead for optionaires and others who manage to get through college are not encouraging. But compared with the outlook for young people in the nonaffluent society, the optionaires are still ahead.

Once again a point made earlier is germane. If you are on top, you can always move down, but those at the bottom have no place to go. The unemployed computer specialist can probably find a job as a salesman in a computer store or can work in a related area of electronics. The lawyer who cannot find a place with a firm, nor enough clients to open his own office, can pursue other options, such as administrative jobs in government and business. (And these days the young lawyer may strike a bonanza if he specializes in bankruptcy proceedings.) If all else fails, the computer specialist and the lawyer can take jobs in nonspecialized fields temporarily; their college training and self-assurance will help them win out over those who lack such attributes.

The frustration that comes from being underemployed is considerable. Being forced to accept nominal pay for routine work that does not make use of one's skills, training, and intellectual faculties is discouraging as well as a waste of human resources. But this problem is of a different magnitude from the frustration that comes when a person is unable to find any job at all. For many young people in the nonaffluent society today, the prospect of chronic unemployment looms on the horizon.

CHAPTER SEVENTEEN

Not Enough Jobs

Unemployment became a major issue in the United States when it visibly affected the nation's prime working group—experienced white males between the ages of 25 and 55. People were accustomed to reports about job difficulties for blacks, women, the young, and the old; but when experienced white male workers started losing their jobs in considerable numbers during the 1974 recession, pushing the national unemployment rate as high as 8.9 percent, that was news.

It was also news when experienced workers from the nonaffluent society began roaming the country in search of work in the tradition of the 1930s. Although new migrants had been on the road for years and no one had chronicled their work odysseys (they were assumed to be hippies in search of new life-styles), the advent of men in their thirties and forties leaving home because they could no longer find jobs there sent reporters on their trail.

In 1975 *The New York Times* ran an article on Americans who had hit the road in search of paychecks. A 32-year-old electrician who had earned more than $400 a week in the past drove his truck through Arizona, Colorado, Nevada, Washington, and Wyoming looking for work. He came out with one prospect—a job that might open up in another month in a nuclear power plant in Washington State. In Boston, where 300 members of Millwrights Union Local 1211 were out of work, the union's business manager said: "There's no work in Massachusetts. I've got men in Houston and men in Minnesota and some will be going off to Syracuse, New York. They go off in a car pool of five or six and then live in an apartment together. . . . It's a real hardship, but it comes to the point where families have to break up to put food on the table."[1]

Much of the job migration was toward the Southwest. "The migrants can be seen arriving at bus stations and by car in Houston and Dallas, and pulling up in camper trucks and house trailers at places like Globe, Arizona, where the grapevine has—sometimes erroneously—said that jobs may be available. . . . Alaska is still drawing job hunters, despite repeated warnings by state officials that the chances of new arrivals finding work on the Alaska pipeline are negligible," said *The Times*. When Continental Trailways Bus Company offered a 50-percent discount to the unemployed for two months during 1975, more than 28,000 people used the discounts. The northeast-to-southwest routes were the most popular. "We found that people who took advantage of the fare traveled about six times farther than the average customer," a company official said.[2]

Migrants kept moving, although employment specialists said there were no real boom areas, with the possible exception of Texas, Oklahoma, and Alaska, parts of which were then benefiting from oil and energy work.

But most people out of work stayed home, awaiting an upturn in the economy that would restore their jobs. Some experienced workers took jobs at lower pay that did not make use of their work skills—when they could find such jobs.

In upper Minnesota the closing of a giant United States Steel Corporation plant in the early 1970s, along with a declining shipping industry in the area, plunged many residents there into poverty. The new unemployed were largely descendants of Swedes, Finns, and Germans who had migrated to Minnesota a hundred years earlier in search of the dream.

The news that immigrants to America were not all as rich as they had been touted to be was of interest to Europeans who were struggling with their own economic recessions. In 1975 Simon Winchester, a British correspondent for the London-based newspaper *The Guardian*, went to Minnesota. He visited the food-stamp office of the Welfare Department in Duluth, which served the region where the steel plant had closed two years earlier, and reported to the British on the "Stamp of Sudden Poverty."

"The room teemed with children," Winchester said. "Not the boisterous, all-American children of the sort you see in prosperous suburbs . . . but sullen, pasty-faced children with scrawny necks who have neither enough to do, nor to eat." He reported that Jim, a 44-year-old man of Nordic descent who had lost his job as a mill worker, now worked ten hours a day parking cars in a downtown garage, earning $450 a month. With a wife and two children he was barely making it. His wife, Sara, "dowdy and extremely tired, her snow boots leaking from a crack in the sole," was applying for food stamps.

The social worker showed Winchester the figures: "Her husband brings back $450. The taxes he pays whittles it down to $380. Gas and electricity cost $90 in January—the family lives in a trailer. . . . They have to pay $200 a month mortgage on their trailer and $30 to rent a place to park it. That leaves them $60 a month for food and clothing."[3]

The closing of the steel plant in Minnesota had no relationship to expanding a national park or preserving trees (as in the controversy over the redwoods described in Chapter 14), so there was no one to blame. Under the philosophy of the unfettered open market, when a plant no longer made enough profit to justify its existence, it closed. If the region that had once been sustained by jobs from that plant now became poverty-stricken (and if it remained a depressed area like some New England mill towns that never recovered from the textile industry's exodus to the South), that was not the responsibility of the company that closed the plant. Nor was it the responsibility of the state where the people lived, or of the federal government. The responsibility was that of the workers who lost their jobs; it was their responsibility to find other jobs on their own.

Under the mandate of individual responsibility, it would be wrong for the factory that closed or the government to help the unemployed. All the unemployed had to do was look elsewhere and they would find good jobs on their own; if they didn't find jobs, it meant they hadn't looked very hard.

The Humphrey-Hawkins Bill

All along there were critics of the work theory outlined above, people who thought the government should take some responsibility for helping the unemployed find jobs; and that government, in conjunction with big businesses, should engage in long-range economic planning to try to prevent thriving industrial areas from turning into ghost towns.

When World War II ended, so did the war industries; but at the same time, servicemen were returning home in great numbers, clamoring for jobs. Some job specialists feared that without government help in finding jobs, as well as national economic planning to ease the transition to a peacetime economy, there would be widespread unemployment. In 1945 a full-employment bill was introduced in Congress. The bill said that every American had a right to a job; if he or she couldn't find one, then the government should make a commitment to finding or creating jobs for "all Americans able to work and willing to work."

The bill caused a furor in Congress. In the land of Horatio Alger, the right to a job was interpreted as the right to look for a job, not to find one—certainly not the right to any help from the federal government. Senator Robert Taft of Ohio insisted that the term "right" be changed to "opportunity." In the watered-down version of the bill that passed in 1945, the word "full" was deleted from the title.[4] Senator Taft assured his conservative colleagues that they could vote for the final version without qualms because "there is no full employment bill anymore."[5] (What the bill did accomplish, however, was the formal acknowledgment, for the first time in American history, that the government had a role to play in economics.)

Thirty years later some liberal congressmen tried again to put through a full-employment bill. The initiator was Augustus Hawkins, congressman from the Watts district of Los Angeles —the predominantly black, low-income area that had erupted into four days of rioting in 1965—and the first black congressman from west of the Rockies. Hawkins introduced his full-employment bill in Congress in 1974; Senator Hubert Humphrey of Minnesota soon sponsored an identical bill in the Senate. The bill, in its numerous versions, became known as the Humphrey-Hawkins bill (officially, the Full Employment and Balanced Growth Act).

"The Employment Act of 1946 is amended to declare that all Americans able, willing, and seeking work have the right to useful paid employment at fair rates of compensation," the bill stated.[6] Most unemployed people want jobs, not welfare, Humphrey and Hawkins stressed in promoting their bill. It called for long-range economic planning to help people find jobs in both the private and public sectors, with the government being the employer of last resort. The goal, over a four-year period, would be to lower the national rate of unemployment to 3 percent (later upped to 4 percent).

Once again the bill created a furor. Technology and the rise of multinational corporations had altered the employment picture considerably since 1946, but the underlying belief that Americans who really wanted jobs could find them on their own remained intact—at least among people who had little contact with the nation's unemployed and encountered no job problems in their own circles.

When hearings on the bill were held in 1975, economist Arthur F. Burns, then head of the Federal Reserve Bank, objected to the bill's proposal that the government should pay "fair rates of compensation" for the jobs it provided. Burns thought any jobs created by the government should have wages that were "unattractive, deliberately set that way to provide an incentive for individuals to find jobs themselves." Where these jobs might be found at a time when eight million Americans were unemployed, Burns did not say.

As the recession of 1973–75 lifted and unemployment rates dropped—among experienced white, male, adult workers—so did the national interest in unemployment. In the years that followed, the Humphrey-Hawkins bill seemed likely to die of neglect. Instead, its cosponsor, Senator Humphrey, died. The bill was resuscitated and passed in 1978, more as a memorial to the late senator than as a full-employment bill. The provision mandating the government as employer of even last resort had been deleted. The act did state, for the first time in the nation's history, that Americans had a right to a job. It also acknowledged that the government should be involved in economic planning and set economic goals for the nation; but the act provided neither the funds nor the machinery to reach those goals.

When Congressman Hawkins filed a nine-point indictment against President Carter in the summer of 1979 for failing to implement the Humphrey-Hawkins Act,[7] most newspapers and television stations did not even bother to report his charges. The official national unemployment rate was then a rosy 5.7 percent, although many economists and businessmen kept warning that another recession was unfolding. But if the president and Congress seemed unconcerned, why should people with jobs give it a thought? Besides, if the breakdown of the official jobless rate showed that unemployment was 10.8 percent for blacks, 15.3 percent for teen-agers, and 30 percent for black teen-agers, wasn't that normal? Blacks always had job problems, and young people didn't need jobs as much as older people. Anyway, young people would become older adults in a few years, and then they would find jobs easily. Or would they?

NONAFFLUENT YOUTH AND UNEMPLOYMENT

Youth unemployment increased during the 1970s, and the problems it posed refused to go away even though some people tried to argue them out of existence. One approach was to insist that there *was* no youth-unemployment problem.

This view was set forth in an article, "Young People Without Jobs—How Real a Problem?" published in *U.S. News and World Report* in 1977. According to the article, teen-agers had no job problems at all; to the contrary, unskilled jobs were going begging nearly everywhere. The real problem was mollycoddled youngsters who were too lazy to go out and look for work, teen-agers who expected high-paying plums to be tossed into their laps while they sat at home watching television.

The magazine's staff interviewed people in several parts of the country. A vocational counselor at a high school in Houston, Texas, said of teen-agers: "They are looking for prestige jobs, and they just can't be president of a bank when they're a junior in high school." A teacher in New Canaan, Connecticut, told a reporter: "I don't find an awful lot of youngsters willing to do odd jobs. They don't feel they have to work. They don't think in terms of starting at the bottom because they figure: 'My Dad's an executive; why should I dig ditches?' "

The West Coast was the exception. "It's a different story on the West Coast, apparently," the article reported. An employer in a state employment office in Los Angeles said, "Kids are waiting in line for jobs at fast food places. Jobs go very quickly." An executive for Kentucky Fried Chicken outlets declared, "We have twenty kids waiting in line for each of these jobs, at the minimum wage."[8]

But a report from the East Coast confirmed the worst suspicions about the softness of today's youth. In New York City the director of a private employment agency was asked if the work ethic was really dead. "I'm sure of it," he replied. "Today it's get as much as you can for as little as you can." In his view, the basic problem of many teen-agers was that "they just don't want to work."[9]

In the same city where that employment executive worked, a different picture had emerged a month earlier, when New York City began taking summer-job applications from teen-agers who came from families below the poverty level, part of a federally funded program. On the first day that applications were accepted, 20,000 teen-agers applied. At one community agency on the West Side, teen-agers began lining up at one o'clock in the afternoon and stayed in line overnight. It was a chilly night, so at 3:00 A.M. the young people in line were allowed to enter a nearby school so they could keep warm while they waited for the agency to reopen. Reporting on the incident, *The Nation* commented:

> The unemployed in the United States—particularly today, when popular political movements are at a low ebb and the country seems in a drugged sleep—suffer silently; they are isolated, unorganized, and often feel personally responsible for their idleness. As a result they go unnoticed. The urban youngsters who are discarded by society even before their mature lives have begun, and who are thus condemned to a hopeless dog-eat-dog existence, make headlines only when they mug the elderly or sell hard drugs to their fellows at the age of 14. So the appearance in one day of 20,000 of them looking for work—almost certainly to supplement their families' desperately low incomes—can still come as a surprise, although it is the surprise itself that is dismaying.[10]

How can two views of teen-agers in the same city at the same time be so different? Part of the answer is that they describe two separate segments of the teen-aged population—optionaires on the one hand and young people from the bottom of the non-affluent society on the other.

Here a word should be said in defense of the attitudes of teen-agers described in the *U.S. News* article. Raising a generation of affluent youth to expect unlimited career opportunities and then criticizing them for having high expectations is like training a watchdog and then complaining because he barks at strangers who appear on the front porch at midnight.

The *U.S. News* article was based on information about option-aires and borderliner teen-agers, who were assumed to be typical of American youth. Implicit in that article were the assumptions that all teen-agers attend high school and that they live with parents who are making it financially; if these teen-agers look for work, they want part-time work, to have extra spending money, to save for luxuries like their own cars, or to increase their college funds.

These assumptions do not fit all teen-agers, especially hundreds of thousands of young people from the nonaffluent society. In 1975, 40 percent of 16- and 17-year-olds looking for work wanted full-time work, as did 77 percent of those who were 18 and 19. More than 3.1 million Americans dropped out of high school between 1965 and 1973. Their rates of unemployment were significantly higher than the national average. In 1974–75, 25.3 percent of dropouts aged 16 to 24 were unemployed; among non-white dropouts, the unemployment rate for the same age group was 61.4 percent.[11] These dropouts, along with teen-agers who graduate from high school at 17 or 18 but do not go on to college, want and need full-time jobs. In many cases they are married and have children to support long before they are 20.

The argument that young people do not need jobs as much as older people does not hold up for this population; and the related argument, that as soon as teen-agers become adults they will find jobs easily, falls down for most youths. One of the first questions a prospective employer asks is about previous work experience. The person who has a blank employment record for the preceding years and no acceptable excuse (such as attending high school or college, serving in the army, or, if female, having babies) is unlikely to be hired. People who had prolonged periods of unemployment as youths may find it impossible to get back into the job market later without special help.

Optionaires from the top of the affluence pyramid may be exceptions. The Harvard dropout who spent two years on drugs, a year on a rural commune, and three years roaming Southeast Asia in search of truth may be able to slip back into an Establishment job at age 27, after half a decade of unemployment; his family will be so delighted to have him back in the fold that they will pull whatever strings are necessary to secure a good job for him. But the typical youth in the nonaffluent society enjoys no such advantages; his employment record—or lack of it—may count for more than a high-school diploma when he goes in search of work; without previous jobs, he is often out of luck.

Those who dismiss youth unemployment as unimportant overlook the appreciable role that young people play in the labor force. Nearly half the people who seek work at any one time are under 25. As one labor specialist put it, "Youth unemployment is frequently a euphemism for unemployment in general, because such a large segment of the work force are youths."

The President Attends a Summit Conference

The American belief that anyone who wants to work can find a job is so deeply ingrained in the national psyche that it took outside reinforcement to convince its citizens, even temporarily, that youth unemployment was a problem.

In May 1977 (during the same week that the *U.S. News and World Report* article on lazy teen-agers appeared), President Jimmy Carter attended a summit conference in London. There the leaders of seven Western nations declared that youth unemployment was a significant problem of international scope.[12] President Valéry Giscard d'Estaing of France said, "The problem of unemployment, and especially of unemployment among the young, is a basic challenge to our whole economic system."[13]

What caused this international interest in jobless youths? It was not so much the increasing rates themselves, for they had been rising throughout the 1970s; rather, it was the impact of statistics showing similar trends everywhere. Each separate nation could have blamed the lack of jobs for its young people on the party in power, if the same situation had not appeared in dozens of countries. The message was unmistakable.

Early in 1977 the International Labor Organization (ILO) in Geneva reported that seven million people under the age of 25 were now unemployed in the twenty-four nations of the Organization of Economic Cooperation and Development (OECD), a coalition that includes the world's wealthiest democratic industrial nations, including the United States and Japan. In these nations young people comprised 40 percent of the unemployed, although they represented only 22 percent of the population. In the nine Common Market countries of Europe, the unemployment rate among people under 25 had more than doubled since 1973. By 1977, one out of every three of the five million people unemployed in Common Market countries was under 25 years old.[14]

Among teen-agers the rates were even higher in most countries. Australia, long a favorite emigration route for Britons in search of economic opportunity, had a 15.6-percent unemployment rate among teen-agers, compared with an average of 3.9 percent throughout the 1960s.[15] In America, the general unemployment rate was 7.3 percent in 1977, but among 16–19-year-olds it was 19 percent. That same year Sweden, Italy, France, Denmark, and Belgium had all reached or exceeded America's high ratio of teen-age-to-adult unemployment.[16] And while 28,000 teen-agers in Britain had been unemployed in 1968, nine years later more than 200,000 British teen-agers could not find jobs.[17]

Economists offered several reasons for the high rates of unemployment. One was the baby boom of the postwar years. According to that line of reasoning, more youth were looking for work now than in the past, or in the future; therefore, youth unemployment was only a temporary problem that we must put up with for a few more years. But other labor specialists saw the baby boom as just one of many contributors to the problem. They pointed out that even if the youth population shrank appreciably in the 1980s, seven million young people out of work in the late 1970s would pose a serious problem for the future. "As these people become middle-aged workers, what's going to be the impact of their never having had a suitable first job?" asked an OEDC analyst in Paris. Peter Melvyn, an ILO researcher, asked, "Do we sacrifice a generation? What's going to happen to these people?"[18]

Another argument put forth to explain youth unemployment was a shortage of jobs. Since young people lack job experience, they will naturally be among the last hired when a job crunch comes and there are more people applying for jobs than there are jobs. This situation concerned the summit conference leaders because of its possible political ramifications. Young people who are dissatisfied take to the streets in protest more quickly than older people. Leaders of Western nations were concerned that continued youth unemployment might turn their countries more to the left. Some countries, such as France and Italy, were already feeling the effects of growing youth unemployment. A month after the summit conference, the *Wall Street Journal* reported:

> In France, where 49% of the 1.1 million jobless are under age 25, politicians say voting by unemployed youths played a big role in the upset scored by leftists in recent municipal elections. The government, one official says, worries that if the jobs problem isn't solved, these youths will swing to the Communist-Socialist bloc in the general election next March. So the government recently introduced, and parliament approved, some special measures aimed at getting young people employed. However, the left has branded the measures as insufficient.[19]

In Italy the jobless rate among young people was identified as one of the forces that was leading the country to the left. Soon after the summit conference, *Time* reported: "Danger: Not Enough Youth at Work," and said of Italy:

> There, official statistics place youth unemployment at 36.8% of all unemployed. But some Italian experts say the real percentage is probably closer to 65%, and soars to 80% for people under 30. Violence has flared, chiefly among frustrated students who know they will not be able to get jobs when they graduate. Riots this spring in major Italian cities have killed two policemen and two students. In Naples, where young people probably account for fully half the total of 250,000 unemployed, some 30,000 protesters marched through the center of the city last month demanding government job programs.[20]

In the United States, President Carter, who had campaigned in part on promises to reduce unemployment, did take some steps in 1977 to decrease youth unemployment. In the months before the summit conference there had been brisk activity among government and private groups alike to help draft legislation for youth-jobs programs; the Ninety-fifth Congress received seventeen youth-employment bills during its first two months.

At that time 3.5 million Americans between the ages of 16 and 24 were officially unemployed, and another 1.5 million had part-time jobs but wanted full-time work. Two of the proposals that

Carter's staff studied called for the creation of a million jobs for youths (see Chapter 18). The bill that the administration supported and pushed through—The Comprehensive Youth Employment Act of 1977—was more modest; it created jobs and training for a total of 243,000 young people. Programs included a young-adult Conservation Corps for 16–23-year-olds from all income brackets; a jobs program for low-income youth 16 to 19 years old, in community and conservation projects; and a jobs and training program for low-income youth from 16 to 21, along with some funds for "innovative and experimental" youth-job programs. Part of the programs would be administered under CETA, the existing Comprehensive Employment and Training Act.

Predictably, the Right said the programs went too far and the Left said they did not go far enough. But, as noted earlier, during 1978 and 1979 the administration and the general public lost interest in unemployment, including the problem of jobless youths. When disaffected youths without jobs in Italy and France did not cause those countries to go socialist in the next election, the worry about the political repercussions of unemployed youths was allayed. With Americans smarting from inflation and laying the blame on government spending, the administration in Washington looked for ways to cut domestic spending and began chipping away at the CETA programs. The passage of the Humphrey-Hawkins Act seemed to have changed nothing but the paper it was printed on.

A Human-Interest Story

In January 1979, while snowstorms deluged the Northeast, a young man of 18 who was looking for work collapsed on a road outside of Cincinnati, Ohio. Men in a passing salt truck rescued him, and the incident made the news. The youth, William Cain, said he had been to about a hundred places looking for work since November. He walked because he couldn't afford a car, and buses didn't serve the places he needed to go. When the news of his determination to find work brought job offers from several local businessmen, the story—with its happy ending—went out over the AP wire service as a human-interest story.[21]

No connection was made between Cain's plight and that of other young people. But if chance and the media had not brought

Cain's situation to the attention of local businessmen, would the outcome have been different? How many more months would he have tramped around in search of work? If he didn't find a job, would he have decided to leave home and seek work in a sunnier climate where jobs were said to be easier to find—namely, in the Far West or the Sunbelt states? If so, where would he have stayed when he climbed off the bus in Los Angeles or Phoenix without much money? Would he have found a job in either city?

The answers are not important in terms of this individual—he did find a job near home; the point here is that Cain's situation before he collapsed is typical of what youths throughout the country are facing, especially those in the large industrial cities of the eastern half of the United States. His situation is typical of young people who are likely to become new migrants if they fail to find work near home after prolonged searches.

PLACING THE NEW MIGRANTS

In the last two parts we have lost sight of the new migrants, but they have not disappeared; now it is time to rejoin them and place them within the wider context of our society.

Where do the new migrants fit in? Clearly they are members of the nonaffluent society. In all but a handful of cases they grew up in that society and they are destined to remain there. Their problem is to find a job and a place in the mainstream of the nonaffluent sector.

The new migrants belong with all the other unskilled youths who cannot find jobs or can only find them at rock-bottom wages. They belong with the children of displaced coal miners in Appalachia and with the children of midwestern farmers who can no longer compete with agribusiness and are forced to sell their farms. They belong with the children of factory workers whose parents are facing layoffs, and with children of low-echelon white-collar workers in cities that keep eliminating such jobs to balance their teetering budgets. They belong with unemployed youth in all these categories who stay home—at least until their job prospects appear hopeless.

The new migrants also belong with the unemployed youth of nonwhite minorities—with blacks, Hispanics, American Indians, Filipinos, and others whose young people face high levels of unemployment. The movements for racial equality and ethnic consciousness in the 1960s had many positive results, building pride and positive group identification among members of racial minorities. Civil-rights legislation and the antipoverty program helped many people in these groups have better jobs and housing facilities. But these advances did not wipe out poverty and unemployment. Extreme poverty still rages in inner-city ghettos and barrios; unemployment rates are astronomical there, especially among the young. But the unemployment problem of these young people goes beyond skin color. An underlying cause is a lack of jobs.

To continue viewing the unemployment problems of minority youth as primarily a racial issue will not do much to help them find permanent jobs. Unskilled minority youth, like the new migrants, are part of a widespread youth-unemployment problem. If by some magic ritual we could make all racial prejudice disappear overnight, in the morning the unskilled, poorly educated black teen-agers would still not be able to find jobs on their own. Nor would they find them the following day. Those who eventually did find jobs would rarely be offered more than the minimum wage, and the jobs would offer such limited advancement that when these workers reached their peak earnings they would still be drawing salaries near the poverty level.

To make significant changes in job opportunities for youths in the nonaffluent society, we must confront problems whose roots touch all unemployed youth, including the new migrants.

Part Four

CHANGES

CHAPTER EIGHTEEN

Jobs for Youth

Prelude

Presenting a problem is easier than trying to solve it. A rash of
evidence can be mustered to show the need for change in any
number of areas; but having defined a problem, we face the complexities inherent in the solution of any major social issue.

There are small-scale solutions, and there are larger ones that
take into account the underlying causes and try to change the
situation that created the problem in the first place. In the case
of youth unemployment, the small solutions might include
setting up training programs and making more jobs, perhaps
concentrating on the geographical areas with the highest unemployment rates. The larger solutions might involve grappling
with causes such as machines that replace workers; massive transfers of job overseas; the insistence that increasing production is
the only way to create jobs, even if more goods are already manufactured than can be sold; and a national policy that gives the
profit motive precedence over all other concerns.

One view of change holds that several small changes will add
up to a large enough change to solve the problem. Another view
says it is useless to make small changes until you attack the
underlying causes of the problem; furthermore, according to this
view, small changes are actually dangerous, because they pacify
people and impede progress toward crucial, significant changes

that get at root causes and provide a sweeping solution that will solve the problem permanently.

The remainder of this book will deal with the need for changes in employment and other interrelated areas; so it is appropriate now to clarify the author's perspective on change. It is also time to switch gears stylistically and use the first person when I express my own views.

Neither of the views on change outlined above is satisfactory from my vantage point. Several small changes, such as job training and job creation, will not by themselves end growing youth unemployment if the larger causes are ignored. But the other extreme—refusing to work on the problem until one can offer a sweeping change that gets at the root causes—is equally shortsighted: In the short run it may result in suffering for those who are denied the benefits of small reforms; in the long run, when and if the larger change is achieved, a lack of previous small changes may result in chaos.

It is naïve to believe that a nation's needs for jobs and services will automatically be met once a major change occurs—such as ousting a corrupt head of state or a despised regime. The new regime inherits the old problems. If small reforms that provide people with basic needs—such as jobs, housing, food, and medical care—have preceded the larger change, the new head of state or political party will have a far better chance of succeeding—and of remaining in power. Other larger changes can then be made in time.

Small and large changes are not antagonistic; instead, they complement each other. Both are essential to any blueprint for improving the lives of a nation's people.

A consideration of jobs for youth leads us back to a policy that has served as the foundation for upward mobility in the twentieth century—higher education.

IS HIGHER EDUCATION THE ANSWER?

As technological advances mushroomed after World War II, higher education assumed a central place in the American dream. "You must go to college in order to succeed" was the message to the masses. States expanded their college systems and students flocked in to take advantage of the opportunities offered. As the nation became concerned about the widespread poverty among the nonwhite population, education was hailed as the great panacea, the method through which minority youths could climb the ladder to success.

From 1960 to 1974 enrollment in two-year colleges grew from 660,000 to 3,257,000.[1] These students—white, black, and brown—came largely from the nonaffluent society, which was according to plan, because the community colleges they attended were set up with them in mind. Community colleges charged little or no tuition, they were situated in cities where the students lived (eliminating the cost of living away from home), and they were usually open to any student who finished high school, regardless of grade-point average. Ways were also devised to allow motivated high-school dropouts to enter community colleges. These colleges operated, and still operate, on principles of democratic egalitarianism, giving children from poor and working-class backgrounds the chance to achieve the American dream by training for a specialized or professional job.

California has the largest and most comprehensive college system in the country—in fact, the world. Under its master plan, students who do well in the two-year community colleges can go on to state colleges or universities, receiving scholarship help if they come from low-income homes. The people who set up the college system in California thought of every eventuality except one: that many of the students they trained, and whose expectations they raised, might not be able to find jobs that fit their newly acquired skills and training.

That possibility was out of the orbit of American thinking in the 1960s—with minor exceptions. A few Cassandralike critics, familiar with the employment scene, warned that the nation was setting a lot of young people up for a fall by raising expectations that could not be fulfilled in the labor market.

One such critic was Harry Brill, a specialist in labor who is now associate professor of sociology at the University of Massachusetts. In 1964 Brill published an article in *The Nation* entitled "Educating Youth—The Cruel Solution." He argued that providing higher education for more and more young people so they could hold white-collar jobs or enter a profession would aggravate unemployment by producing more trained people than the country could use.

"Except insofar as they keep the younger generation in school, and thus for a time out of the labor pool, intensified training and education will fail to solve youth's unemployment problems," said Brill. Rejecting the theory that the unemployed were jobless because they lacked the qualifications for existing jobs, Brill said, "A simpler explanation is that youth is jobless because the jobs are not there."[2]

Such warnings were ignored. The shortage of specialized jobs did not come to public attention until well into the 1970s when sizable numbers of optionaires began to face unemployment after college graduation. The business option, as we saw in Chapter 16, is serving as a temporary reprieve for many optionaires and borderliners—and for some people on the lower rungs of the socio-economic ladder, although their chances of making it in business are slimmer.

Fifteen percent of all jobs in the United States are classified as professional, but nearly half of all young people aspire to them, mainly through higher education.[3] A lot of young people are doomed to disappointment.

Does this mean that, for their own good, we should discourage people in the nonaffluent society from going on to college? Should we firm up class lines and direct all children of blue-collar workers and the poor into practical occupations such as institutional cooking, assembly-line work, or auto mechanics, and reserve the universities for optionaires whose parents can afford to send them to first-rate private prep schools? Not at all. The college option should remain open to self-motivated students from the nonaffluent society; some of them will make it into the professions or get higher-level white-collar jobs through staunch effort and persistence. Likewise, in the case of students who show academic promise, it would seem reasonable for teachers to encourage them to go on to college, if the teachers are also willing to take responsibility for acquainting the students with possible methods of financing (show them how to work the system) and for giving them some idea of the competition they will face in the professional job market.

What the oversupply of college graduates does mean is that we should stop viewing college as the answer to joblessness. Higher education is not a panacea for the unemployed; we cannot solve the job problems of unskilled youths by sending them all to college. What they need are jobs.

JOB CREATION AND JOB TRAINING

If there are not enough jobs for all the young people who want and need them, why don't we create jobs for them? This possibility was explored during the 1970s by specialists who studied the youth-unemployment problem with an eye to practical solutions. Sar Levitan, a manpower specialist who is professor of economics and director of the Center for Social Studies at George Washington University, favored the job-creation approach. At a conference on teen-age unemployment, sponsored by the Congressional Office of the Budget in 1976, Levitan said:

> [Except] for a minority of youth who need special assistance to find and retain jobs, it would seem that all the help most teenagers needed to function effectively in the workforce was enough jobs to go around. In the labor markets with large deficits, it's only to be expected that the inexperienced will be shoved to the end of the line and some will give up completely. My prescription for the day is that the best way to reduce unemployment—for youth as well as adults—is to create jobs.[4]

Who Should Create Jobs?

If more jobs must be created, who should do it? The standard answer of businessmen and the conventional economists who serve them is that the private sector should do it indirectly. If industry has more capital available, this argument goes, it will expand its operations. Production will increase, more jobs will be created, workers will consume more products, and the entire economy will benefit. According to this view, the government's role in job creation should be to give business and industry special tax incentives (lower their tax rate), and then keep its hands off the business sector, so it will be free to expand production.

Former President Gerald Ford used this reasoning in 1976 when he vetoed a job bill that would have created 600,000 jobs. Calling the bill "an election year pork barrel," Ford said the best way to create jobs was to pursue "balanced economic policies that encourage the growth of the private sector without risking a new round of inflation"[5]—that is, give business a bigger tax break.

There are problems with this approach. First, there is no assurance that business and industry will use the money they save from tax breaks to expand their production. If the government gives tax breaks to businesses with no strings attached, leaving the spending of the extra capital to the expertise of experienced business executives, those executives may choose to spend the money for other purposes. They may buy businesses unrelated to their major product—established businesses that come equipped with a full corps of employees. Oil and steel companies, for example, may buy taco and pizza franchises, department store chains, dog food companies, and other businesses, instead of increasing production in oil or steel. This situation, which is common today, does not encourage the growth of the private sector; it merely consolidates it into fewer hands.

Second, although some industries, including the largest, will use tax savings at times to increase production, this will not necessarily increase jobs. To the contrary, in some cases increased production may decrease the number of jobs in a given factory, if the higher level of production is achieved through the purchase of labor-saving machinery.

To illustrate, suppose that a business is given a million-dollar tax break to help it increase production during a recession. The company immediately invests a million dollars in four new machines. Each machine works faster and more efficiently than ten workers combined formerly did, and one skilled worker can oversee the four machines. The company has indeed increased its production (and its profits), but it has also decreased employment—in this instance by thirty-nine employees. In business terms this would be called efficiency and progress; in human terms, and in its eventual political effects, the money spent may have a different effect. Some would call it labor-destructive.

The crucial distinction between capital-intensive and labor-intensive increases in production was stressed in a report, *Youth Unemployment: Causes and Cures,* published by the British Youth Council (BYC) in March 1977. The report dealt with youth unemployment in Britain and in other Common Market countries, but its message was equally applicable to the United States. Geared to practical solutions, its authors urged countries to specify that industries which receive tax cuts to bolster the economy must show that this money was used for labor-intensive measures.

At the same time, however, the BYC report took note of the complications here in terms of the world market for the products these industries manufacture. For example, if Britain were to purposely remain labor-intensive in her automobile and television industries in order to keep workers on the job, while West Germany, the United States, and Japan became increasingly capital-intensive, reducing their labor forces through automation in order to cut production costs, Britain's cars and television sets would cost more to produce, so they could no longer compete effectively on the international market. The BYC report commented: "It will be much more difficult to restructure British industry in such a way as to provide genuine employment for all who need it, unless our major industrial competitors adopt similar practices."[6]

On top of the capital-intensive-versus-labor-intensive dilemma, another specter stalks the world market—overproduction. If you can't sell all the products you are already capable of manufacturing, then where is the sense in increasing production? Yet the conventional answer to the question of job creation is that business alone can create jobs—by increasing production. More will be said about overproduction in Chapter 20. Suffice it to say here that increasing production is not *the* answer to the current employment problem, although business, in tandem with government, can play a role in job creation.

Government's Role in Job Creation

Government not only needs to be involved in national and international economic planning about industry and its products; government can also play a vital role in helping to create jobs —in public services and in the private business sector.

Labor specialist Harry Brill sees the government as the major creator of jobs during hard times. His interest is in public-service jobs, which he believes can improve the nation as well as helping the unemployed.

In times of high unemployment, the government should be the employer of first resort, Brill told me in 1977. The private sector has shown an inability to create jobs on a large scale, he said. In the private sector, where profit guides the operation, a company may throw numerous people out of work anytime it closes down a plant because it is not making a high enough margin of profit, or relocates in some other area where costs, particularly labor costs, will be lower, he said. In public-service work, where a profit is not required, the emphasis can be on jobs for the unemployed and on services that will improve the quality of life.

Only the government can provide good public transportation, clean air, and other environmental projects that will create jobs and improve the lives of its people, Brill said. Industry will not be interested in such projects, because they don't make a profit. "But we don't ask whether the police force or the fire department shows a profit. We accept the need for such services and pay people to perform them." There are many more services that society needs and could pay people to perform.

Brill disagreed with the criticism that many government-created jobs, such as raking leaves and weeding flower beds, are useless "make-work" tasks devised to give jobless people something to do. Middle-class people perform such tasks to keep their own yards and gardens in order and consider it worthwhile, he pointed out; keeping public parks and gardens in good condition is likewise useful work.

Seconding Levitan, Brill said: "The only answer to joblessness is jobs."

The New York Plan

Other labor specialists see a role for business as part of government job programs. They recommend setting up job apprenticeships in industry under the aegis of government—with the government covering most of the costs—as part of programs that also include strong public-service components. One of the most comprehensive proposals of this nature was prepared by the New York State Division for Youth at the end of 1976 to help the Carter administration develop a jobs bill.[7]

The New York plan recommended an Office of Youth Initiatives (OYI) in the Executive Office of the President, which would oversee the Youth Office's four components: two public-service programs operating in the public or nonprofit sector; one program of apprenticeships in business and industry; and a work/study component that would allow young people to work part time while going to school. The program would be for young people aged 16 to 22.

The business component, called Opportunities in Private Enterprise (OPE), would set up apprenticeships in small businesses and internships in larger corporations. Here the New York plan followed the European practice of stressing on-the-job training for youths in industry and related fields. Past programs of this type failed in America, said the authors of the New York plan, because the employers had to absorb all the costs and risks involved. This would not be the case with the OPE plan.

> With the federal government subsidizing 80 percent of the labor costs of youth participant employees, leaving participating firms with only training and other ancillary costs, there are strong incentives for substantial business participation in OPE. . . . Experimental local programs now in operation reveal that skilled managers and craftspeople in such fields as auto mechanics, computer and related electronics systems, environmental control and protection, equipment repair and building restoration welcome the opportunity to train subsidized apprentices; but existing federal programs provide insufficient incentives for either workers or employers.[8]

The two proposed public-service components followed some of the ideas suggested by Brill. The National Youth Service (NYS) would support projects by state and local governments and by nonprofit groups. Approved on a project-by-project basis for a specified time, they would extend local human and environmental services in the manner of England's Job Creation Program. The Programs of National Priority (PNP) would cover larger ongoing programs under federal agencies in areas such as mass transit, housing, and environmental conservation. They would, like the OPE component, be supported on an 80/20 basis, with the federal program supplying 80 percent of the funds, and the public or nonprofit agency supplying 20 percent. (The work/study component would be wholly subsidized by the program.)

The Santa Barbara Plan

Another plan, somewhat similar in scope in all but one component, was devised at the same time as the New York plan, by the Citizens Policy Center in Santa Barbara, California, a private group.[9] Their three-pronged proposal called for Youth Basics, New Apprenticeships, and National Service. Youth Basics, for young people who lacked basic reading, writing, and mathematics skills, would combine classroom learning with on-the-job training. New Apprenticeships would provide on-the-job training at a more intense level for people who had mastered basic skills. (Graduates of Youth Basics could go on to New Apprenticeships.) As in the New York plan, apprenticeships would be available in the private as well as the public sector.

The Santa Barbara plan stressed the importance of bringing organized labor into the programs. There should be a stipulation that no adult workers would be displaced by youth trainees in these programs, the authors said, and some persons from organized labor could be hired as staff members within each of the programs.

The last prong of the Santa Barbara plan differed from New York's. This was for a proposed National Youth Service, in the tradition of the Civilian Conservation Corps of the 1930s, that would offer unemployed young people from 16 to 22 a chance for a year's socially useful work, in their own communities or in a residential service program elsewhere. It would be open to all young people, regardless of their economic circumstances.

"It is imperative that the program serve a variety of young people and not be focused on one class, racial or ethnic group," said the Santa Barbara proposal. "By being responsive to the three categories noted above, the program would have a much better chance of being 'pluralistic' and receiving a wide range of support."[10]

The New York plan, taking the opposite view, was set up specifically for low-income youths. "For both policy and fiscal reasons," it explained, "it is advisable to target a substantial proportion of all program components on youth who would otherwise have been unemployed and in areas of high unemployment generally. . . . And with unemployment so acute among distinct groups of youth, it is even more difficult to justify a program without appropriate criteria for participation." In other words, the New York plan was geared primarily to nonwhite youth in inner-city ghettos, the population with the highest unemployment rate in the nation.

The view of the New York plan is not surprising, because it was written by a state agency whose staff was directly involved in setting up programs for unemployed youths. The authors knew the difficulties that black and Puerto Rican youths from inner-city slums faced when they looked for work in the private sector. They also knew that New York City was having serious financial troubles and that the national mood was to push for lower taxes by cutting back on public services. So it seemed logical to spend what money there was on the people who needed help the most.

But the Santa Barbara plan's argument that a program which serves a variety of young people will receive wider public support raises an important consideration. It takes us back to the discussion of blue-collar alienation in Chapter 13, about workers who resented being taxed to pay for antipoverty programs from which they and their families were excluded because their incomes were above the poverty level. These workers' children often needed job help too, and today their need is even stronger.

The factory worker's son who drops out of high school in the tenth grade and drifts for a year or two will generally need help in reentering the labor market, whether he is white, black, or brown. Left on his own, he is likely to remain unemployed or end up permanently in the secondary labor market of part-time, temporary work at low wages. If the factory worker's son is ineligible for government job training because his father's salary is not quite low enough to meet the poverty requirements, that family may harbor deep resentments. They may resent not only the government that excludes them but also the people who are poor enough to qualify; in short, they may resent poor blacks and Hispanics whom they view as getting special treatment for which they—nonaffluent whites—foot the bill. At some point their resentment could explode into another "white backlash" and sabotage the programs set up to help the poor.

In order for job-creation and job-training programs to receive popular support from congressmen and their constituents, these programs must cover all young people who need job help, not just those from the poorest families. We need to implement the law (the Humphrey-Hawkins Act) and find ways to make jobs for everyone who wants to work.

Regional strategy, concentrating on the areas of highest unemployment, is one method with possibilities.

REGIONAL STRATEGY

Several countries, including the United States, have already used regional strategy on a limited basis to combat unemployment. During the 1973–75 recession, France, Britain, the Netherlands, and Italy gave special help to regions of their countries where unemployment was highest; this help was usually along traditional lines, giving tax credits and other incentives to businesses, and wage subsidies to workers who might otherwise have been laid off.[11] The United States has used a type of regional strategy in recent years, by giving cities with the highest unemployment rates the most money for job creation and related services.

Far more could be done with regional strategy. Here I see three divisions: the old, economically depressed regions; the slums of large cities; and the burgeoning regions to which people are currently migrating in large numbers.

The Old Regions

The old regions are areas that can no longer provide enough work to support their populations. They might be former industrial areas, such as Appalachia, upper Minnesota, or some old New England mill towns, where the decline of a major industry meant the end of steady work for most people—and for their growing children in future years. Such regions may once have been agricultural, but were unable to compete with large-scale farming (agribusiness), which could grow the same products at lower costs through mass production and the use of machinery and the latest methods.

It will take a combination of government planning in conjunction with agriculture and industry to figure ways to bring new jobs into these areas. In some, a whole new industry may be feasible; in others, smaller projects in business or agriculture, or perhaps a plan to encourage tourism—e.g., helping to build needed tourist accommodations and publicizing the region—may be an answer. But whatever is worked out to rejuvenate an old region, it is essential that such planning include people who live in these areas as well as outside experts. Otherwise the result could be similar to what happened after World War II, when the United States shipped great quantities of dried split peas to Italy to feed the hungry: It was an excellent plan in every way, except that the Italians, unfamiliar with split-pea soup, wouldn't eat it.

The Urban Slums

Industrial centers are swelled by migrants who come in from depressed areas expecting to find good jobs in factories and other businesses in the big cities. When more people come in than industry can use, or when a recession hits, the migrants may find themselves not only out of work but also without the support system of the old region—relatives, neighbors, friends, and a little livestock that provided food back home.

Detroit, Chicago, Pittsburgh, and Cleveland are but a few of the cities in the foundry sections of America to which large numbers of people migrated during and after World War II to take factory jobs. These people now face job difficulties, and their children, when grown, form the principal stream of the new migrants. In cities that are main entry points for immigrants from other countries—New York City and Los Angeles in particular—the problem is twofold, because immigrants from other countries as well as internal migrants are seeking unskilled and semiskilled jobs. Many of these people go on welfare eventually and their children grow up in the slums, imbibing the defeat of their parents at an early age.

London faces this same double problem. Along with British migrants to the city, it has large numbers of immigrants from the former colonies. During the 1950s, black immigrants from the West Indies came to England at the invitation of the British government, which, in those good years, wanted immigrants because they would do the low-paid "menial" jobs that Britons turned down as long as better-paying jobs were available. But when an economic downturn caused a scarcity of jobs, native whites became willing to take such jobs. Now London and other industrial cities in Britain have their predominantly black slum sections, reminiscent of New York City's Harlem and with similar high unemployment rates.

To teen-agers in the slums of London or New York, jobs are a top priority, more important than counseling, urban renewal, or relief measures. They want to work so they can be financially independent and have money to spend like other teen-agers. And they are also thinking, if only vaguely at that age, of what their job futures will be as adults. (Teen-agers living in city slums are by no means all black or brown, but nonwhite teen-agers constitute a significant number of the "hard-core" unemployed youths in depressed urban areas.)

Regional strategy can help develop jobs for teen-agers in our cities. The British Youth Council report recommends locally based, small-scale enterprises in inner-city areas, to be set up through the public and private sectors. For example, local governments could set up "sites and small workshop units based on crafts, renovation, and repairs."[12] In the United States there are movements in a few cities to organize people in low-income areas to refurbish their own neighborhoods and create jobs there; OCCUR in Oakland, California, is one such project. The key ingredients for these grass-roots projects are neighborhood acceptance, local participation in planning and operating the project, and government funding—mainly federal at the present time, because local governments everywhere are facing budget crises these days.

But our largest cities are so overcrowded, and the number of nonspecialized jobs they can support is so inadequate to meet the demand, that the third regional strategy—building up jobs and services in new areas—could hold out much promise for unemployed youths and for the nation as a whole.

The New Regions

In the United States, as we saw in Chapter 9, there has been a widespread move toward the Sunbelt states and the Far West during the past decade. So many people have migrated to these regions that they are expected to pick up eleven new seats in Congress as a result of 1980 census data. (California, Texas, and Florida will each gain two seats, while Utah, Oregon, Washington, Arizona, and Tennessee gain one each. The states losing representatives because of their dwindling populations are New York, Ohio, Illinois, Pennsylvania, Michigan, and South Dakota.) [13]

In one sense this migration is a city and regional planner's dream, because large numbers of people have left northeastern megalopolises that were sagging with overpopulation and have settled in the less-populous parts of the country. There is a better balance now. But without careful planning to facilitate these shifts of population, the results could be a nightmare: Phoenix,

Houston, Denver, and San Jose could become the new Detroit, Pittsburgh, Cleveland, and Newark in terms of overcrowding and unemployment. Los Angeles has already gone that route, becoming so gargantuan that it resembles eastern industrial cities in many ways; part of the Sunbelt migration is made up of Los Angeles citizens who are fleeing eastward to escape the congestion, high crime rates, and pollution in their area.

How can the growth of unwieldy megalopolises be prevented in the burgeoning regions of the South and West? One way would be to encourage migrants to settle in smaller towns, by providing housing and job opportunities for them. At the present time, however, the opposite policy is being followed in many small towns in these regions: Instead of accepting new residents as a necessary outgrowth of the western/southern migration, some small towns have passed growth limitation ordinances to try to keep the town's size and character the way it was in "the good old days."

From what I have seen of such action in the West, the main impetus to restrict growth does not come from residents who arrived forty or more years ago (their towns are already much bigger than when they came) ; the impetus comes from people who settled there during the 1960s and early 1970s. Some arrived with fantasies of a utopian small-town or rural existence where there would be plenty of space to raise the children and lead a wholesome life. Predominantly optionaires, they may see themselves as environmental pioneers because they install solar heaters in their houses and follow ecologically sound practices in their daily lives. They would be shocked to find themselves described as selfish.

But perhaps these preservers of small-town values should not be judged harshly at this point, because where have they heard another view? Who has asked them: What about poor and working-class people in our largest cities? If they move, should they be forced to exchange a city slum on the East Coast for a city slum on the West Coast because you, and others like you, seek to preserve the small-town flavor of America's past—a flavor, incidentally, that writers such as Edgar Lee Masters, Sherwood Anderson, and Sinclair Lewis thought was sour in the first place?

Trying to limit population growth makes sense to me in cities of perhaps three million or more residents, not in towns of 10,000 to 60,000 people. It is small and medium-sized towns that residents of our largest cities and suburbs need to move into, if we are to scale down our cities to livable sizes.

The Need for National Planning

To turn the present migration to the Sunbelt states into a positive move for migrants and the nation alike, we need coordinated planning. The first step is to make the public aware that the migration to the West and South is more than a switch in life-styles and values among a smattering of affluent Americans; that it is a mass migration of people from every walk of life. In the coming years the nonaffluent are likely to leave the eastern foundry cities in greater numbers than the affluent, because there are twice as many nonaffluent citizens, and they have fewer resources to fall back on in hard times.

But making the scope of the migration known could be dangerous if this information is not accompanied by news of the second and third steps—that the government is helping the new migrants find jobs and housing in the areas they are moving into. By itself, news of a mass migration could cause panic in the receiving towns and cities, leading to vigilante action against newcomers who arrive without obvious financial resources—as happened in Los Angeles in 1934.

Joint action by government and business could ease the transition and make a better nation. Fewer people would flock into the largest cities of the South and the West if they learned that industries and jobs existed in smaller places, too, and that specialized employment services and temporary housing facilities would be available for them when they first arrived. Such services would be a boon to the new migrants.

CHAPTER NINETEEN

Services for the New Migrants

The proposed jobs-for-youth programs described in Chapter 18 shared one characteristic: They did not mention migrant youth. Likewise, job programs for youths in European countries during the same period also ignored the young migrant. Underlying the proposals and programs of various nations was the assumption that young people all live at home with their parents or in other stable living arrangements. Yet, as we saw earlier, many young people are moving around in search of work, and their transiency adds an additional dimension of difficulty to their quests.

Obviously, more jobs at home could reduce the numbers of new migrants, because fewer youths would leave home in the first place if they could find work near home. The oldest son in a large family who goes on the road at 17 to give his parents one less child to feed might stay put and begin contributing to the family food budget if there were a job at hand.

The programs suggested in the preceding chapter could help cut down the flow of youth migration. Though young people seized by wanderlust might still leave home to see the country, many would return to their families and communities after an interval on the road if there were job opportunities at home. What often happens now is that, after a spell on the road, young travelers return home with the expectation of remaining permanently; but when no job is available to them in the prime labor market, they leave again, this time for good.

Enough jobs at home would reduce youth migration, but it would not eliminate it. Problems between parents and child—seemingly insoluble during the teen years—send many young people on the road. Other young people have no families, hometowns, or personal support systems. Their parents may be alcoholics, in prison, or rootless travelers themselves; some parents have been known to run off to Europe or a California commune and neglect to send their children the address. Some children may have been orphaned or abandoned early in life, brought up in a series of foster homes or state institutions, assigned to relatives who may not have wanted them, or placed in other living arrangements that left them feeling isolated. For such young people the open road may beckon. Somewhere else they hope to settle and achieve the love and stability they were denied as children.

As we saw in Part One, the hope of economic advancement is an equally potent force that causes young people to leave home. With more industries shutting down in the eastern half of the country and local governments cutting back on personnel in human services, we can expect to see more new migrants in the future. They will need temporary housing facilities and help in finding jobs. Older migrants will also need help. Many of the suggestions in the pages ahead could apply as well to those past 30, and in some cases to juveniles who are ready to assume responsibility for their own lives.

Transient Housing

The temporary housing needs of young people can be divided into three categories: traditional-type youth hostels; midrange hostels with employment counseling and other services attached; and shelter care for migrants with special problems. These divisions are not offered as a concrete proposal, but rather as a springboard for discussion and research that could lead to the emergence of temporary housing facilities in our cities.

Traditional Youth Hostels

Cities in the United States need more traditional youth hostels of the familiar type run by American Youth Hostels, Inc., which provide a safe, inexpensive place where young travelers can sleep and eat for a few nights. Most youth hostels in this country are situated outside of cities, meeting the needs of the backpacker or bicycler, which is fine for that group of travelers; but there is still a paucity of facilities in our cities for young American and foreign tourists on student budgets who use public transportation. More hostels have opened in cities in recent years, but they are inadequate to meet the demand.

If youth hostels existed in every city, young people reacting to family conflict, or simply eager to see the country, could travel inexpensively in safety and postpone the decision of whether to return home eventually. Now, a lack of safe, low-cost facilities in cities often throws young people into unexpected crises—sexual assault, robbery, trouble with the police who view them as loiterers and up to no good; or forays into the illegal underworld economy when the search for a cheap room takes them to the part of town where prostitution, drug dealing, fencing operations, and the like flourish, and where people in those businesses may be seeking new recruits. An innocent trip may turn into a catastrophe that makes it difficult or impossible to return home again.

A small percentage of new migrants could also use traditional youth hostels as temporary housing; borderliners who had some money and more skills and self-confidence than most new migrants might find that a three-night stay in a hostel while they hunted for a job was all the transient housing they needed.

(Recently an interest in traditional youth hostels has surfaced in the United States. In 1979 Congressman Phillip Burton of San Francisco sponsored a hostel bill that would authorize grants of up to $200,000 to public or private organizations for opening new hostels or renovating existing ones; it would also set up a commission for a year to study ways of unifying the nation's hostel system and of making sure that new hostels are constructed in areas where they are most needed. The bill passed the House in May 1980.)

Midrange Hostels with Services Attached

Midrange hostels would be the heart of the program for new migrants, serving most of the people described in Part One. They would give single people and families alike a safe place to stay while they attempted to settle in a new community, offering help and guidance with job hunting, permanent housing, and other needs. The time limit might be from a week or less up to two or three weeks, with short extensions in special circumstances.

The recommendations made in the 1947 study *Transient Youth in California* are still valid, especially the one for "Housing facilities for temporary shelter and food with trained supervisors in charge; employment information and help in reaching the proper placement agencies; and counseling services which should include help in the immediate problems presented by the individual, as well as information about and referral to other community facilities and agencies."[1]

One group of migrants that were not included in the 1947 study needs special attention now, however. These are couples or single parents traveling with young children, parents who are in their mid-twenties to early thirties in most cases. Boona Cheema, who coordinates the Berkeley hostel as part of her job as Director of Berkeley Support Services, has noticed an increase in the number of mothers traveling with small children in recent years. In the summer of 1979 the hostel had to turn away two or three such families each night because of its lack of staff and facilities, she said. These families are not all transients—some have lived in the area for several months—but they are all homeless. Some families move in circles from temporary facilities in Berkeley, Oakland, and Richmond, and back again.

Migrant families could be accommodated within the midrange program. They would need separate sleeping arrangements—a room for each family instead of the large dormitories where single migrants would sleep. They would also need space and toys for the children, and child care while the parents were out trying to find work or otherwise stabilizing their lives. But in most particulars, families could use the same facilities as single migrants.

The other notable difference betwen California's transient youth population in 1947 and 1979 is the growing number of young blacks. At the Berkeley hostel, black youths made up close to half of the residents by 1977 and that ratio has persisted. The one difference between black and white transients in Berkeley is that the blacks have not traveled as far or as long in most cases. They, too, may have had conflicts with parents or been told it was time to leave home and get a job; but home is more likely to be east Oakland or San Jose than Philadelphia or Chicago. Their presence underscores the tone of poverty among the transient youth population and makes the lingering vestiges of interest in life-style dwindle into insignificance alongside of economic necessity.

In any large city where a midrange hostel program is set up, the participation of black and other nonwhite youths is likely to be significant. In Arizona, New Mexico, and Texas, more Hispanic than black youths would probably come to the hostels.

In projecting programs for the midrange hostels, a look back at San Francisco's Aquarius House (described in Chapter 7) can provide some ideas. Residents of Aquarius had to set some immediate goals, such as job hunting or taking care of a medical or legal problem, and sign a contract agreeing to spend their days trying to accomplish these goals. Every few days residents renegotiated their contract with a counselor; residents who were not trying to accomplish their goals, or who broke house rules, were asked to leave. Among the residents who stayed with the program (a little more than half), the job placement rate was 40 to 50 percent, a high number for a transient youth population that is largely unskilled and has been programmed for failure, so to speak, by past experience. Aquarius House gave food, lodging, information on where to get services and how to work the system, and it gave moral support; but it also made demands on its residents: It expected the initiative for improving one's life to come from the individual. In essence, it helped people to assume responsibility for their own futures.

The midrange program would cost more to operate than traditional youth hostels because it would keep people longer and provide more services, necessitating not only a larger staff but one with special training and skills—in most cases social-work skills—but it would cost less than the third type of hostel, described below. The only practicable source of funding for midrange hostels at present is the federal government.

Unfortunately, no community wants to spend tax money on housing transient youth; the one service cities are usually willing to provide transients is a free bus ticket out of town. Aquarius House is a good example: Although it operated along lines that most Americans would applaud and was notably successful, the house closed down in 1978 because no public or private agency in San Francisco would give it permanent funding, and there was no federal program for which it qualified.

Midrange hostels would need federal funding, but they could

operate under local auspices in most cases and use existing community services for their referrals when possible. Starting small would be more advisable than a comprehensive program in the vein of the old antipoverty programs that set out to eradicate poverty altogether—and inevitably failed to achieve their goal. Pilot hostel programs in a few cities where the new migrants cluster would enable the staff to iron out the wrinkles and further assess the need for services and the best way to provide them. At the same time, funds could be allocated so that other cities that wanted to set up a hostel program for new migrants in their communities could put together a plan and apply for federal aid.

Shelter Care for Migrants with Special Problems

The third type of facility would be an emergency shelter for people too troubled to fit into the midrange hostel. This program would cost the most to operate, because it would require trained personnel, a higher ratio of staff to residents, and outside professional consultants; but its existence would enable the midrange hostels to function more efficiently at lower cost, by giving them a place to refer deeply disturbed people who took up an inordinate amount of staff time and energy. Along with providing emergency shelter, this program would, when possible, help residents resolve pressing difficulties and figure out a workable plan for the future.

Shelter-care facilities would be designed to serve the mentally ill and others who cannot support themselves, at least not at the time of their stay. Shelter residents might have shorter stays than those in the midrange program because, since they are unemployable and thus eligible for financial assistance, their obtaining permanent housing would not hinge on first finding a job to pay the rent; they could be redirected into a permanent housing facility more quickly. In other cases, the nature of their illness or special situation might necessitate a longer stay.

A sizable number of new migrants, however, fall between the midrange and shelter programs in their behavior and needs: They are too hostile and alienated to fit into a structured framework, yet they are not alcoholics or drug addicts, nor are they patently mentally ill. They are similar in feelings and background to the migrants with whom Thomas Minehan rode the rails in the 1930s, as described in Chapter 3. These new migrants could be accommodated as an adjunct to the midrange or shelter programs, but they would do better in small private hostels with a less structured format, hostels run by alternative agencies, religious orders, or other nonprofit groups. These small hostels, which would need enough funding to hire skilled staff people as well as professional consultants, could use the services of the larger programs, and redirect appropriate migrants to the midrange or shelter programs.

Local and state departments of mental health, along with community social-service agencies, could be involved in planning and running shelter-care facilities, but, as with the midrange hostels, the major funding source would need to be federal. A look at the shelters in Britain run by the Department of Health and Social Services (DHSS) could be a starting point for those drafting legislation for shelters in the United States.

To gain maximum benefit from this plan, the different types of hostels could coordinate their services, forming an umbrella-type organization to exchange information and refer new migrants to the appropriate facility. They could also pool resources on other services, such as where to send new migrants who had found jobs and needed inexpensive permanent housing.

PERMANENT HOUSING FOR FAMILIES AND SINGLE PEOPLE

In most cities new migrants, like other Americans who earn the minimum wage or thereabouts, will have difficulty finding permanent housing that they can afford. Some people see rent control as the answer to rising housing costs, but where it has been tried, as in Britain, the lowest-cost housing tends to disappear altogether; landlords no longer make much profit on this type of rental, so they convert their property to other uses or sell it to a developer who may erect an office building on the site. Rent control would be feasible in time of inflation if it were accompanied by price control and wage control.

Public housing, or government subsidization of rents for people with low incomes, seems a more workable solution at the present time. We do have public housing in the United States, but it is geared primarily to families with children; as in Britain, there is virtually no housing help for the single low-income person who has no special problem other than an economic one.

At a time when both nations are experiencing rising inflation, it is unlikely that either will construct new housing for low-income single people. But much could be done with existing structures. For example, large old houses could be converted into rooming houses with communal kitchens or kitchen privileges. This type of arrangement exists now for university students, often under church sponsorship; it could be used as well for people who don't earn enough to share an apartment. Such housing might need to be partially subsidized by government (a public housing authority could administer the funds), but the houses could be run by nonprofit groups such as churches or civic organizations, and possibly under private auspices as well.

The above suggestion is but one way to house single working people with low incomes; other innovative arrangements can be worked out once a community becomes concerned about housing for this population and seeks to improve it. When we turn to permanent housing for mentally ill street people, however, we face a problem of a different magnitude; here there are no easy answers.

PERMANENT HOUSING FOR MENTALLY ILL STREET PEOPLE

With state mental hospitals on the decline and board-and-care homes primarily suitable for docile, introverted people, and in short supply at that, where can the mentally ill street person be referred for permanent housing? The street as domicile is no long-term solution; it leads to pneumonia and other debilitating illnesses, makes the mentally ill easy prey for thieves, and upsets the local residents.

Howard Levy, a young lawyer who directed Berkeley Support Services for several years in the 1970s, says housing for the mentally ill depends in part on how much the public is willing to spend. Hospitalization costs at least $150 a day, while SSI (Supplementary Security Income—the federal/state pension for the disabled) costs $10 to $15 a day. Levy sees the SSI program as a practicable solution for disturbed street people if more backup services were provided with it. "The problem with SSI now is not what it does but what it doesn't do," he told me.

The monthly check provides enough money for a person to rent a room in a cheap hotel and eat. But some people on SSI are too disturbed to handle their own money—they will spend it all on the day they get it, or lose it, or be relieved of it by the first passing con artist. To prevent this, the SSI program requires a substitute payee to receive and manage the money for recipients who can't handle their own money. But there is no provision in the program to compensate the substitute payee—who in theory is a concerned relative close at hand.

Berkeley Support Services serves as substitute payee for several disturbed street people. One client, "Andrew," came to them in rags, with no money for food. It turned out that Andrew was already on SSI and had a few thousand dollars accumulated in a bank account in his name; but he couldn't touch the money because no one would agree to be his payee, and he couldn't withdraw it himself. BSS became his payee; now they give Andrew his money in small amounts every few days to insure that he will be able to eat throughout the month. Andrew comes to the office regularly and uses it as a day center; it is the one place where he feels comfortable.

Levy believes that the SSI program should make provision to compensate agencies that act as substitute payees and provide other services for recipients—or that the government should provide such services itself; this would make the program viable, and it would still cost much less than hospitalization.

The Hotel Project Model

The Hotel Project experiment described in Chapter 8 has possibilities as a practical solution to the housing needs of disturbed street people on SSI. But such programs cannot simply be tacked on to small hotels in the private sector. It is a matter of economics.

At today's prices, a hotel operator cannot provide decent accommodations and still make a profit on what he can charge people who live on GA or SSI. There is the additional point that people with special problems are more expensive to house than the average tenant; they are more likely to start a fire by accident, misuse the plumbing and break it, or keep their rooms in unsanitary condition. Hotels for this population need to be subsidized whether they are privately run or operated by a nonprofit group in the community. If a hotel is in poor condition, extra money will be needed to repair it, and then to keep it in shape.

Although it is possible to run such programs with private hotel ownership, the margin of profit is so slim, and the operation so fraught with daily difficulties, that it makes more sense to run these hotels under nonprofit auspices such as a church or civic group, or a municipality; they, in turn, could contract with city agencies or other groups to bring in social services on a regular basis. (These hotels could also be called hostels—in the British meaning of the word—because basically they would be rooming houses with support services attached.)

Mental Hospitals: Should They Exist?

Although many disturbed street people can manage with SSI and a well-run hotel project or other community facility, some people will need hospitalization periodically, or, in some cases, permanently. Levy and Cheema both spoke of the folly of trying to close out mental hospitals entirely as a humanitarian measure and substitute community care across the board. It doesn't work out for many chronically disturbed street people, they explained. In the short run, the most disturbed people "fall through the cracks" of the community care system and receive no help (see Chapter 8). In the long run, when the tolerance of the community reaches the breaking point, chronically disturbed people are removed from the street through the criminal-justice system; they end up in prison for a series of minor infractions of the law, but their real crime is being mentally ill. This outcome is not only unfair to the mentally ill; it also places an intolerable burden on the prison system, and on other prisoners.

"Some people in every society will always need to be hospitalized at times because they can't take care of themselves," says Cheema, an Indian from the Punjab region of India and a Unitarian minister by training. "Left alone, they'll die a slow death on the streets, because they have no friends, no support system."

But Cheema is against traditional methods of hospitalization for the street population she works with. She feels that hospitals encourage dependency. "Let these people learn to take some responsibility for their own lives if they can. In the hospital they are waited upon, so when they get back to the community they can't do anything for themselves."

Cheema believes that mental hospitals or others should teach basic survival skills to the disturbed population she works with. "Can you buy your own food? Can you cook it? Can you buy your own clothes? A lot of people never get a chance to find out."

With more help of this kind, she believes that many former mental patients could survive in the community on SSI, in a hotel or in some other living arrangement that offers them backup social services as a support system. Others may need permanent residential care outside the community, she says, perhaps in a rural setting where they would have space to move around, but would be provided with the basic amenities of life.[2]

CAN WE CURE EVERYBODY?

Some may object to the types of arrangements described above for mentally ill street people, because they do not stress rehabilitation or cures. As British social worker June Lightfoot observed, the American social-service system operates on the premise that everyone with problems can be cured through proper treatment. The result is that we spend inordinate amounts of money trying to straighten out people's heads and make them "normal" again, while sometimes neglecting to provide them with basic survival needs. Or we withhold basic services if the person refuses to be cured.

Unfortunately, every story does not have a happy ending, as ardently as we Americans would like it to. Every person cannot be cured. But everyone needs to eat in order to live. In my view, food, shelter, and basic medical care are what society owes people who cannot take care of themselves. It does not owe them a cure, nor can it prevent them from destroying themselves if they are bent on doing so. For a country that prides itself on individualism, the United States has scant tolerance for deviant behavior. A Danish woman once said, when the subject of Americans' passion for therapy and analysis arose, "In Europe, we allow people their differences."

Therapy, like "meaningful work," is a luxury. If a nation can afford to offer therapy to people with serious problems who are motivated to change, that is fine; but to insist on therapy for everyone with problems, whether they want it or not and can benefit from it or not (and to withhold basic survival services if they refuse therapy), is not only a waste of money, it is often ineffective and inhumane.

Again, as in Chapter 8, we need to switch our focus from the needs of the unemployable few back to the majority of new migrants, whose main problem is a lack of work.

HELPING THE NEW MIGRANTS FIND JOBS

Some new migrants may arrive in a community and find a job forthwith through the state employment office or an ad in the newspaper, but most will need special help to relocate in a new community and find work. This is not only because of the problems inherent in transiency, but also because of local prejudice against newcomers.

Throughout history most local units of government have solved the transient problem by driving them out of town. It happened in medieval England, it happened in the United States during the Great Depression, and it happened in San Francisco in 1976 when the city tightened welfare regulations in an effort to force penniless transients to leave town.

When jobs are scarce, local governments that set up or administer job programs for youths are likely to give preference to the children of permanent residents, whose parents presumably vote and pay taxes in that locality. The administrators, or their bosses, may be up for reelection in the future, so their own jobs may depend on their popularity among local citizens.

Local CETA programs, for example, although wholly funded by federal funds, have residency requirements for eligibility. In some cases applicants must present the receipt from their latest gas or electricity bill to prove residency, a requirement that automatically excludes anyone living in a temporary hostel or a hotel room. Homeless people may be ineligible wherever they go.

In drafting future legislation to make jobs for youth, some way of helping transients should be included. This might mean a separate title for CETA, or perhaps job help could be included in legislation mandating transient housing facilities and backup social services in our cities.

The emphasis on federal funding may bother people who are

worried about the central government having too much power, but I take a different view. Citizens pay their largest share of taxes to the federal government as income tax, yet basic community services such as police, fire protection, schools, and the like are supported primarily by local and state funds. So it makes sense for the federal government to pay for other services that cities and counties may feel they cannot afford. Federal funding is particularly appropriate for facilities that house transient youth, because the people served come from cities throughout the nation.

Chapters 18 and 19 have concentrated on practical suggestions for small changes. Now we need to see what is causing the job problems we have been attempting to solve. Here it goes beyond this book's scope to propose concrete solutions, because a look at underlying causes of unemployment catapults us into the midst of some of the world's major problems. But we need to understand these causes and their international connection so that the many people who will need to be involved in future solutions can break through the myths that fetter us, and address the larger picture.

CHAPTER TWENTY

The International Connection

The commerce and trade of the world's nations are so interwoven that no single nation can solve its unemployment problem in isolation. This situation is not new; it has merely intensified in the decades since World War II and increased manyfold in complexity.

For centuries people have looked beyond their own borders to increase their wealth or to make a living. Merchants and manufacturers increased their wealth by developing markets overseas, while the poor earned a living abroad by emigrating.

EMIGRATION: A VANISHING OPTION
FOR THE POOR

Give me your tired, your poor,
Your huddled masses yearning to breathe free. . . .
I lift my lamp beside the golden door![1]

Those lines, which are inscribed on the base of the Statue of Liberty in New York Harbor, expressed not only American policy but the past immigration policies of some other countries, such as Canada and Australia. In the nineteenth century, nations with undeveloped frontiers and untapped natural resources needed countless hands to work the land, build the cities, and develop the resources. They welcomed unskilled immigrants without money who were willing to work. This gave poor people in the older, developed countries an option: If all other ways of making a living failed, or if they aspired to more than lives of grinding poverty, they could emigrate to the new world.

That phase of history is over now. The frontiers and their natural resources are developed, and there is a surplus of labor in the countries that once solicited immigrants; hence immigration policies have been tightened in most countries. As a Canadian immigration official explained in the 1970s, "Just a few years ago we were getting 25,000 immigrants a year, but with eight-percent unemployment of our own, we've cut down to 3,000 and are giving priority to immediate families of established immigrants, engineers, and other highly trained people."[2]

Instead of being an option for the poor and unskilled, immigration is becoming an option for the rich and the highly skilled. Trained technicians are welcome in most countries, and the rich are welcome everywhere.

The rich and their money are emigrating in droves to the United States and other countries in the Western Hemisphere. Sometimes their money emigrates alone. Wealthy Italians and French are investing their money abroad as a precaution against a possible Communist takeover in their native lands; they plan to emigrate themselves at the last moment and be as rich in the new land as they were at home. Wealthy immigrants from the Middle East more often accompany their money—Iranians arriving in the United States in the late 1970s, for example, who knew that a revolution was likely to occur in their country in the near future. In Beverly Hills, California, a section of Los Angeles once famed as the home of the movie stars, the sales of businesses and mansions to Middle Easterners paying cash have become legendary.

In New York City, "Half of the really large apartments with prices in excess of $400,000 are going to foreigners," a real-estate broker there said. "Multinationals, Europeans, see New York as the realm of the 1970s. . . . Because of the tax problems in some foreign countries, some newcomers are buying their apartments in corporate names." Today, an international investment broker in New York suggested, "We ought to change the sign on the Statue of Liberty to make it read: 'This time around, send us your rich.' "[3]

The Temporary Immigrants

With opportunity at its nadir for the poor to emigrate to other countries and seek their fortunes, poverty-stricken people in many lands have accepted a second-best solution. They become temporary immigrants.

Western Europe became the center of temporary immigration. In the early 1970s there were nearly twelve million temporary immigrants in Europe. Most of them worked in northern and western European countries—in Switzerland, West Germany, France, Belgium, Sweden, and Norway. They came from southern European countries and beyond—from Spain, Portugal, Italy, Yugoslavia, Greece, and Turkey.

The temporary immigrant is allowed into another country for a limited period to do a specific job, his contract renewable at the discretion of the host country. He comes in to do the strenuous physical labor that nationals reject in good times because of its low pay and low status. In most cases the immigrant cannot bring his family along or settle permanently in the new land. It is primarily a migration of adult males.

British writer John Berger explored the plight of the temporary immigrants in a book, *A Seventh Man: Migrant Workers in Europe* (1975).[4] Berger saw these workers as an exploited group, an expendable labor force that could be brought in or dismissed at the convenience of the host nation. The temporary immigrants rarely learned new skills abroad, he said; hence when they finally returned home, even if they had saved up enough money to buy a car or television set, or build a house, they faced the same unemployment that caused them to leave in the first place.

In the mid-1970s, as unemployment rose in Western nations, increasing numbers of temporary immigrants were sent home before they had saved enough for a car or a television set. In Italy, for example, in 1975 the number of people returning home was greater than the number leaving, for the first time in history. Germany had laid off 77,000 Italians in the past year, and the Swiss were also cutting back on seasonal Italian workers. Back home in Italy, where more than a million workers were officially unemployed, the returning immigrants faced further competition for jobs from Ethiopians and Somalians as well as refugees from some former Portuguese colonies.[5]

The Commonwealth Immigrants

Another immigration pattern concerns former subjects of colonial rule. Now citizens with commonwealth status, they have
a right to emigrate and seek work in the industrial nations that
once ruled them. In England the immigrants come from India,
Pakistan, and the West Indies; in Holland from Surinam (Dutch
Guiana) and the Molluccas; in France from Algeria; and in the
United States from Puerto Rico, to name some of the major
migrations of former colonial subjects.

In times of labor shortages, the immigrants were welcomed into
many of these lands because, coming from poverty-stricken areas,
they were willing to work for low wages. As unemployment rates
have risen, and as the immigrants have started demanding the
same wages and rights as other citizens, they are not as welcome.
But the governments involved cannot simply revoke their visas
and ship them home, as they can with immigrants from southern
Europe. The added fact that these immigrants usually have dark
skins in nations of light-skinned people has made them convenient targets for far-right groups who play on racial prejudice to
gain political power.

In England, the National Front party has been using immigrants, especially black immigrants from the West Indies, as
scapegoats for the nation's ills. In local elections throughout the
country early in 1977, the Front picked up from 10 to 20 percent
of the vote in working-class districts of many industrial cities.
Reporting on that election, the *Washington Post* commented:

> Britain's virulent inflation, high unemployment and fall-
> ing living standards have hit workers harder than the better-
> protected middle and wealthy classes. The Thursday vote
> suggests that a growing number of workers now blame their
> plight on Britain's immigrants from the Caribbean and
> South Asia. . . . The front is almost a one-party issue,
> calling for the deportation of colored immigrants. It takes
> pot shots at the European Common Market and parades
> waving Union Jacks. But its speeches, its slogans, and its
> jokes are all about race, with an occasional slap at the
> Jews.[6]

In August 1977, London experienced its worst street riots since World War II, when National Front marchers clashed with counterdemonstrators in Lewisham, a working-class borough of southeast London with a growing black population. The 1000 to 1500 National Front marchers, who ostensibly demonstrated to protest increased muggings in the area, were met by an estimated 3000 counterdemonstrators, both black and white, while 4000 policemen tried to keep the peace. In the ensuing riots 111 people were injured and 241 demonstrators were arrested.[7]

Earlier in the day the Bishop of Southwark, an adjoining borough that also has a high incidence of poverty, had led a countermarch of ALCARAF (All-Lewisham Campaign Against Racism and Fascism), causing a National Front leader to say after the riots: "These political priests, the whole ragbag lot of them, will have to go. We want church leaders who will do the job they are supposed to do, which is to look after the morality of the people, not the Third World."[8]

But economics, not morality, was the underlying cause of the riots. It was working-class protestors against poor immigrants, and at the core of their grievances was a similar plea: Stop excluding us from the good life; give us the chance to have more.

OVERSEAS EXPANSION

At the same time that emigration as an option for the poor is diminishing, the development of overseas markets to augment the incomes of the rich is increasing. The old method of direct colonization, which provided captive markets for the colonizers' products as well as a sure supply of raw materials from the countries they occupied, has been discredited. But a different arrangement for overseas expansion—the multinational corporation—has proved equally profitable.

The Multinationals

Today, multinational corporations sell their products across the globe. America is a leader in this type of enterprise, but Britain, Holland, West Germany, France, Switzerland, Italy, Canada, Sweden, and Japan also have their multinationals. These corporations differ from old-style traders in that they often manufacture a good portion of their products abroad as well as selling them there. Many overseas factories of the multinationals are situated on the same continents where colonialism once flourished —Asia, Africa, and Latin America. A major attraction is cheap labor.

Scores of American corporations have transferred their manufacturing facilities from the mainland to Third World countries, which means a shrinking number of jobs at home for industrial workers. From the companies' point of view, why pay American workers several dollars an hour, and go through union hassles as well, when an abundant supply of docile workers elsewhere will do the same work for a fraction of the pay?

In a study of multinationals, *Global Reach: The Power of the Multinational Corporations* (1974), Richard J. Barnet and Ronald E. Müller document the mass exodus of manufacturing from the United States into countries with cheap labor. In the electric industry, for example, "Between 1957 and 1967 GE built 61 plants overseas. A number of these moves followed closely upon strikes and other labor difficulties. . . . By 1974 about 75 percent of the assets of the American electric industry were located overseas." In other industries at that time "about one-third of the total assets of the chemical industry, about 40 percent of the total assets of the consumer goods industry . . . about one-third of the assets of the pharmaceutical industry, are now located outside the United States. . . . Some of the largest U.S. corporations and banks such as Gillette, Pfizer, Mobil, IBM, Coca-Cola, and the First National City Bank earn more than 50 percent of their profits overseas."[9] (In 1980 many of these percentages would be considerably higher.)

It's too bad that our American workers are losing so many jobs by these overseas transfers, some might argue, but don't we have a moral obligation to help the poor in developing countries? they ask. Isn't it our duty to bring industry and the benefits of modern technology to these countries and help them raise their abysmal standard of living?

The entry of the multinational corporations into developing countries is not helping the people, say the authors of *Global Reach*. Using Latin America as their field of study, they argue that the multinationals are hindering rather than helping the countries in which they set up their factories.

In the area of capital, for example, most of the money used to set up new factories of multinational subsidiaries comes from the nations they go into. "From 1960 to 1970 about 78 percent of the manufacturing operations of U.S.-based global corporations in Latin America was financed out of local capital."[10]

International banks that open branches in undeveloped countries also look to local coffers for most of their loans, while charging their borrowers high interest rates. "A retired executive of one of the three largest multinational banks recalls for us that in the late 1950's and early 1960's, his bank always tried to use 95 percent of local savings for its local loans and no more than 5 percent of its dollar holdings." Another banker revealed that "while we earn around 13 to 14 percent on our U.S. operations, we can easily count on a 33 percent rate of return on our business conducted in Latin America."[11]

Another popular practice of global firms in Latin America was to undervalue exports (pretend to make less profit, so you could pay lower taxes) while overvaluing imports. In Colombia, for example, researcher Constantine Vaistos found that American and European drug subsidiaries reported an average profit of 6.7 percent to the Colombian tax authorities during a year when their actual average profit was 79.1 percent. But for imported Librium and Valium, Colombians were charged, respectively, 65 and 82 times the established international market price.[12]

The result of such practices is that the profits of global corporations in poor countries are made at the expense of the people who live there. The very rich in such countries may benefit by working in tandem with the multinationals, but the poor grow poorer. And most people in Latin America are poor.

Barnet and Müller did not question the sincerity of top corporation executives who say they are helping these Latin American countries by establishing factories there. To the contrary, "In talking with top managers of global corporations in oak-paneled offices and private dining rooms high above Central Park or nestled in a suburban New Jersey wood, we were struck by their invincible faith in their power for good."[13]

But when the researchers interviewed eight field managers who were stationed in the Latin American countries where their factories were located, not one of these managers believed that their operations were helping the people there. All displayed "a high level of awareness" of the problems their corporations were causing the local economy, and they all expressed "in some degree a certain moral distaste for some of the practices in which they were engaged. . . . A number of local managers expressed frustration with the home office's insistence that they engage in what one termed 'extralegal practices.' But there was always a ready rationalization. 'If we don't engage in these practices, our competitors will, and where does that leave us in two, three, or five years down the road?' "[14] A German executive working for a global corporation in Latin America told them, "It is true for most people that things are getting worse and we are not helping matters."[15]

Another aspect of global corporations that troubled Barnet and Müller was the desire of management to supersede the nation-state—that is, to make their corporations beholden to no country's law and thus free to control the world's commerce at will. A. W. Clausen, president of the Bank of America, looked forward to "an international corporation that has shed all national identity";[16] George Ball, chairman of Lehman Brothers (and former U.S. undersecretary of state), saw the nation-state as "a very old-fashioned idea and badly adapted to our present complex world";[17] while Carl A. Gerstacker, chairman of Dow Chemical Company, dreamed of buying an island owned by no country, so the company could operate "beholden to no nation or society. . . . We could even pay any natives handsomely to move elsewhere."[18]

"By what right," asked Barnet and Müller, "do a self-selected group of druggists, biscuit makers and computer designers become the architects of the new world?"[19]

Alvin Toffler, author *of Future Shock,* is also troubled by the desire of the multinationals to replace the nation-state. In a later book, *The Eco-Spasm Report,* Toffler said:

> The very notion of democracy presupposes that the people of a country can control their own economic life. When this ceases to be true, for whatever reason, they become colonies.
>
> In this sense the richest countries of the world are sliding into the status of colonies. . . . What is increasingly possible today is a new, far more slippery kind of colonialism, a super-colonialism in which national economies are subordinate not to other nations but to the workings of a transnational economic system or network over which they have no control.[20]

INCREASED PRODUCTION: THE
CONVENTIONAL ECONOMIC SOLUTION

The goal of multinational corporations and banks is worldwide profit maximization. The heads of these corporations can continue to regard themselves as humanitarians because whenever they go into another country, they help increase that country's industrial production; and in conventional economic theory, increased production is considered the answer to every nation's problems. The conventional economists, who advise businesses and governments alike, evaluate a country's economy in terms of how much goods it produces; to them nothing is more important than a country's Gross National Product (GNP).

Even John Maynard Keynes, the British economist who recommended government spending as the way out of the Great Depression, based his theory on increased production. When savings are depleted during a severe recession, he said, the government should put money into circulation through public projects, to "prime the pump"; then available capital will build up, businesses can increase their production, and the system, now repaired, will run smoothly again.

John Kenneth Galbraith is the economist who attacked the theory that increasing production always improves a nation's well-being. In his book *The Affluent Society* (1958) Galbraith argued that when a country could not produce enough goods to satisfy the basic needs of its citizens for food, clothing, and shelter (as in the days of Smith, Ricardo, and Malthus), it made sense to concentrate on the increased production of goods above all else; but when a country was more than able to meet the needs of its people (in terms of its capacity to produce goods), as in the case of the United States, when it was in fact an affluent society, it no longer made sense to keep pushing increased production as the nation's number-one goal.

Galbraith introduced the theory of social balance, which he defined as "a satisfactory relationship between the supply of privately produced goods and services and those of the state."[21] Production of more goods increases the need for more services; for example, if we produce more automobiles, we will need more highways, traffic control, and parking spaces. But in the United States this social balance is out of whack, said Galbraith. The country keeps producing more goods—often goods of marginal

utility, for which citizens feel no need until an advertising campaign creates a desire for them—while the money for needed
services in cities and states is hard to come by. The result is a
devastation of our cities and countryside that affects everyone, he
said.

Galbraith argued for a better balance between the production
of goods and the social services provided by the state. By implica-
tion he urged economists to take cognizance of this changed situation and adjust their systems to include social as well as
monetary values.

Although Galbraith's book was primarily about the United
States, his argument that the capacity now exists to produce
enough goods to satisfy everyone's basic need for food, shelter,
and clothing appears to have some validity for other nations as
well in terms of the world's ability to produce enough goods to
supply everyone. Millions of people still die of starvation and
malnutrition every year, but the problem is more one of economic distribution than of an inability to produce enough food
for them. People die because they lack the money to buy food.
Relief agencies may distribute free food to starving people during severe famines or other emergencies, but usually you need
money to get food, or the seeds, equipment, and land to grow
it; and to have money, you need to be able to make a living.
Which brings us back to the question of whether increased industrial production of goods is the only way to improve the lives
of people in a given country.

An African Textile Mill

The late British economist E. F. Schumacher said no—increasing production, by itself, wasn't the answer. Schumacher was one
of that small group of maverick economists like Galbraith who
challenged the conventional economic wisdom. The way to help
the developing nations become self-sufficient, said Schumacher,
was to encourage the use of "intermediate technology"—that is,
small-scale projects that made a virtue of employing the local
people. In his essay "2 Million Villages," Schumacher made his
point by describing a visit to a textile mill in Africa:

The manager showed me with considerable pride that his
factory was at the highest technological level to be found

anywhere in the world. Why was it so automated? "Because," he said, "African labor, unused to industrial work, would make mistakes, whereas automated machinery does not make mistakes. The quality standards demanded today," he explained, "are such that my product must be perfect to be able to find a market." He summed up his policy by saying, "Surely my task is to eliminate the human factor."[22]

The mill's equipment and raw materials all had to be imported, and the sophisticated equipment demanded that all higher management and maintenance personnel be imported. By the standards of the conventional wisdom, this mill was a sound project: It increased production and the country's GNP as well as helping its balance of payments on the iternational market. The fact that the mill created virtually no jobs for African workers and that the foreign goods shipped into the country in exchange would be consumed by a tiny elite (of which the manager was one), because most people were too poor to buy them, would be irrelevant to the calculations of trained economists. But politically this textile mill, which helped the rich become richer while the poor remained poor from lack of a way to make a living, was like one more piece of dynamite stored up for a future explosion, an explosion of the have-nots that could ultimately affect both the nation's GNP and the mill itself.

Selling Shirts on the World Market

Increased production remains the standard solution to unemployment, although, as we have just seen, this solution may be illusory. The example of what happened to Sri Lanka illustrates another problem that may arise when increased production alone is viewed as the answer to a nation's economic woes.[23]

Sri Lanka (formerly Ceylon), the island at the tip of India, has a high rate of unemployment and considerable poverty. After wide-scale riots there in 1971, the Western nations decided they had better help Sri Lanka make more jobs for its people or the country might be wooed successfully by the Soviet bloc. Economists analyzed the country's situation and recommended establishing a garment industry there. The World Bank lent the country $20 million to establish the industry, and Western shirtmakers came in to teach the managers and workers how to cut the fabric and use the newly purchased sewing machines to make quality shirts that could compete on the world market. Labor is cheap in Sri Lanka, so the shirts would sell for less than those made in Europe or the United States.

All went according to plan until the Sri Lankans tried to sell their shirts. Then they discovered that the same Western nations that had encouraged them to make shirts for the international market did not want to buy them. The sale of Sri Lankan shirts might adversely affect the garment industries of those nations, where labor costs are higher.

Sri Lanka ran into the free-trade-versus-protection controversy: Should countries restrict imports or charge tariffs on foreign goods to protect their own manufacturers, or is it better to allow goods to enter freely and let those who can compete most effectively win out? Should quotas be worked out to give every country the chance to sell some shirts, or does economic reality dictate that whichever country can capture the market for a given commodity should do so? In the context of the free-trade-versus-protection controversy, if one country wins, another has to lose.

Part of the problem is overproduction. More shirts are being manufactured in the world than there are customers to buy them. Millions of other people may be in dire need of more shirts, but, unless they have the money to pay for them, they will not function as consumers of shirts, because no company increases its profits by giving away its shirts, nor does a country help its balance of payments that way.

As long as countries view their economic development primarily in terms of increasing production, there will be controversy over who sells what to whom, and the likelihood of international dissension will remain high. This is an old story. But other effects of spiraling production, made possible by our massive technological breakthroughs, are causing a new problem that earlier generations never heard of—environmental overload.

The Destruction of the Environment

Another reason for deemphasizing the production of goods as the primary way of making a living is the havoc it is wreaking on our planet. Polluted waters and smoggy air have become commonplace in and around industrial areas throughout the world. As economist Robert Heilbroner puts it, "We are running out of the sheer absorptive capacity for the dangerous byproducts of an ever-growing industrial output. . . . There was a time when every act of production, by adding a needed bit to the skimpy pile of social wealth, justified itself without question. But as our air darkens and our lakes putrefy, as our population continues to swell and our reserve of resources shrink, that easy equation of *more* with *better* is no longer possible to make."[24]

Heilbroner, Galbraith, and Toffler all recommend a further conversion to a service-oriented society. This does not mean that production should stop altogether or that industrial nations should return to rural village economies, as a handful of environmental purists suggest; it means trying to achieve a better social balance between goods and services. Toffler sees two benefits from the shift: "First, a service society can help us solve many accumulated social, community, and environmental problems bequeathed to us by the unrestrained economic growth policies of the past two decades. Second, a service-oriented society is less dependent on high inputs of energy and resources than is a traditional industrial society."[25]

When a garment factory in Manhattan closes down or moves to Korea because shirts made at home are too expensive to compete on the world market, it means that more young people who might have become garment workers are likely to end up as new migrants. The same is true of garment factories that close in Manchester, England—or steel mills or automobile factories that shut down in any nation. We cannot escape the international connection of jobs and commerce in the modern world.

Nor in the long run can we escape the need to put the production of goods in perspective and stop worshipping growth per se.

CHAPTER TWENTY-ONE

Horatio Alger, Farewell

A nation that no longer needs the full-time labor of all its people does not have to be in trouble; instead, the nation could consider this cause for rejoicing. This was the belief in the 1950s when machines began replacing workers at an astonishing rate. Now people would have more time for leisure pursuits, the theorists said, time to develop their spiritual and intellectual sides, time to become fuller human beings who could help build an even better world.

But it didn't turn out that way. We never reconciled the moral imperative "If you don't work, you don't eat" with the reality of not enough jobs to go around. The Protestant work ethic, combined with the dream of unlimited opportunity for all, kept us from reassessing the job situation in the light of technological changes and making the necessary adjustments.

People without jobs were accused of not wanting to work, of preferring welfare to jobs. In fact, the work imperative is as strong among the jobless as among those who receive regular paychecks, if not stronger. Most adults want to work; they do not want to be dependent on welfare or charity. When tomato-picking machines began putting farm workers out of jobs in California, the pickers did not rejoice at the prospect of relaxing on the dole; they mounted a campaign to try to stop the development of machines that were taking away their jobs, jobs that many an optionaire would consider boring, menial labor.[1]

Plenty of people from all walks of life would enjoy a moratorium from work in youth or middle age, a period when they could relax, travel, and do as they pleased. And we all need vacations. But there are few adults who do not want some kind of work to structure their life around. This goes beyond the need for money and a moral imperative to work; it is a matter of needing something to do, some activity that gives direction and purpose to life. Even boring work may be better than doing nothing at all full time.

Ultimately, we will need to develop different kinds of jobs, and a greater variety of job arrangements: for example, shorter hours; job sharing; longer vacations; more adult education to help people develop new interests they can pursue if they retire early; programs open to teen-agers that will give them satisfying experiences while keeping them off the regular job market a year or so longer. Numerous other innovative arrangements could be devised and tried if people put their minds to it.

We already have the technological capability to create jobs for all, but two stumbling blocks keep us from making the necessary transition: the myth of the American dream and inflation. In this final chapter we will consider both impediments to change, starting with inflation and working back to the need to relinquish the dream—the central thesis of this book.

THE INFLATION MENACE

When inflation is rampant, few people will want to share jobs or work shorter hours if it means less pay; conversely, government and business will not agree to full-time pay for less work during a period of inflation. Other arrangements would involve government spending for programs or pensions, again unacceptable during inflation, a time when people are pushing to decrease existing government spending, not add to it. Therefore, before we can make significant changes, we must solve the problem of inflation.

What is causing inflation? The nation's top economists disagree. Just as Supreme Court justices naturally interpret the law according to their individual social and political beliefs, so economists fit the causes of inflation into their own economic theories: Conservative economists blame government spending and call for a balanced federal budget, while liberal economists blame high profits and massive spending and call for controls on prices and wages. I would not attempt to fathom inflation's complex web of causality, except to suggest that some of the points stressed in this book—our expectation of continuous upward mobility and our worship of riches—are intimately tied up with the causes of our current inflation. Changing the dream may thus have the secondary benefit of helping to lessen inflation.

In 1958 John Kenneth Galbraith wrote, "Discrimination against the public services is an organic feature of inflation."[2] That observation has been borne out with a vengeance in the current crisis, and not only in the United States. Canada and Britain both dumped labor governments in 1979 and elected Conservatives who pledged to cut domestic government spending.

The situation is curious. Scores of nations are facing a similar crippling inflation at the same time, so even an untrained observer might suspect a link between the various inflations; yet in most countries domestic spending is getting the blame.

In the United States, social services—especially to the poor—are being cut back, and the government is viewed by many as a robber who is stealing part of everybody's paycheck. This anti-government feeling reached its climax in 1978 in California, with the passage of Proposition 13.

Inflation and Proposition 13

For more than a decade a real-estate executive named Howard Jarvis had been leading a movement to cut property taxes in California; although his initiative got on the ballot regularly,* it failed, because Californians did not want to give up the local services that property taxes support. But in 1978, with inflation rampant, Proposition 13 (the Jarvis-Gann initiative) won a sweeping victory.

Jarvis, who assured Californians that his measure would only cut the fat from government, emerged as a folk hero. He was photographed with James Ware, who had won the Republican primary for state controller by endorsing Proposition 13. Ware said jubilantly, "Like Howard Jarvis, I've been on the ballot for

---

* Under California law, if enough citizens sign petitions, a proposed law change can appear on the next ballot as an initiative measure.

15 years. Now, we're both part of a new revolution to save the American dream."

But victory was not as sweet as expected. Instead of trimming the fat off government, it was the lean that went, because the people with the knives were not about to trim themselves away. Public libraries were closed a few days a week, city-run day camps and summer schools were canceled, day-care centers for children of working mothers were closed, as were some neighborhood medical clinics. These closures did not bother people who had enough money to pay for private services in these areas, but even the most ardent supporters of Proposition 13, it turned out, did not want to close down the police and fire departments in their cities in order to cut the cost of government.

Cities and counties had to apply to the state for relief, which lessened local control. And although property owners did have a little more money to spend, with escalating inflation this money did not change their financial picture much, unless they owned vast amounts of property.

What people were really rebelling against when they voted for Proposition 13 was the rising price of ground beef, the fact that, no matter how much money they earned, they never got rich the way one was supposed to in America. What had happened to the promises of the dream?

It was appropriate that Proposition 13 occurred in California, the land at the end of the frontier where people had once rushed in from all corners of the globe expecting to pull gold nuggets out of the earth and became millionaires overnight. The state where the American dream—a dream of money, money, and more money—had appeared to be a sure thing. Now they wondered— could the dream still happen?

Robert J. Ringer says "Yes!" in his 1979 best-seller *The Restoration of the American Dream*. Ringer's message has much in common with the theme of his earlier book, *Looking Out for Number One*, but his style is distinctly different; the earlier, snappy, anecdotal style is replaced with a dignified tone that befits the high priest of libertarianism. Preaching that government is the evil that keeps Americans from achieving their dream of riches, Ringer recommends phasing out all taxes and gradually eliminating government services and government employees. Essential workers, such as postmen and firemen, "would be legitimate private employees performing the same functions as before, only better, less expensively and more efficiently than in the old government-employment days." Ringer urges Americans to "Make an unwavering commitment to become fiercely independent and individualistic."[3]

The Restoration of the American Dream may be inspirational to people who share Ringer's beliefs and ideals, but the book offers no effective plan for establishing his anarchic utopia. Ringer is such a staunch individualist that he opposes all group action—even joint action by conservatives to restrain the government.

Prices continued to rise in 1979, and although many big businesses and some speculators made enormous profits, most people were worse off, because wage increases were not as great as price increases. At the end of 1978 President Carter had asked business and labor to restrict their increases voluntarily in order to help fight inflation; but in the first quarter of 1979, profits earned by businesses increased 26.4 percent over the same period a year earlier, while labor raises, for the most part, kept within the suggested 7-percent guideline.[4]

With the people in an antigovernment mood, the president did not invoke price and wage controls, as some economists urged. The people got less government—and more inflation.

The Role of Government

How much should the government govern? Americans still yearn for small government, for the town meetings of old New England where every citizen could participate directly and Washington was a distant image that people thought about every four years. They love tales of the old West where, according to legend, one "good guy" sheriff was personnel enough to restore law and order in a town and keep it that way. Small government sufficed when there were few people, and land and resources were plentiful. But today the United States is a complex nation with a large population, and it requires a complex government in order to function.

But what about waste, inefficiency, and corruption in government? Aren't there legitimate complaints against the government, and shouldn't we try to correct them? Certainly. The machinery of government—any government—does have a tendency to become large and unwieldy; at times it is inefficient; sometimes it is corrupt. Government needs to be watched constantly. It also needs to be checked and evaluated periodically, so programs that aren't working can be removed, red tape can be spliced, and services can be streamlined. Old services may need to go in order to make room for new ones of greater urgency.

In one sense the government is like a large house that becomes cluttered through long and active use. Sensible people do not burn down their house because it is cluttered and move into a small tent in hopes of avoiding future clutter. Instead, they clean out their house periodically.

What we need to strive for is not less government but better government. A return to the laissez-faire economy recommended by Ringer would not bring most citizens an increased chance to earn a better living; to the contrary, it would decrease their opportunities by enabling those with the greatest financial resources and political clout (the big corporations and banks) to grow even larger and more powerful. The Constitution gives us the machinery with which to impeach a president who tries to grab too much power; but where is the machinery to oust the head of a conglomerate who assumes the role of dictator in formulating national policies that will enrich himself and his associates while impoverishing others?

Who Pays the Bill?

It costs money to run social programs. Earlier chapters have stressed the need for a variety of programs to help the new migrants and other people in the nonaffluent society find jobs and decent places to live. These programs will not make a profit, so the business sector will not be interested in running them. Nonprofit organizations lack the financial resources to operate large-scale programs. Only one institution is capable of running long-range social programs—the government, which was set up in part to help promote the general welfare of its citizens. But where will the government get the money to pay for these programs?

The answer should be obvious by now, in the context of this argument. People pay to support their government through taxes, and the tax rate is geared to one's ability to contribute. In theory, our graduated-income-tax laws already provide for this; in practice, the system does not always operate that way.

Wage earners are forced to pay their fair share of taxes, because taxes are deducted from their paychecks; if all their income goes for living expenses, as is the case with virtually everyone in the nonaffluent society, there is none left over for tax-shelter investments. At the same time, middle-income citizens—those around the base of the affluence pyramid, and some with incomes considerably larger—may pay higher taxes than many of the rich and super-rich if they do not search avidly for loopholes. But those in the middle resent the unfairness of the situation.

It is this type of inequality that taxpayers should revolt against. If the top rates are too high now to be realistic, as some argue, they should be lowered somewhat—and collected without fail. (The obscene housing prices in California and many other states would surely be lower if our tax structure did not encourage people to invest and speculate in real estate as a method of escaping taxes.)

But as long as the dream of riches remains the dominant goal, and the wealthy are held up as role models of success—with their tax evasions considered smart instead of immoral—there is little chance of significant tax reform. Nor can other important changes occur while we cling to the myth of unlimited opportunity and venerate the super-rich.

A TIME FOR CHANGE

Personal expectations keep rising throughout the world. At the same time, technological innovations keep increasing the world's ability to produce enough basic goods for all and eradicate poverty. Everyone should be better off. Instead, poverty perversely remains, and the divisions between rich and poor grow wider.

We are pursuing outmoded economic goals. The philosophy that championed rugged individuals in competition for the land and resources of the frontier, with the winner taking all, belongs in the archives of history.

It is time to say, "Horatio Alger, farewell." The hallowed dream of millions for everyone who works hard enough is obsolete. There is, quite simply, not enough wealth or natural resources on earth for every person to be rich, or even affluent, no matter how hard we all work; nor is a higher standard of living for all likely to spread across the United States or any other country in the future through improved technology and increased production of goods. In order to give everyone the chance to make a living and escape poverty, we will have to scale down our conception of how rich is rich enough.

The United States did attempt to eradicate poverty and lessen the income gap during the 1960s, but there was no corresponding drive to lessen the concentration of wealth. We assumed that there was plenty for all. Today, only those who bury their heads in the sand (or remain in executive suites far from the masses of population) can still believe that fairy tale.

Lowering Our Expectations

People at every income level, except the very bottom, need to lower their expectations. Now when a leader exhorts the people to lower their expectations for the common good, he speaks to those in the middle and lower income ranges, because they constitute the majority; he does not exhort those in the highest income brackets to buy one less luxury car or beachfront retreat. The wealthy are exempted from retrenchment. This has got to change.

People in the middle and lower income ranges will not be convinced that they should tighten their own belts as long as others live in opulence. If we are to lower our expectations, then those in the top income brackets must also reduce their standard of living (and the number of their investments) and learn to find satisfactions in life that do not depend on having more money and power than other people. We can no longer afford to allow enormous holdings of personal and corporate wealth to accumulate and multiply.

Changing Our Perceptions of Success

Another significant change must occur before people in the nonaffluent society will relinquish the dream of riches—a change that strikes at the core of the dream. We must stop ranking people as failures if they do not make enough money to become affluent.

Labor specialist B. J. Widick summed up workers' grievances about this attitude of the affluent society in *Auto Work and Its Discontents:* "They [workers] do have a grievance against society, with its middle-class values, and that is the general contempt in which factory workers, in particular assembly-line workers, are held, making it doubly difficult for blue-collar workers to maintain a sense of personal pride and dignity."

Workers are placed in a double bind: They are regarded as inferior if they remain in the nonaffluent society; but when they try to climb up, as the dream encourages them to do, they find that the affluent society has no place for them.

As earlier chapters have stressed, far more people want professional jobs than the country can use in that capacity. Higher pay and greater intellectual stimulation motivate this aspiration in part, but the desire for status—the determination to be ranked as somebody in the community—is an equally strong goad.

It is time to stop preaching upward mobility as the only way to go, time to give recognition to people who are satisfied (or at least willing) to stay where they are—and who perform much of the labor that keeps our society going. By pretending to be a classless society, we rob the working classes of status and dignity.

A Different Dream

Now that there are no more frontiers or undiscovered continents for rugged individuals to conquer, we need a different dream. The challenge facing the United States and other Western nations in the coming century is whether they can end dire poverty, put limits on individual and corporate wealth, and usher in full employment without also inaugurating the totalitarian excesses that have so often accompanied attempts to effect such changes in communist nations. An equitable balance between the rights of the individual and the needs of the community and nation has yet to be worked out in most countries in either power bloc, but it is essential that we work toward this goal.

On the international level, cooperation and compromise are the key words of the future, if we are to prevent the holocaust of a nuclear war.

The multiple changes that occurred in our age have rendered both capitalism and communism in their traditional forms obsolete as adequate economic solutions for the centuries ahead. We are sorely in need of new comprehensive economic theories, carefully formulated plans of the magnitude of those put forth by Adam Smith and Karl Marx in the past, but based on the world in which we now live.

Meanwhile, the new migrants wend their way from city to city in search of opportunities that do not exist for them. Without help from their governments, and encouragement to lower their expectations, the new migrants will remain wanderers, part of a growing army of unemployed youths in Europe and the United States who have become surplus commodities in their own countries. Their presence mocks the Alger myth, and undermines their nations' priorities.

When countries with the capability of putting men on the moon and developing hydrogen bombs declare that it is impossible for them to devise methods of employing all their people who want to work, then something is clearly amiss with their systems and values. It is time for changes.

The end of the American dream may seem sad, even tragic, to some people. But it need not be a time for mourning. In the United States we have come through our childhood as a nation and lived through a stormy adolescence in the past two decades. Perhaps we are ready for a new dream, a mature dream that does not center on individual desires for grandiose wealth and the power to play God. It could be that in the century ahead, a different dream can serve us just as well or better.

Notes

Full citations are given in the bibliography for materials marked as follows:

    *B = Books
    *R = Reports, Papers, Documents, Pamphlets
    *M = Magazine and Newspaper Articles

2. The Land of Opportunity
(pp. 8–21)

1. The observer was Cadwallader Colden. Quoted in Wyllie, p. 12, *B.
2. Tocqueville, p. 41, *B.
3. Quoted in Wyllie, p. 22, *B.
4. All manuals listed are discussed in Wyllie. Those interested in the self-help books of the nineteenth century will find Professor Wyllie's book a gold mine of information.
5. Wyllie, p. 127.
6. Ibid., p. 56.
7. Ibid., p. 49. Quoted from *The Money Maker,* ed. Henry Livingston (New York: 1868) , p. 35.
8. Wyllie, p. 50. Quoted from Ida C. Murray, "Small Things That Won My Success," *Ladies' Home Journal,* vol. 24 (1907) : 66.
9. Wyllie, p. 123.
10. Alger, *Struggling Upward and Other Stories,* pp. 203 and 205, *B.

11. Alger, *Strive and Succeed*, p. 52, *B.
12. Ibid., p. 146.
13. Ibid.
14. Hofstadter, *Social Darwinism in American Thought*, Ch. 2, "The Vogue of Spencer," pp. 32–50, *B.
15. See Matthew Josephson, *The Robber Barons*, *B, for details about how Vanderbilt and other multimillionaires of the late nineteenth century amassed their fortunes.
16. Collier, pp. 22–23, *B.
17. Ibid., p. 29.
18. Details of this strike come principally from Yellen's *American Labor Struggles*, 1936, *B. This labor-history classic is available in paperback.
19. See Josephson's foreword to the 1962 edition of *The Robber Barons*, p. vi, *B.
20. Yellen, p. 5, *B.
21. Reprinted in *The New York Times*, July 22, 1877. Quoted in Yellen, p. 12, *B.
22. Yellen, pp. 21–22, *B.
23. *The New York Times*, July 24, 1877. Quoted in Yellen, p. 24, *B.
24. *The New York Times*, July 28, 1877. Quoted in Yellen, p. 25, *B.
25. Yellen, p. 25, *B.
26. Allsop, p. 113, *B.
27. Ibid., pp. 112–13.
28. Ibid., pp. 119–20.
29. Information about the hobo and his life comes principally from Nels Anderson, *The Hobo*, *B.
30. Anderson, p. 70, *B.
31. Ibid., p. 72.

3. Westward Ho!
(pp. 22–36)

1. For the history of California agriculture and its many land grabs in the nineteenth century, see Chapter 2, "Land Monopolization," in McWilliams, *Factories in the Field*, *B.
2. For more information, see Chapters 5 and 6 in McWilliams, *Factories in the Field*, *B.
3. Steinbeck, *The Grapes of Wrath*, p. 35, *B.
4. For more information about government-sponsored relief programs during the Depression, see Josephine Brown, *Public Relief 1929–1939*, *B.
5. Brown, p. 260, *B.
6. Allsop, pp. 131–32, *B; see also McWilliams, *Factories in the Field*, pp. 310–11, *B.

7. McWilliams, *Factories in the Field*, p. 311, *B.
8. Brown, p. 261, *B.
9. Information about Outland's study comes from George Outland, "The Education of Transient Boys," *M. See also George Outland, *Boy Transiency in America*, a compilation of the articles on boy transiency that Outland published during the 1930s, *B.
10. Outland, p. 501, *M.
11. Ibid.
12. Minehan, p. xvi, *B.
13. Ibid., p. 73.
14. Ibid., p. 148.
15. Ibid., p. 59.
16. Ibid., p. 165.
17. Ibid., pp. 21–23.
18. Ibid., p. 24.
19. Ibid., p. 27.
20. Ibid., p. 28.
21. For more information about California between World Wars I and II, see McWilliams, *California: The Great Exception*, *B.
22. See California Committee for the Study of Transient Youth, *R.
23. Ibid., p. 10.

4. *The New Migrants*
(pp. 37–51)

1. Results of the Baumohl-Miller study were published in Baumohl and Miller, *R.
2. Ibid., p. 23.
3. Ibid., pp. 57–58 and 59–60.

5. *Job Hunting in the City*
(pp. 52–66)

1. Information about the San Francisco Travelers Aid special program for transient youth in 1966–68 comes from the author's interviews with Marjorie Montelius, Director of San Francisco Travelers Aid, and from papers by Montelius: "Youth in Flight," *R, and "Demonstration Project on Transient Young Adults in San Francisco," *R.
2. Montelius, "Youth in Flight," p. 2, *R.
3. Ibid., p. 1.
4. Author's interviews with Cathie Greene, casework supervisor at Travelers Aid, San Francisco.
5. *San Francisco Chronicle*, Oct. 30, 1975. Report of a four-year study

at the University of Texas, headed by Norvell Northcutt. (Reprinted from the *Washington Post*.)

6. Information about Dick Baltz and the outreach job office he ran in the Tenderloin for the California Department of Employment's Employment Development Division (EDD) comes from author's observations of that office during 1975–78 and from interviews with Baltz. (In 1979 Baltz became supervisor of intake for the EDD in San Francisco and Robert Martin took over the Tenderloin office. The EDD's outreach office in the Haight-Ashbury district, run by Martin, had closed down in 1978 along with Aquarius House, in whose basement the office had been housed.)

7. Author's interviews with Robert Martin, who ran an outreach job office for the California Department of Employment in the Haight-Ashbury district. (See preceding note.)

6. *Welfare and Other Social Services*
(pp. 67–81)

1. Torchia, *M.
2. Author's interview with Steve Mooser, former staff member at Berkeley Support Services.
3. Craib, *M.
4. Information about the Charity Organisation Society in Britain comes from Mowatt, *B. Information about the American Charity Organization Society comes from Komisar, *B.
5. The leader was Josephine Shaw Lowell. Quoted in Komisar, p. 31, *B.
6. Mowatt, p. 75, *B.
7. Mowatt, *B. See pp. 117–18 and pp. 127–28 for Barnett's views, his split with the COS, and citations to his writings and biography.
8. Haight-Ashbury Switchboard, "Office Procedures," p. 1, *R.
9. Ibid.. "Survival Manual," *R.

7. *A Place to Stay*
(pp. 82–98)

1. Author's interviews with Howard Levy, former director of Berkeley Support Services.
2. Details about the summer of 1967 come from Smith and Luce, p. 139, *B, and from author's interviews.
3. Details about Amsterdam and its treatment of transient youth come from author's interviews with Wil van Lake, Tourist Information Office (Vereninging voor Vreemdelingenvekeer, or VVV); Haim Jans, Administrator, Hans Brinker Student Hostel; Jetty

de Rooy, Director, Social Advice and Information Center (Maat-
schappelijk Advies-en Informatienburo, or MAI); Helmut van
Renesse, Young People Advisory Center (Jorgen Advises, or
JAC); and Alyda Hoenderdahl, Administrator, Crisis Intervention Center, "Singel"; and from *Living Guide to Amsterdam*,
1974–75·

4. Haight-Ashbury Switchboard, "Survival Manual," p. 1, *R.
5. Aquarius House, *R.
6. Lindsay, *M.
7. Author's interview with Peter Field.
8. Author's interviews with Cathie Greene, Travelers Aid.
9. Author's interview with Irene Kudarauskas, Director, Travelers Aid
   Drop-in Center for children in the Tenderloin.

8. Reaching the Unemployable

(pp. 99–111)

1. California Community Mental Health Services Act of 1968, popu-
   larly called the Lanterman-Petris-Short Act after its sponsors.
2. For information on how California saved nearly $40 million be-
   tween fiscal years 1970 and 1974 by closing down three mental
   hospitals and providing scant funds for community mental-
   health programs and services for former mental-hospital patients,
   see California, Legislature, pp. 30–31, *R. In January 1974, the
   California legislature overrode Governor Ronald Reagan's veto
   of a bill requiring legislative approval prior to any more hospital closures.
3. For more information on how local resistance to neighborhood
   residential facilities for the mentally ill causes board-and-care
   homes to choose docile ex–mental patients, see Aviram, *M. See
   also their book about the mentally ill in community-based shelter
   care, Segal and Aviram, *B.
4. Segal, *M.
5. Ibid., pp. 388–89.
6. Ibid., p. 394.
7. The results of this study are discussed in Spears, *M, and Pittel,
   *M. A book by Pittel and Miller based on this study, *Dropping
   Down: The Hippies Then and Now* (unpublished), analyzes
   their data.
8. Author's interview with Dr. Stephen Pittel.
9. Spears, p. 15, *M.
10. Author's interview with Phyllis Hunt, public health nurse, City of
    Berkeley.

9. Changing Patterns of Migration

(pp. 112–18)

1. "Population's Historic Shift," *M.
2. "Americans on the Move," *M.
3. Morris, *M.
4. "Americans on the Move," p. 64, *M.
5. *San Francisco Sunday Examiner and Chronicle,* April 17, 1977, Sec. A, p. 3.
6. Carroll, *M.

10. Down-and-Out in Britain

(pp. 119–37)

1. "All About the kids," Report of the Soho Project, 1974, mimeo.
2. Author's interviews with staff members of New Horizons; see also New Horizon Youth Centre, *R.
3. "Squatters Handbook," July 1974, mimeo.
4. Author's interview with Cathy Coyne.
5. "CHAR Campaign Charter," p. 2, *R.
6. "Tooley Hotel—Southwark," *R.
7. *Homeless Poor of London,* published by the Charity Organisation Society, 1891. This report is discussed in Mowatt, p. 74, *B.
8. See "CHAR Campaign Charter," *R. CHAR also publishes pamphlets and booklets relating to homelessness and the problems it engenders.
9. Author's interview with David Brandon and his research staff.
10. Described in "Postulates to Be Tested in Long Interviews," n.d., mimeo.
11. "CHAR Campaign Charter," p. 2, *R.
12. Waugh, p. 26, *R.
13. Great Britain, *R. The report includes information about the Gleaves case.
14. *New York Times,* Aug. 8, 13, 16, 1973; Jan. 14, July 21, 1964. See also the chapter on the Houston murders in Chapman, *B.
15. *Directory of Projects,* *R.
16. Author's interview with David Carrington, field worker for the National Association for the Care and Resettlement of Offenders, known as NACRO.
17. Mills, *B.
18. Ibid., p. 2.
19. Author's interviews with Bob Blyth, director of the Blenheim Project, and other staff members.

11. *The Advantages of Being an Optionaire*
(pp. 141–55)

1. *News,* April 29, 1979. Bureau of Labor Statistics, Department of Labor.
2. "Money Income in 1977 of Householders in the U.S." Census Bureau, Department of Commerce.
3. "Worker Experiences in the Population, 1977," Special Report, Bureau of Labor Statistics, Department of Labor.
4. Sharpe, p. 19, *M.
5. *San Francisco Chronicle,* Jan. 8, 1976, p. 17.
6. Sheehy, p. 58, *B.
7. Ibid.
8. Roth, *B.
9. Ove M. Wittstock, owner, Layton's Store, Berkeley.

12. *"They Don't Want to Work Anymore"*
(pp. 156–60)

1. Erikson, pp. 156–58, *B.
2. Ibid., p. 157.
3. Karl Marx and Friedrich Engels, "The Communist Manifesto," reprinted in Mendel, p. 23, *B.
4. William Hamilton, "The Now Society" (cartoon), *San Francisco Chronicle,* Feb. 26, 1976.
5. Steinbeck, *Cannery Row,* p. 6. *B.

13. *Two Alienations*
(pp. 161–77)

1. Roszak, p. 1, *B.
2. Ibid., p. 49.
3. Ibid., p. 240.
4. Reich, *B.
5. Ibid., p. 25.
6. Ibid., p. 52.
7. Ibid., p. 66.
8. Rossman, p. 12, *M.
9. "Getting Your Head Together," p. 57, *M.
10. Peter L. Berger, p. 23, *M.
11. Chinoy, p. 1, *B.
12. Purcell, *B. See Chapter 9, "Aspirations for His Children," pp. 153–64.
13. Ibid., p. 157.

14. Herman Miller, *Income of the American People* (New York: Wiley, 1955), pp. 31–33. Miller's findings are discussed in Aiken, pp. 5–6, *B.
15. Tyler, p. 207, *B.
16. Sexton, p. 31, *B.
17. Ibid., p. 52.
18. Ibid., p. 55.
19. Rosow, p. 9, *R.
20. Krickus, p. 113, *B.
21. Ibid., p. 113.
22. Reich, p. 19, *B.
23. Ibid., p. 219.
24. Ibid., p. 310.
25. Pittel, p. 9, *M.

14. Combat on the Domestic Front
(pp. 178–86)

1. Photo in the *San Francisco Chronicle*, April 14, 1977, p. 28.
2. *San Francisco Chronicle*, April 15, 1977, p. 1.
3. Ibid., April 23, 1977, p. 12.
4. Rubenstein, p. 4, *M.
5. *San Francisco Chronicle*, April 15, 1977, p. 11.
6. Rubenstein, p. 4, *M.
7. Ibid., p. 4.
8. Laqueur, pp. 5–6, *B. Information about the Wandervögel comes principally from Laqueur's book.
9. Ibid., p. 116.
10. Ibid., p. 117.
11. Heer, p. 66, *B.
12. Ibid., p. 69.
13. Stanley High, *The Revolt of Youth* (New York: Abingdon Press, 1923). Quoted in de Graaf, p. 28, *M.
14. De Graaf, p. 28, *M.
15. Gengler, *Kampfflieger Rudolph Berthold*. Quoted in Waite, p. 51, *B.

15. The Rise and Fall of Meaningful Work
(pp. 189–202)

1. Reich, p. 19, *B.
2. Henry Ford is quoted in Al Nash, "Job Satisfaction: A Critique," in Widick, ed., p. 67, *B.
3. Robert Reiff, "Alienation and Dehumanization?" in Widick, p. 45, *B.

4. Ibid., p. 47.
5. Patricia C. Sexton, "A Feminist Union Perspective," in Widick, p. 22, *B.
6. Al Nash, "Job Satisfaction," in Widick, pp. 79 and 81, *B.
7. Wallace, p. 2, *M.
8. Ross, *M.
9. Robinson, pp. 10–11, *M.
10. Ringer, *Looking Out for Number One*, p. 117 and 216, *B.
11. Greene, *M.
12. Korda, p. 4, *B.
13. Ibid., p. 58.
14. Advertisement in *New York Times Book Review*, Oct. 2, 1977, p. 37.
15. Advertisement in *Saturday Evening Post*, Jan./Feb. 1978, p. 1.
16. Advertisement in *San Francisco Sunday Examiner and Chronicle*, April 16, 1978 (comics section).

16. Optionaires and the Business Route
(pp. 203–13)

1. Orison Marden, *The Young Man Entering Business* (New York: Crowell, 1907), p. 110. Quoted in Wyllie, p. 143, *B.
2. "Slim Pickings for the Class of '76," *M.
3. "For Historians It's a Buyer's Market," *M.
4. Maeroff, *M.
5. "Scandal in Med School Admissions, *M.
6. *Lifelong Learning*, course catalog of adult-education courses offered through University Extension of the University of California at Berkeley. Catalogs analyzed for their business and management offerings are: Spring 1970, Fall 1974 and Spring 1979 (Bay Area issues).
7. Advertisement in *San Francisco Chronicle*, June 11, 1978, Sec. A, p. 8.
8. Advertisement in *Focus*, magazine of listener-supported television station KQED in San Francisco, May/June, 1977, p. 17.
9. Anders, *M.
10. Rosenberg, p. 1, *M.
11. Ibid., p. 8.

17. Not Enough Jobs
(pp. 214–27)

1. *San Francisco Chronicle*, Dec. 27, 1975, p. 10. (Reprinted from *The New York Times*.)
2. Ibid., p. 10.
3. Winchester, *M.

4. U.S. Congress, p. 3, *R.
5. Ginsburg, p. 139, *M.
6. U.S. Congress, p. 4, *R.
7. "Law Enforcement," *M.
8. "Young People Without Jobs," *M.
9. Ibid., p. 95.
10. "Waiting for Jobs," *M.
11. Edelman, pp. 4 and 5, *R.
12. *The New York Times,* May 8, 1977, p. 16.
13. Ibid.
14. "Why It's Hard to Cut Youth Unemployment," *M.
15. See Beatrice G. Reubens, "Foreign Experience," in U.S. Congressional Budget Office, *Teenage Unemployment: What Are the Options?* p. 53, *R.
16. Ibid.
17. Mack, *M.
18. Morgenthaler, p. 40, *M.
19. Ibid., p. 40.
20. "Danger: Not Enough Youth at Work," *M.
21. "Thaw in the Job Market," *M.

18. Jobs for Youth
(pp. 231–46)

1. "Slim Pickings for the Class of '76," p. 47, *M.
2. Brill, p. 297, *M.
3. Edelman, p. 5, *R.
4. U.S. Congressional Budget Office. *Teenage Unemployment Problem: What Are the Options?* p. 64, *R.
5. *San Francisco Chronicle,* Feb. 20. 1976.
6. British Youth Council, p. 74, *R.
7. Edelman, *R.
8. Ibid., p. 8.
9. Boone, *R. See also the Citizens Policy Center report, *The Quiet Crisis,* which adapts the Center's national policy proposals to California. *R.
10. Boone, p. 2, *R.
11. See U.S. National Commission for Manpower Policy, "Recent European Manpower Policy Initiatives," *R.
12. British Youth Council, p. 79, *M.
13. "Sunbelt West to Gain House Seats," *M.

19. Services for the New Migrants
(pp. 247–59)

1. See California Committee for the Study of Transient Youth, *R.
2. Author's interviews with Boona Cheema.

20. The International Connection
(pp. 260–72)

1. "The New Colossus," a sonnet by Emma Lazarus.
2. Selden, *M.
3. Goldman, *M.
4. Information on the temporary migrants comes primarily from Berger, *B., and Berger, John, *M.
5. *San Francisco Chronicle,* June 8, 1977, p. 6.
6. Ibid., May 7, 1977, p. 8. (Reprinted from the *Washington Post.*)
7. Mather, *M.
8. Ibid., p. 2.
9. Barnet and Müller, pp. 41, 17, 50, *B.
10. Ibid., p. 153.
11. Ibid., p. 154.
12. Ibid., p. 158.
13. Ibid., p. 185.
14. Ibid., p. 186.
15. Ibid., p. 187.
16. Ibid., p. 56.
17. Ibid., p. 19.
18. Ibid., p. 16.
19. Ibid., p. 25.
20. Toffler, p. 76, *B.
21. Galbraith, *The Affluent Society,* p. 201, *B.
22. Schumacher, p. 194, *B.
23. See transcript of "The Shirt Off Your Back," television documentary of *World,* WGBH, Boston, 1979.
24. Heilbroner, pp. 303 and 305, *B.
25. Toffler, p. 84, *B.

21. Horatio Alger, Farewell
(pp. 273–82)

1. Chavez, *M.
2. Galbraith, *The Affluent Society,* p. 209, *B.
3. Ringer, *The Restoration of the American Dream,* p. 280, *B.
4. "Huge Profits Anger the White House," pp. 1 and 16, *M.

Bibliography

BOOKS (*B)

Aiken, Michael; Ferman, Louis; and Sheppard, Harold. *Economic Failure, Alienation and Extremism*. Ann Arbor: University of Michigan Press, 1968.

Alger, Horatio, Jr. *The Store Boy, or The Fortunes of Ben Barclay*. In *Strive and Succeed;* introduction by S. N. Behrman. New York: Holt, Rinehart & Winston, 1967.

————— *Ragged Dick, or Street Life in New York*. In *Struggling Upward and Other Stories;* introduction by Russel Crouse. New York: Crown, 1945.

Allsop, Kenneth. *Hard Travellin': The Hobo and His History*. New York: New American Library, 1967.

Anderson, Nels. *The Hobo: The Sociology of the Homeless Man*. Chicago: University of Chicago Press, 1961.

Barnet, Richard J., and Müller, Ronald E. *Global Reach: The Power of the Multinational Corporations*. New York: Simon & Schuster, 1974.

Becker, Howard P. *German Youth: Bond or Free*. New York: Oxford University Press, 1946.

Berger, John. *A Seventh Man: Migrant Workers in Europe*. Photographs by Jean Mohr. New York: Viking, 1975.

Brown, Josephine C. *Public Relief, 1929–1939*. New York: Holt, 1940.

Chapman, Christine. *America's Runaways*. New York: Morrow, 1976.

Chinoy, Eli. *Automobile Workers and the American Dream*. Introduction by David Riesman. Garden City, N.Y.: Doubleday, 1955.

Collier, Peter, and Horowitz, David. *The Rockefellers: An American Dynasty*. New York: Holt, Rinehart & Winston, 1976.

Domhoff, G. William. *The Higher Circles: The Governing Classes in America*. New York: Random House, 1970.

—— *Who Rules America?* Englewood Cliffs, N.J.: Prentice-Hall, 1967.

Erikson, Erik H. *Identity: Youth and Crisis*. New York: Norton, 1968.

Fisher, Alan A. "The Problem of Teenage Unemployment." Ph.D. dissertation, University of California, 1973. (Available: U.S. Dept. of Commerce, NTIS No. PB-223 914.)

Form, William H. *Blue-Collar Stratification: Autoworkers in Four Countries*. Princeton, N.J.: Princeton University Press, 1976.

Galbraith, John Kenneth. *The Affluent Society*. New York: New American Library, 1958.

—— *The Great Crash, 1929*. Boston: Houghton Mifflin, 1955.

Gardner, Ralph D. *Horatio Alger, or The American Hero Era*. Mendota, Ill.: Wayside Press, 1964.

Harrington, Michael. *The Other America: Poverty in the United States*. New York: Macmillan, 1962.

Heer, Friedrich. *Challenge of Youth: Revolutions of Our Times*. Translated by Geoffrey Skelton. London: Weidenfeld and Nicolson, 1974.

Heilbroner, Robert L. *The Worldly Philosophers: The Lives, Times, and Ideas of the Great Economic Thinkers*. 4th ed. New York: Simon & Schuster, 1972.

High, Stanley. *The Revolt of Youth*. New York: Abingdon Press, 1923.

Hofstadter, Richard. *Anti-Intellectualism in American Life*. New York: Knopf, 1963.

—— *Social Darwinism in American Thought*. New York: George Braziller, 1959.

Josephson, Matthew. *The Robber Barons 1861–1901*. New York: Harcourt Brace, 1962.

Kearney, Robert N. *The Politics of Ceylon (Sri Lanka)*. South Asian Political Systems series. Ithaca, N.Y.: Cornell University Press, 1973.

Kerouac, Jack. *On the Road*. New York: Viking, 1957.

Komisar, Lucy. *Down and Out in the USA: A History of Public Welfare*. Rev. ed. New York: Franklin Watts, 1977.

Korda, Michael. *Success! How Every Man and Woman Can Achieve It*. New York: Random House, 1977.

Krickus, Robert J. "White Working Class Youth." In *Man Against Work*, Lloyd Zimpel, ed. Grand Rapids, Mich.: Eerdmans, 1974.

Laqueur, Walter Z. *Young Germany: A History of the German Youth Movement*. Introduction by H. R. Crossman. London: Routledge & Kegan Paul, 1962.

McWilliams, Carey. *California: The Great Exception*. Salt Lake City, Utah: Peregrine Smith, 1976.

—— *Factories in the Field*. Salt Lake City, Utah: Peregrine Smith, 1971.

Mayes, Herbert R. *Alger: A Biography Without a Hero.* New York: Macy-Masius, 1928.

Mendel, Arthur P., ed. *Essential Works of Marxism.* New York: Bantam, 1977.

Mills, Richard. *Young Outsiders: A Study of Alternative Communities.* Reports of the Institute of Community Studies. London: Routledge & Kegan Paul, 1973.

Minehan, Thomas. *Boy and Girl Tramps of America.* New York: Farrar and Rinehart, 1934. Reprint: Seattle: University of Washington Press, 1977.

Mowatt, Charles Loch. *The Charity Organisation Society, 1869–1913: Its Ideas and Work.* London: Methuen, 1961.

Orwell, George. *Down and Out in Paris and London.* London: Penguin, 1966.

———— *The Road to Wigan Pier.* London: Penguin, 1962.

Outland, George E. *Boy Transiency in America.* Santa Barbara, Calif.: Santa Barbara State College, 1939.

Parker, Richard. *The Myth of the Middle Class: Notes on Affluence and Equality.* Introduction by G. William Domhoff. New York: Liveright, 1972.

Pliven, Frances Fox, and Cloward, Richard A. *Regulating the Poor: The Functions of Public Welfare.* New York: Pantheon, 1971.

Purcell, Theodore D. *Blue Collar Man: Patterns of Dual Allegiance in Industry.* Cambridge, Mass.: Harvard University Press, 1960.

Reich, Charles A. *The Greening of America.* New York: Random House, 1970.

Reitman, Ben L. *Sister of the Road: The Autobiography of Box Car Bertha.* New York: Harper & Row, 1975.

Ringer, Robert J. *Looking Out for Number One.* New York: Funk & Wagnalls, 1977.

———— *The Restoration of the American Dream.* San Francisco: QED, 1979.

Roszak, Theodore. *The Making of a Counter Culture: Reflections on the Technocratic Society and Its Youthful Opposition.* Garden City, N.Y.: Doubleday, 1969.

Roth, Philip. *Portnoy's Complaint.* New York: Random House, 1969.

Rubin, Lillian B. *Worlds of Pain: Life in the Working Class Community.* New York: Basic Books, 1976.

Saunders, Nicholas. *Alternative London/4.* London: Saunders and Wildwood, 1974.

Schumacher, E. F. *Small Is Beautiful: Economics as if People Mattered.* Introduction by Theodore Roszak. New York: Harper & Row, 1973.

Segal, Steven P., and Aviram, Uri. *The Mentally Ill in Community-Based Sheltered Care.* New York: Wiley, 1979.

Sexton, Patricia Cayo, and Sexton, Brendan. *Blue Collars and Hard Hats: The Working Class and the Future of American Politics.* New York: Random House, 1971.

Sheehy, Gail. *Passages: Predictable Crises of Adult Life.* New York: Bantam, 1977.

Smith, David E., and Luce, John. *Love Needs Care: A History of San Francisco's Haight-Ashbury Free Medical Clinic and Its Pioneer Role in Treating Drug-Abuse Problems.* Boston: Little, Brown, 1971.

Steinbeck, John. *Cannery Row.* New York: Bantam, Pathfinders, 1972.

———— *The Grapes of Wrath.* New York: Bantam, 1972.

Terkel, Studs. *Hard Times: An Oral History of the Depression.* New York: Avon, 1971.

Tocqueville, Alexis de. *Democracy in America.* Introduction by John Stuart Mill. Vol. 2, 1840. New York: Schocken, 1961.

Toffler, Alvin. *The Eco-Spasm Report.* New York: Bantam, 1975.

Tyler, Gus. "White Workers/Blue Mood." In *The World of the Blue Collar Worker,* Irving Howe, ed. Based on the Winter 1972 issue of *Dissent.* New York: Quadrangle, 1972.

United States Catholic Conference, Campaign for Human Development. *Poverty in American Democracy: A Study of Social Power.* Washington, D.C.: U.S. Catholic Conference, 1975.

Waite, Robert G. L. *Vanguard of Nazism: The Free Corps Movement in Postwar Germany, 1918–1923.* New York: Norton, 1969.

Wallich-Clifford, Anton. *No Fixed Abode.* London: Macmillan, 1974.

Warshaw, Stephen, and Leahy, John W., Jr. *The Trouble in Berkeley.* Berkeley, Calif.: Diablo Press, 1965.

Widick, B. J., ed. *Auto Work and Its Discontents.* Foreword by Eli Ginzberg. Policy Studies in Employment and Welfare, no. 25. Baltimore: Johns Hopkins University Press, 1976.

Wolfe, Tom. *The Electric Kool-Aid Acid Test.* New York: Farrar, Straus, and Giroux, 1968.

Wyllie, Irvin G. *The Self-Made Man in America: The Myth of Rags to Riches.* New York: Macmillan, Free Press, 1966.

Yellen, Samuel. *American Labor Struggles: 1877–1934.* New York: Monad Press; distributed by Pathfinder Press, 1974.

REPORTS, PAPERS, DOCUMENTS, PAMPHLETS (*R)

Aquarius House. "Client Follow-up Study—Phase One." Mimeographed. San Francisco, 1976.

Baumohl, Jim, and Miller, Henry. *Down and Out in Berkeley: An Overview of a Study of Street People.* Berkeley: City of Berkeley/University of California Community Affairs Comm., 1974.

Berkeley, "Report of the Ad Hoc Committee to Study Transient Youth." Rowena Jackson, chairman. Mimeographed. City of Berkeley, 1971.

Boone, Dick, and Franco, Nancy. "Position Paper on a National Youth

Program." Mimeographed. Santa Barbara: Citizens Policy Center, Dec. 1976.

British Youth Council. *Youth Unemployment: Causes and Cures.* Report of a working party. London: March 1977.

California Committee for the Study of Transient Youth. *Transient Youth in California: A National, State, and Local Problem.* Prepared by Miriam R. Resnik. San Francisco: 1948.

California, Legislature. "Senate Select Committee on Proposed Phaseout of State Hospital Services." Final Report. Senator Alfred E. Alquist, Chairman. Sacramento: 1974.

Cavanna, Roger; Priestly, Tom; and Solomonson, Julie. *Telegraph Avenue Study: Vending.* Phase Two. Mimeographed. Prepared for course IDS 241, Dept. of Landscape Architecture, University of California, fall 1972.

"CHAR Campaign Charter." London: Campaign for the Homeless and Rootless, n.d. (leaflet).

Citizens Policy Center. Open Road/Issues Research. *The Quiet Crisis: A Report on Unemployment Among Young Californians.* Santa Barbara: 1977.

Directory of Projects: For Adult Offenders, Alcoholics, Drug Takers and Homeless Single People. London: National Association for the Care and Resettlement of Offenders. (Yearly.)

Edelman, Peter B., and Roysher, Martin. "Responding to Youth Unemployment: Toward a National Program of Youth Initiatives." A policy paper. Mimeographed. Albany: New York State Division for Youth, 1976.

Great Britain, Department of Health and Social Security, *Working Group on Homeless Young People.* London: DHSS, 1976.

Haight-Ashbury Switchboard. "San Francisco Survival Manual." Published anually by the Haight-Ashbury Switchboard and other organizations.

———— "Office Procedures." Mimeographed. 1972 rev. ed.

Montelius, Marjorie. "Demonstration Project on Transient Young Adults in San Francisco." Mimeographed. San Francisco: Travelers Aid Society, 1968.

———— "Youth in Flight." Paper read at Travelers Aid Association's Fifteenth Biennial Convention, April 29, 1968, in Detroit, Mich.

New Horizon Youth Centre. *Annual Report, 1973/1974.* London: 1974.

Pawlak Vic. *Conscientious Guide to Drug Abuse.* 4th rev. ed. Phoenix, Ariz.: Do It Now Foundation, 1973.

Rosenberg Foundation, San Francisco. *Annual Report, 1973.* With an essay on transient youth by Jim Baumohl.

Rosow, Jerome M. "The Problem of the Blue-Collar Worker." Memorandum for the Secretary of the U.S. Department of Labor. Mimeographed. Washington: 1970.

"Tooley Hotel—Southwark: A Report by the Southwark Forum."

Mimeographed. London: Campaign for the Homeless and Root-less, 1973.

U.S. Congress, Senate. *Congressional Record,* 94th Congress, 2nd sess., May 3, 1976.

U.S. Congressional Budget Office. *Budget Option for the Youth Un-employment Problem.* Background Paper no. 20. Washington: March 1977.

———— *Policy Options for the Teenage Unemployment Problem.* Back-ground Paper no. 13. Washington: Sept. 1976.

———— *Public Employment and Training Assistance: Alternative Ap-proaches.* Budget Issue Paper. Washington: Feb. 1977.

———— *The Teenage Unemployment Problem: What Are the Options?* Report of a Conference held April 30, 1976. Washington: 1976.

U.S. National Commission for Manpower Policy. *The Challenge of Rising Unemployment: An Interim Report to the Congress.* Report no. 1. Washington: Feb. 1975.

———— *The Economic Position of Black Americans: 1976.* By Andrew F. Brimmer. Special Report no. 9. Washington: July 1976.

———— *Recent European Manpower Policy Initiatives.* By Charles Stewart. Special Report no. 3. Washington: Nov. 1975.

———— *Reexamining European Manpower Policies.* Special Report no. 10. Washington: Aug. 1976.

Waugh, Sarah. *Needs and Provisions for Single Homeless People: A Review of Information and Literature.* A report funded by the Department of the Environment (Great Britain). London: Cam-paign for the Homeless and Rootless, 1976.

MAGAZINE AND NEWSPAPER ARTICLES (*M)

"Americans on the Move." *Time,* March 15, 1976, 54–64.

Anders, Corrie M. "Home Sales: Hot Job Market." *San Francisco Ex-aminer,* Aug. 26, 1979, BAZ sec., 33.

Aviram, Uri, and Segal, Steven P. "Exclusion of the Mentally Ill." *Archives of General Psychiatry* 29 (July 1973) : 126–31.

Berger, John. "Europe's Expendable Work Force." *The Nation,* Oct. 18, 1975, 369–72.

Berger, Peter L., and Berger, Brigitte. "The Blueing of America." *New Republic* 164 (April 3, 1971) : 20–23.

Brill, Harry. "Educating Youth—the Cruel Solution." *The Nation,* March 23, 1964, 296–97.

Carroll, Rick. "14,000 Jam a Job Office." *San Francisco Chronicle,* Jan. 27, 1976, 1.

Chavez, Cesar. "The Farm Worker's Next Battle." *The Nation,* March 25, 1978, 330–32.

Craib, Ralph. "New Rules Trim S.F. Welfare Rolls." *San Francisco Chronicle,* Nov. 29, 1975.

"Danger: Not Enough Youth at Work." *Time,* May 30, 1977, 64–65.

"For Historians It's a Buyer's Market." *San Francisco Chronicle,* Jan. 3, 1977, 3. (Reprinted from the *Washington Post.*)

"Getting Your Head Together." *Newsweek,* Sept. 6, 1976, 56–62.

Ginsburg, Helen. "Congressional Will o'-the-Wisp," *The Nation,* Feb. 5, 1977, 138–43.

Goldman, John J. "A Bastion for Wealthy Foreigners." *San Francisco Sunday Examiner and Chronicle,* May 29, 1977, "Sunday Punch" sec. (Reprinted from the *Los Angeles Times.*)

Graaf, John de. "Perils of Counterculture." *East-West Journal* 6 (Sept. 1976) : 28–29. Originally published in *North County Anvil* 17 (March/April 1976) .

Greene, Bob. "Let Us Now Praise Greedy Men." *San Francisco Sunday Examiner and Chronicle,* Sept. 25, 1977.

"Huge Profits Anger the White House," *San Francisco Chronicle,* March 21, 1979.

"Law Enforcement." *The Nation,* June 30, 1979, 772.

Lindsay, Robert. "$50,000 American Dream." *San Francisco Chronicle,* Oct. 26, 1976. (Reprinted from *The New York Times.*)

Mack, Joanna. "Youth Out of Work." *New Society* (London) , April 27, 1977, 117.

Maeroff, Gene I. "College's Quest for Philosophy Teacher Provides a Lesson in Academic Hiring." *New York Times,* April 2, 1979, sec. A, 13.

Mailer, Norman. *The White Negro.* San Francisco: City Lights Books, n.d. Originally published in *Dissent,* 1957.

Mather, Ian; Glass, Charles; and O'Lone, Kevin. "111 Hurt in the Bloody Battle of Lewisham." *Observer* (London) , Aug. 14, 1977, 1–2.

Morgenthaler, Eric. "European Youth, Hard Hit by Unemployment, Are Posing Major Political and Social Problem." *Wall Street Journal,* June 21, 1977, 40.

Morris, Willie. "The Glorious Sunbelt Comes into Its Own." *Family Circle,* Feb. 1977, 66–67 in West Coast Edition.

Newmayer, John. "Five Years After: Drug Use and Exposure to Heroin Among the Haight-Ashbury Free Medical Clinic Clientele." *Journal of Psychedelic Drugs* 6 (Jan./March 1974) : 61–65.

"The New Migration—of Money." *Newsweek,* May 3, 1976, 65–66.

Outland, George. "The Education of Transient Boys." *School and Society,* Oct. 13, 1934, 501–04.

Pittel, Stephen. "The Drug Culture: Understanding Its People." *Menninger Perspective* 2, Oct./Nov. 1971, 4–9.

"Population's Historic Shift." *San Francisco Sunday Examiner and Chronicle,* Jan. 9, 1977, 1.

Robinson, Eugene. " 'Flight' School for Rising Tycoons." *San Francisco Chronicle,* Oct. 24, 1977, 10–11.

Rosenberg, Marcy. "Statistics Foreshadow Employment Crunch for DP Grads by 1985." *Computerworld,* April 9, 1979, 1.

Ross, Mitchell T. "Tom Robbins: The Soft Cover Literati." *San Francisco Chronicle,* Feb. 28, 1978, 15.

Rossman, Michael. "Coming Down: Where Do You Go After You've Been So High?" *California Monthly* (University of California Alum. Assoc. mag.) , Dec. 1975, 12–15.

Rubenstein, Steve. "Tall Trees and Angry Loggers." *San Francisco Chronicle,* April 30, 1977, 4.

"Scandal in Med School Admissions." *San Francisco Chronicle,* April 24, 1978, 1. (Reprinted from *The New York Times.*)

Segal, Steven P.; Baumohl, Jim; and Johnson, Elsie. "Falling Through the Cracks: Mental Disorder and Social Margin in a Young Vagrant Population." *Social Problems* 24 (Feb. 1977) : 387–400.

Selden, Ina. "Returning Emigrants." *San Francisco Chronicle,* June 8, 1977, 16. (Reprinted from *The New York Times.*)

Sharpe, Ivan. "Amazing Stampede for a Lowly $90 Job." *San Francisco Chronicle,* Jan. 25, 1976, 19.

"Slim Pickings for the Class of '76." *Time,* March 29, 1976, 46–49.

Spears, Larry. "Where Have All the Flower Children Gone?" *California Monthly* (University of California Alum. Assoc. mag.) , Dec. 1975, 13, 15.

"Sunbelt West to Gain House Seats." *San Francisco Chronicle,* Aug. 1, 1979, 1. (Reprinted from *The New York Times.*)

"Thaw in the Job Market." *San Francisco Chronicle,* Jan. 26, 1979.

Torchia, Joseph. "Surviving the Tenderloin." *San Francisco Chronicle,* Oct. 5, 1977, 38.

"Waiting for Jobs." *The Nation,* April 23, 1977, 301.

"Why It's Hard to Cut Youth Unemployment." International Labor Organization, *ILO Information* 5 (1977) : 1 in U.S. ed.

Winchester, Simon. "Stamp of Sudden Poverty." *Guardian* (London) , Feb. 7, 1975.

"Young People Without Jobs—How Real a Problem?" *U.S. News and World Report,* May 9, 1977, 94–96.

Index